INDIAN POLITY

INDIAN POLITY:

A VIEW OF
THE SYSTEM OF ADMINISTRATION IN INDIA.

GEORGE CHESNEY

GYAN

Published by

Gyan Publishing House
5, Ansari Road
Daryaganj, New Delhi-110002
Phone: 011-47034999, 9811692060
E-mail: books@gyanbooks.com

Distribution Network
gyanbooks.com
India, USA, Canada, UK, Australia, France

ISBN: 978-81-212-8666-4 (PB)
First Published, 1868

2nd Impression 2023

Printed at: Gyan Press, Delhi.

INDIAN POLITY
Author: George Chesney

THE SYSTEM

OF

ADMINISTRATION IN INDIA

INDIAN POLITY

A VIEW OF

THE SYSTEM OF ADMINISTRATION IN INDIA

BY

GENERAL SIR GEORGE CHESNEY, K.C.B., M.P.

COLONEL COMMANDANT ROYAL ENGINEERS

Οὐ μόνον ἄρα δυνατὸν, ἀλλὰ καὶ ἄριστον πόλει νόμιμον ἐτίθεμεν

(Thus the system we have proposed is not only practicable, but is also best for the state)

PLATO, the *Polity*, Book V. 457

THIRD EDITION

LONDON
LONGMANS, GREEN, AND CO.
AND NEW YORK: 15 EAST 16th STREET
1894

PREFACE

TO

THE THIRD EDITION

The long period, nearly a quarter of a century, which has elapsed since the last edition of this book was published, has made that work out of date in every sense, especially because the numerous reforms, civil and military, which it advocated, have in the interval been in great measure carried out. The book has therefore been rewritten throughout—except the historical introduction in Chapter II.—and treats of the new and greatly altered conditions, political and administrative, which have now to be dealt with.

While this edition is thus a new book, the old title has been retained, as remaining appropriate to the subject. Reform of the Indian administration is still as much needed as ever, but reform addressed to new circumstances, and needing new methods. With the progress of time, the problems which present themselves for solution, while as ever many and various, become ever more delicate and complex.

The opportunity has been taken to bring under

review the Home Government of India, as well as the administration in that country.

The acknowledgments of the author are due to the publishers for the completeness of the elaborate map attached to this edition, which is, he believes, the first to show in one view all the administrative divisions of British India.

LONDON:
November, 1894.

PREFACE

TO

THE SECOND EDITION

THE reforms in Indian administration during the past two years, have included certain proposals put forward in the first edition of this work, and involve considerable alteration now, in order to bring the descriptive portion into accordance with existing facts. The rapid development of policy in regard to public works which has taken place during this time, and the new aspect presented by the financial condition of the country, have rendered it necessary to re-write in part the concluding chapters.

That reconstruction of the Indian army, which was before strongly advocated, has still to be entered upon, although the necessity for an entire change in its organisation becomes every day more apparent. The part of the work which refers to that subject is, therefore, reprinted almost without alteration.

LONDON:
June, 1870.

PREFACE

TO

THE FIRST EDITION

THE FOLLOWING PAGES have for their twofold object to furnish an outline of the system under which British India is ruled, and to bring to notice some points in that system which appear to call for improvement. Ten years have already elapsed since the direct government of that country was assumed by the Crown, and its affairs made matters of Imperial interest. The time, then, has arrived when the whole course of Indian administration may fitly be reviewed, as a preparation towards modifying it where policy and wisdom recommend, instead of leaving its reform to the pressure of chance; and on this head some considerations are offered which, it is believed, if simple, are also original. The attempt has also been made to show clearly that the defects now most prominently apparent are, so to speak, accidental ones, arising out of the fortuitous manner in which our Indian Empire has grown up, and which only require the exercise of some administrative vigour to remove. When this is clearly apprehended, the path of reform is made easy.

The writer on Indian subjects is at every point met by the difficulty of adapting his treatment to the very slight acquaintance of them possessed by most readers, without making it tedious to the better informed. But as for the distaste which it is usual to assert is felt for Indian affairs, the author can only say that, so far as personal experience is a guide, the interest expressed about them appears often to exceed the knowledge possessed on the subject. Nor is it surprising, in view of the rapid transition through which India has lately passed, that even those personally connected with the Indian service should have only the most indistinct notions as to the functions its members perform. The want thus felt it is hoped the present volume may supply.

With respect to the Indian Army, for example, it may be surprising to hear, after all the discussion of late years, that its real reform has yet to be undertaken; that what has been done so far is at best only a provisional arrangement, suited for a temporary emergency. Yet such is the conclusion which is inevitable from a consideration of the facts. And this is but one of the problems before Indian administrators, and which for their solution demand a closer knowledge of the subject than is usually to be found. Some of these questions will certainly before long engage public attention; and as a contribution towards the discussion which will then arise, it is hoped that these pages may not be without their value, especially as regards the important subject of the share to be granted to the natives of India in the administration of that country.

HARROW-ON-THE-HILL:
May, 1868.

CONTENTS

CHAPTER I

GEOGRAPHICAL SUMMARY

CHAPTER II

OUTLINE OF INDIAN HISTORY

CHAPTER III

RISE AND DEVELOPMENT OF BRITISH RULE IN INDIA

CHAPTER IV

THE PRESIDENCIES

CHAPTER V

THE PROVINCIAL GOVERNMENTS

CHAPTER VI

THE SUPREME GOVERNMENT

CHAPTER VII

THE LEGISLATIVE COUNCILS

CHAPTER VIII

THE CENTRALISED DEPARTMENTS

CHAPTER IX

DISTRICT ORGANISATION

CHAPTER X

THE NON-REGULATION PROVINCES

CHAPTER XI

EXTENSION OF NATIVE AGENCY IN CIVIL ADMINISTRATION

CHAPTER XII

RISE AND DEVELOPMENT OF THE INDIAN ARMY

CHAPTER XIII

BRITISH OFFICERS OF THE INDIAN ARMY

CHAPTER XIV

ARMY ORGANISATION

CHAPTER XV

INDIAN ARMY PROMOTION

CHAPTER XVI

NATIVE OFFICERS

CHAPTER XVII

PUBLIC WORKS: ORGANISATION AND DEVELOPMENT

CHAPTER XVIII

IRRIGATION WORK

CHAPTER XIX

RAILWAYS

CHAPTER XX

FINANCE

CHAPTER XXI

THE HOME GOVERNMENT OF INDIA

CHAPTER XXII

GENERAL CONSIDERATIONS

INDIAN POLITY

CHAPTER I

GEOGRAPHICAL SUMMARY

CHAP. I. Area.

THE peninsula of India is about 1,900 miles in length from north to south, and of about the same breadth in its widest part, nearly due east and west. British India comprises also the extensive region east of the peninsula which bears the general name of Burma. The whole area of India, including the territory beyond the north-west boundary of geographical India which is now under British rule, contains about 1,800,000 square miles, which is somewhat larger than that of Europe without Russia. Its population is 289 millions, nearly one-fifth of the estimated population of the globe, that of Europe without Russia being about 240 millions.

Mountains.

The Himalaya Mountains, with the various chains extending from them east and west, cut off India from the rest of Asia. The central portion of the range to which this name is given extends for about 2,000 miles, with a breadth of several hundred miles, from the plains of India on the south to the table-lands of Central Asia on the north. The main chain of this, the greatest mountain range on the surface of the earth, extends for a long distance farther, both east and west.

CHAP. I.

Another mountain chain connected with the Himalaya extends from it southward and westward along the basin of the Indus to the Arabian Sea, while from the eastern extremity a tangled mass of mountain country spreads into Burma and along the east coast of the Bay of Bengal. It is this geographical isolation from the rest of Asia and its projection into the sea, which determine the climate of India and explain also why its people and their past history should be distinguished by special and unique characteristics.

The great plains.

The north of India is for the most part a vast unbroken alluvial plain, extending southwards at each extremity; at the western along the basin of the river Indus and its tributaries to the Arabian Sea; to the eastward along the basin of the Ganges and its tributaries. The plain of the Upper Indus, before its junction with the other rivers of Punjab, although generally flat, is well raised above the level of the rivers which flow through it, and is generally a great arable district. Lower down, with a reduced rainfall, the margin of cultivation on each bank of the river is small. On approaching the sea the slope of the country diminishes, and the Indus finds its way to the sea through a network of channels. Sind, the delta of the Indus, like Egypt, is almost rainless, but artificial irrigation renders it very productive. Sind is cut off from the rest of India on the east by the rainless and waterless tract known as the Indian Desert, a continuation of the plain of Upper India. The basin of the river Ganges, which, after issuing from the Himalaya and its tributaries, runs in its upper course from west to east, forms the great plain of the North West Provinces and Oudh, which constitutes the greater part of the country known as Hindustan. This country also being well raised above the level of the rivers is generally free from inundations, it has a moderate rainfall and is for the most part arable land. The basin of the Lower Ganges

CHAP. I.

is more tropical in character, and rice cultivation gradually supersedes that of corn. About two hundred miles from the sea the Ganges forms its delta, due to the diminished slope of the country. The waters in the various branches, as of the other rivers which flow into the head of the Bay of Bengal, are now above the surface of the country and are retained in their course by artificial embankments. The Brahmaputra, which issues from the Himalaya to the north of Assam, joins the Ganges below the apex of the delta, forming with it the great river Meghna, which flows into the north-east of the Bay of Bengal. The lower portion of the basin of the Ganges is a vast mudbank, the deposit of that river. The process of recovery from the sea is still visibly going on, soundings at the mouth of the Hugli—one of the branches of the Ganges—changing in a few yards from a depth in which ships may anchor to two thousand fathoms, a difference which affords some indication of the time which the deposit must have taken to reach its present level.

Rivers.

Of the great rivers of Northern India, the Indus and the Brahmaputra take their rise to the north of the Himalaya mountains, and after a course of many hundred miles enter the plains of India on the north-west and north-east respectively. The Ganges, and its great tributary the Jumna, have their sources in glaciers on the southern slopes of these mountains. The Indus is navigable for large boats as far as Attock, in the north of Punjab, and the Brahmaputra is traversed by large steamers throughout the whole length of the valley of Assam. The Jumna and Ganges are also navigable for boats to Delhi and Hardwar, and were for long the great highways of local commerce, but are now in course of being superseded in this respect by railways.

The plains of Northern India (Hindustan) are bounded on the south by the Vindhya range—hills in

CHAP. I.

Table-land of Dekhan.

comparison with the Himalaya, but mountains according to the British standard—extending almost across India from Gujarat on the west to the edge of the plains of Orissa and Behar on the east. This is the watershed of Central India, the river Narbada which flows into the Arabian Sea near Broach; the Sone, a large tributary of the Ganges on the north; and the Mahanadi which flows into the Bay of Bengal, all rising on a plateau about 3,300 feet above the sea within a few miles of each other. The Vindhya chain is the northern boundary of an irregular and elevated plateau with an average elevation of about 1,500 feet, but rising in parts to as much as 5,000 feet. This table-land, called the Dekhan (or south country), is roughly triangular in form, the Vindhyas forming the base, while the sides run parallel to the two coasts of the peninsula, but approaching much nearer to the western than to the eastern coast. This table-land is tilted towards the east, the western boundary being much more elevated. On the latter side the Ghats (boundary walls of the table-lands) rise precipitously within a few miles of the coast below to an average height of 3,000 feet; on the east side the Ghats, which are here less precipitous and seldom higher than 1,500 feet, fall into the plains at a distance of from 50 to 150 miles from the Bay of Bengal. Towards the south of the peninsula the table-land develops into the still more elevated plateau of Coorg and the Nilgiri Mountains, attaining a height of about 8,000 feet. If the level of the ocean were to rise 1,000 feet, the whole of India would be submerged except the triangular table-land of the Dekhan.

Climate.

A country so extensive and of such diversified surface necessarily presents great varieties of climate. Calcutta at the mouth of the Hugli is just within the north-west tropic, but all Hindustan lies beyond it. Sheltered from the icy north winds by the Himalaya, and with a comparatively low elevation, Northern

India experiences a much less degree of cold than other parts of Central Asia in the same latitude, and enjoys a temperate climate in the winter months. In Southern India the temperature is more uniform throughout the year, although neither the climate nor the general aspect of the country are in accord with the popular notions generally held about them, which have been derived from the accounts of earlier visitors whose experience was limited to the seaboard, and who describe India as a region of luxuriant vegetation and equable moist heat. The greater part of India, especially the great plain of Hindustan, is deficient in timber; the climate is dry rather than damp, and there are great varieties of temperature in the course of the year. In tropical India, on the other hand, the climate on the east coast varies but little. It is never cold, but the sea breeze and proximity to the ocean—the great absorber of caloric—prevent excessive heat. But throughout India the characteristic of the summer months is a high temperature which in the low-lying plains is greater as the distance increases from the ocean, till the highest point is reached in Punjab and the desert-bound plains of Sind, where there is no moisture to absorb the solar radiation. Here the bare baked soil throws back the solar rays into the air and the temperature reaches a height unknown to the dwellers on the coast. Vegetation disappears; furious hot dry winds blow all day; the short night brings little relief or fall of temperature; while at frequent intervals fierce dust storms sweep across the plains, making the day dark as night. After a time, as these dry winds are succeeded by calms betokening the great climatic change, life becomes almost insupportable to the European, and is one of suffering even for the indigenous inhabitants.

Periodic rains.

The heated surface of the land has now set up a great indraught of air from the ocean to the southward, deflected by the motion of the earth from a south into a south-west wind—the south-west monsoon, which sets in on the coast towards the latter end of May and reaches the plains of Upper India by the middle of June. This blows with little intermission until the month of September. A strong wind on the seaboard, attaining often to the force of a gale, it discharges its volume of vapour on the Western Ghats, the mountains of Assam, and the east coast of the Bay of Bengal in a deluge of rain, several hundred inches falling in a few weeks. Parting thus with the greater part of its moisture, the monsoon carries a moderate rainfall to the tracts beyond. Over Bengal, where no high land intercepts its course, the monsoon gives a very copious rainfall, and deflected into a south-east wind by the comparatively low air pressure over the basin of the Upper Ganges, it supplies the annual rainfall to the plains of Hindustan, lessening as the wind parts with its moisture, until at Delhi the average rainfall is reduced to about twenty inches. Further to the north-west the influence of the monsoon becomes still slighter, and the Upper Punjab depends more on the winter than on the summer rains for its annual supply. The cooler surface of the Himalaya intercepts the moisture still borne by the wind which passes over Hindustan, giving here also a great rainfall; the southern slopes of the Himalaya during the monsoon are for the most part wrapped in clouds of mist. On the east coast of the peninsula, where the south-west monsoon comes from the landward, it brings little or no rain, the moisture having been intercepted by and deposited on the higher inland country. The wet season elsewhere is therefore a dry season on the Coromandel coast. The rainfall over this part of India comes from the regular north-east trade wind of the northern hemisphere, which is re-established during the months of European winter, and blowing across the Bay of Bengal arrives on the west coast of the bay laden with moisture.

Rainless tracts.

The south-west monsoon which to the southward of Sind arrives charged with vapour, blows on that country from the direction of the dry land of Arabia, and brings little moisture. Sind, therefore, is almost rainless, and the country beyond it a desert.

With the coming of the rain, nature as well as man revives; vegetation springs into life over the land, and husbandry everywhere begins; navigation is re-established on the swollen rivers; village life is gay with marriage festivals. On the table land of the Dekhan, the rain falling upon a light soil is followed by rapid evaporation; the air continues to be comparatively dry, and with the low temperature due to the elevation makes this the coolest and most agreeable season of the year, for the Dekhan does not share in the winter cold with the parts of India lying beyond the tropic. In Northern India and in Bengal the alluvial soil becoming saturated with moisture, the relief from evaporation is wanting, and except when it is actually raining, this season is usually extremely hot and oppressive; it is also the most unhealthy season from the liability to chills due to the moisture and frequent change of temperature, as sunshine is succeeded by storms.

Cold season.

Towards the end of September the south-west monsoon has expended its force, and is succeeded on the ocean by the regular north-east trade wind; a dry westerly wind sets in over the north of India, growing daily cooler, and giving a season of delightful weather, short in Bengal but longer as you go north, the climate in Upper Punjab being not unlike the winter of Southern Europe. Here, although a fall of snow is almost unknown, the temperature often falls at night to freezing point for many nights together. Everywhere the smiling country is now covered with a sheet of cultivation. The rice crop in Bengal is gathered about the beginning of the year; the wheat crops in Upper India are har-

CHAP. I.

vested in March or April, the season being later as the country tends to Punjab, where the corn is not reaped till May. Then, as the crops no longer absorb the solar rays, and the sun, rising daily higher in the heavens, beats down upon the naked soil, which reflects its rays back into the air, a sudden access of heat takes place; the Indian hot weather sets in again with its parching hot winds and dust, and another season of discomfort must be endured until the welcome rain returns.

CHAPTER II

OUTLINE OF INDIAN HISTORY

CHAP. II.

Aboriginal races.

THE existing races of India are descended for the most part from peoples beyond its borders. Little is known of the history of the original inhabitants who at some remote period occupied India, who have left no written records, and who were either absorbed into the ranks of their conquerors, or, driven by them from the plain country, are now represented for the most part by the various tribes in occupation of the wooded uplands of Central India, the Khonds, Gonds, Santals, Bhils, and others, still speaking in great measure their own dialects, and possessing various inferior degrees of civilisation.

Aryan migration.

The first extended foreign occupation of Northern India was made by the Aryan migration of a branch of the Indo-Germanic family originally cradled in Central Asia, which first settling in Punjab, gradually spread over the greater part of India; their language Sanskrit, which, however, in its classical form was possibly confined in use to the sacred books and learned class, a language closely allied to the Greek and Latin, and even more perfect than the former to express subtle shades of thought and feeling; their religion like that of the early Greeks and Latins, embodying the deification of the elements and heavenly bodies. Their dead as with those races were committed to the funeral pile. To the primitive social conditions in force among them at

CHAP. II.

the time of the first immigration, when the head of the household was husbandman, warrior, and family priest, succeeded the institution of the four castes described in the Institutes of Manu, compiled perhaps about two thousand years ago; the priests or Brahmans; the warrior class (including the ruling princes), Rajputs or Kshattriyas; the agricultural classes, and the Sudras, presumably the aboriginal conquered races. The early legendary epics, composed perhaps at a later date, but relating to an earlier period, describe a state of general war, the conquests over the aboriginal races and war amongst the Aryans themselves. The division of tongues which exists to this day is evidence of the formation of separate kingdoms, which for long periods must have been independent of and usually hostile to each other, and holding little inter-communication. Seven principal Aryan tongues now obtain in as many different parts of the country, derived, it is believed, either directly or in sequence from one primitive language, Prakrit—based upon and closely allied to Sanskrit—the spoken language in common use among the first Aryan settlers. These languages are Bengali, in Bengal; Oriya, the language of Orissa; Hindi, in force over the Upper Gangetic plain; Punjabi; Sindhi, the language of Sind; Gujarati, that of Gujarat; and Marathi, spoken over that part of the Dekhan which was conquered by the Aryans—a country now known as the Central Provinces and part of the Bombay Presidency. The differences of language which have thus arisen, and in the written characters of these, are indicative of the isolation from each other of the different nations of India which must have long prevailed.

Aryan languages.

Buddhism.

Buddhism took its rise in India probably about 500 B.C. Buddha, its founder, was prince of a country north of Benares, and passed his early period of asceticism in Behar, the western portion of the present province of Bengal. A reaction from the excesses of Brahmanism, a protest against the supremacy of the Brahmans, a gospel universal to men as opposed to the distinctive privileges claimed by caste and race, Buddhism became the official religion of Northern and Western India and spread over the greater part of civilised Asia. It is still the faith of China, Ceylon, Siam, Burma, and Thibet, having a greater number of votaries than any other religion. But in India its vestiges remain only in ruins and inscriptions, and in the small sect of Jains. Even when Buddhism was dominant in India, Brahmanism was never crushed out; in Bengal and Southern India it appears to have remained always powerful, and about the ninth century a general Brahmanical revival took place, under which Buddhism was driven out or suppressed, and which has brought down Hinduism to the state in which we now find it.

Brahmanic revival.

The Hindu religion, as interpreted by a learned Brahman, is a refined theism; as practised by the uneducated classes, it is a polytheism of indefinite extension, with innumerable deities, and embracing the devil worship practised by the lowest classes, and often by others. The organisation of four castes formulated in the Institutes of Manu has long been succeeded by a state of things under which every vocation forms a caste by itself, and embraces divisions and sub-divisions almost innumerable. In one sense Hinduism is absolutely rigid. As a man is born, so must he be, and his children, and children's children after him. Intermarriage between castes being impossible, a Brahman or Rajput can be descended only from one of that caste respectively. But it is in some respects the most flexible of systems; caste upon caste has been added from among the races which have come under Aryan rule, and deity upon deity introduced into the Hindu pantheon, and the process is still going on to this day. Caste, as now understood, is as much a matter of social

CHAP. II.

usage as a religion, and serves to mark off trades and occupations of all kinds into separate classes. There is a further separation arising from geographical distribution; there are different castes of Brahmans and Rajputs in different parts of the country which do not intermarry, and so with all classes and professions. The most prominent caste observance is in regard to food. Hindus can eat only with people of their own caste, and their food is defiled if touched by any but themselves, or persons of a higher caste, and the lower the caste the greater the punctilio often shown on this head. The foreigner or follower of any other faith—including of course the Christian and the Parsi—is an outcast to all, and for all but the very lowest class it is pollution to touch his food.[1]

The Dravidians.

The Aryan occupation of India did not extend in any large degree to the south of the peninsula. That part of the country was first occupied in strength, and the aboriginal population subdued or driven for refuge to the forests and mountains, by a race probably from beyond the sea, whose origin is lost in obscurity, but which from the test of linguistic affinity may be thought to be allied to the Scythian family of peoples. To this race the name of Dravidian has been given, and five distinct languages of the Dravidian family are spoken in the south of India, over the whole of what is now called the Madras Presidency, Mysore, and parts of the Bombay Presidency and the State of Hyderabad—Tamil, Malayalam, Telugu, Canarese, and Tulu. This distinction of languages indicates that here, as elsewhere, the country must have been divided for a long period into as many separate states, independent

[1] It needs hardly be said that caste observance, based on considerations of personal pollution, necessarily abounds in inconsistencies, without which, indeed, the business of life would be impossible. It would be an insult for an Englishman to send, say, a present of fruit to a native gentleman on a plate from his own dinner service, but fruit and sweetmeats pass freely in baskets between all classes, although these baskets are the handiwork of a class which is practically outcast, the lowest of the low.

of and generally hostile to each other. The Dravidian race, however, became closely connected with the Aryan people of the north in the very important respect that they all embraced the Hindu religion. How this came about is shrouded in mystery. Had the Aryans overrun the south of India, the Dravidian race would naturally have been brought within the expansive fold of Hinduism in separate and appropriate, but inferior, castes; but Brahmanism being from the nature of the case a matter of birth, the fact that the Brahmans of the Dravidian race are among the most powerful and influential in India, and that nowhere is orthodox Hinduism in higher repute than in Southern India, is difficult to account for. A reasonable solution of the problem is found if we assume that during the Buddhist ascendency Aryan Brahmans migrated to Southern India, and, intermarrying with the Dravidian race, raised their offspring to their own dignity of Brahmans. Flexibility is the note of Hinduism, and explains at once the spread of that religion throughout India and its imperturbable vitality against the efforts of the champions of other faiths. If this fusion took place between the high-caste immigrants and the people of the country, their descendants would soon become merged in the population of the Dravidian countries, adopting their language while transmitting the knowledge of the sacred books in their own classical language—a state of things we find existing to-day. The Brahman in the south has the dark complexion of the Dravidian race; their learned men, like the Brahmans of Benares and elsewhere in Northern India, are Sanskrit scholars, but they have inherited the Dravidian tongue of the people to whom they belong.

Separation of the Indian peoples,

Another illustration of what was probably the effect of the Buddhist domination is afforded by the rupture of languages on the dividing lines between Bengal and Behar. Ordinarily, when two contiguous countries

CHAP. II.

speak different languages, it will be found that some physical barrier divides them, or that the two peoples have sprung from different races, and that either the conquering race has stopped short at what has become the dividing line, or that the contiguous countries have been occupied by separate races advancing from different directions. But here the same race of colonists overspread both tracts, yet the line of language division is a purely artificial one drawn across a level, open plain, through which flows a river, the common highway of both countries. Yet, in passing only a few miles across this invisible line of demarcation, a different language is met with. A reasonable inference seems to be that whereas Behar was the birthplace of Buddhism, and for long its stronghold, the ejected Brahmans may have migrated to Bengal, with the result of a complete stoppage of intercourse between the two tracts, maintained long enough to admit of the difference of language arising, a change which might come about comparatively soon at a time when the knowledge of letters was confined to a special learned class.

Scythian immigrations.

The first Aryan invaders of India remained in occupation of the country for many hundred years, the long period diversified by almost constant warfare with the original inhabitants and between the different Aryan peoples themselves, while dynasties rose and fell, and the various kingdoms which the conquerors built up expanded or contracted with the varying fortune of war. During this period Buddhism, which had become for a time the dominating religion, gave way in turn to the revived ascendency of Brahmanism. The conquests of Alexander the Great extended only to Punjab, and the kingdom he established in the north of that country under one of his lieutenants was before long recovered by the Indians, but was eventually overrun by a conquering race of Scythians from the north, whose irruption probably took place about the beginning of the Christian era. The Scythian occupation of India extended at least as far as the Jumna; the invaders established a permanent kingdom in Punjab, and a large part of the present inhabitants of that country are probably descended from these races. The Scythians embraced the Buddhist religion, and it is probably through them that this faith extended to the countries of Asia beyond, in which it has become permanently established.

While in possession of a refined instrument of thought in the Sanskrit language, in which have been handed down, besides the famous Institutes of Manu, beautiful hymns to the Aryan deities, and among later writings some interesting dramas, the Hindus were destitute of historical perception, or any appreciation of chronological accuracy. The so-called epics are extravagant fables; throughout the long period of Hindu rule the use of the critical faculty was wholly absent from its literature, and the succession of events can be inferred only from the myths in which they are suggested with the help of scanty vestiges of inscriptions still remaining. It is not until the Mahomedans appear on the scene that the history of India in any proper sense begins; and if the annals recorded by them are little more than a gloomy succession of wars and revolutions, during which the social condition of the people made little progress, still the historians of the Mahomedan period had a sense of the value of accuracy and of dates, and of the duty to the future of bequeathing the history of the past. From their advent the course of events has been faithfully represented, often in befitting detail.

Mahomedan invasions of India. The Arabians.

On the rise of Islam, the Arabians when overrunning Western Asia in the victorious progress of their arms and faith, made incursions into Sind in the early part of the seventh century, but were in turn dispossessed by the Hindus, and a systematic invasion and conquest of India by the Mahomedans was not begun until the

CHAP. II.

eleventh century. By that time the whole of Western Asia had become Mahomedan, and powerful kingdoms had been founded on the ruins of the old Greek and succeeding Tartar dynasties. The Arabian empire in Asia, however, soon broke up, and the first systematic Mahomedan invasion of India from the north-west was made by Mahmud of Ghazni, the capital of a kingdom inhabited mainly by Persians and Afghans (or Pathans), the ruler himself, and probably a large part of his officers and troops, being however Turki, a people of barbaric origin from Northern Asia, but which from intermarrying with the peoples of the countries conquered by them had lost the original facial characteristics of their race, and had acquired the aquiline and high-bred features of the Persian or Pathan nobles.

Pathan empire of India.

The Mahomedan conquest of India may be regarded as consisting of two well-marked periods. The first, the Afghan or Pathan conquest begun by Mahmud, was continued by his successors. The course of events comprises a series of preliminary invasions, the conquest of a portion of India and its annexation as an outlying province of the conqueror's kingdom beyond the mountains, and then the rupture of this province from the rest of the empire and the establishment of an independent Mahomedan kingdom under the usurper in India. Two hundred years passed before this last development was effected. The kingdom thus established gradually expanded into an empire embracing the greater part of India, with its capital at Delhi. This empire had hardly been established when it began to run the regular course of Oriental monarchies. Portions of it from time to time became detached from the centre as the governors of provinces took advantage of a weak monarch to rebel against him and carve out independent kingdoms. The Oriental system of government especially favours this mode of disintegration. The provincial governor holding both the full administrative and military authority, and the troops in his employ being practically raised and paid by himself, the means for carrying out a revolt are always ready at hand; while the system of polygamy is naturally provocative of family strife. The sons of a king by different wives are habitually opponents and rivals of each other; to each a party of turbulent nobles and intriguers about the court and camp attach themselves, aiming to increase the discord and foment the jealousies always existing between the rivals. Of the prince in charge of a distant province nothing good will be said at court in his absence; his army will be magnified, and every movement of it reported as an incipient rebellion, until, when his recall or supersession is ordained from headquarters, he is driven to rebellion as the only means of deliverance from danger. This is one illustration to explain the sequence of perpetual wars, conspiracies, rebellions, and massacres which make up the annals of the time, and the vicissitudes undergone by the emperor as well as by the other rulers who had created minor kingdoms in various parts of the country. Under a strong man the empire would be re-established and extended again to comprise a great part of the peninsula; under a weak or unsuccessful one it sometimes dwindled away until it contained only a few square miles of the country round Delhi. The Pathan period, counting from the first invasion of Mahmud, lasted for about five hundred years (1000 A.D. to 1500 A.D.). During this time India was the natural resort of soldiers of fortune and adventurers of all sorts from the various races beyond the mountains on the north-west, attracted by the chances of advancement afforded by the country, or driven there by the persecution and severities by the Moguls who were overrunning the rest of Asia.

Influence of Persian literature.

Western Asia in the time of Mahmud was perhaps the most civilised part of the world, and the first Mahomedan invaders of India brought with them a much

CHAP. II.

higher standard of learning and letters than was possessed at that time by the nations of the West. Although constantly overrun by foreign races, the Persian genius has always succeeded in dominating the customs and languages of their conquerors. Persian poetry is still the classic, and the Persian language the *lingua franca* of the East, and in more general use than even French has been at any time in Europe. The emperor's court and camp was a polyglot assemblage of Indians, Persians, Turkis, and adventurers of all sorts, and amongst these arose the Urdu, or camp language, a compound of Hindi with a large infusion of Persian and Arabic words—the modern Hindustani now generally spoken in Upper India and some parts of the Dekhan. Hindustani is written in both Persian and Hindi (Sanskrit) characters; although it has a regular grammatical construction, it possesses but limited powers of expression, has no literature, and in fact hardly deserves to be called a language. Persian, however, was always the official language of the Government during the Mahomedan rule, and continued to be so during the earlier days of British rule; its employment in all the official records of the courts of law and revenue over the greater part of India was abolished only a few years ago. At the present time Hindustani may be regarded as the official language of India, so far that it is the dialect used for the drill-books and official records of all the Indian armies, and in this and other ways has become widely spread throughout the country; and in most provinces every English official must acquire a certain degree of acquaintance with it; but the proceedings of the law and revenue courts throughout the country are now everywhere recorded in the vernacular language of each province respectively.

Mogul empire.

After lasting for five hundred years, the Persian-Afghan rule in India was in turn overthrown by the Mogul (Turki) conquest. Early in the thirteenth century the Moguls, a savage and barbarous horde from Northern Asia, overran the western countries of the continent, sweeping away the dynasties established there and destroying the civilisation which had been established on the basis of the Arabian conquest. Coming under the all-powerful influence of Islam, the conquerors soon embraced that faith, while their Mogul (or Tartar) characteristics became absorbed in those of the conquered people, and a restored civilisation grew up on the ruins of the old. A great Turki or Mogul kingdom having become established in Central Asia, invasions of India from it naturally followed. Almost from the first settlement of the Moguls in the countries beyond the mountains, large numbers passed on into India to take service in the armies of the emperor and other ruling princes, and so became merged in the population of that country; and isolated incursions into and invasions of India occurred throughout the three centuries from 1300 to 1600 A.D.; but the permanent Mogul occupation was not accomplished until the sixteenth century, under the monarch Baber, a great and accomplished soldier and statesman, the founder of what is known as the dynasty of the Great Moguls. The usual sequence followed—the separation of India from the provinces beyond the mountains, which fell to another branch of the family. The sovereignty of India alone was first held by the great Akbar, grandson of Baber. Under his three descendants in the direct line the conquest of India, both of the different independent Mahomedan kingdoms which had been formed during the decadence of the Pathan empire, as well as the old Hindu principalities which had been left unconquered by the latter, or had recovered their independence, was gradually extended. The complete conquest of India, however, was barely effected when, on the death (A.D. 1707) of Aurungzib, the great-grandson of Akbar, in his eighty-ninth year, the last capable monarch of the line, the

CHAP. II.

Mogul empire broke up in a cataclysm of civil wars and insurrections.

Rise of the Sikhs.

Foremost among the new rivals for power were the Sikhs and Marathas. The former, originally a religious sect in Punjab—an offshoot from Hinduism—developed into a strong military monarchy, which eventually obtained possession of that country.

Maratha empire.

The Marathas, the people of Western and Central India, first came into notice as a political and military power about the middle of the seventeenth century. At the outset a rising of the agricultural classes under Brahman leadership against the imperial authority, the movement expanded until the Maratha rule became the most powerful in India; it soon split up into a confederacy of separate states, each under the rule of an adventurer who achieved his position by his sword, often at war with each other, but when united overrunning the greater part of India. The country now entered upon a period of turmoil and anarchy, exceptional even in that long-troubled country. Upper India was further desolated by a fresh cycle of invasions from beyond the frontier, and the inevitable course of another conquest of the country by an incursion of hardier races from the north was on the point of being consummated, when the English appeared on the scene.

State of India before appearance of English.

At this time the political distribution of the country was as follows, although it was subject to almost continual variation, according to the fortunes of the perpetual wars and massacres of which it was the scene. The empire was practically dissolved, the emperor was held a prisoner at Delhi by the Marathas. The Sikh monarchy was established in Punjab, extending as far west as the Indus. The Maratha confederacy, although driven out of Punjab after a short occupation of that country, were still the most powerful military body in India. They occupied a large extent of territory in Hindustan, which they governed in the name of the emperor, as well as all that part of Central and Western India which is inhabited by the Maratha-speaking races; they made frequent incursions of plunder still further south and east, and claimed the right to levy tribute from every state in India. The present principalities of Gwalior, Malwa, and Baroda, which formerly were a part of the Maratha confederacy, still remain as separate states. Oudh, and a large portion of that part of Hindustan now known as the North-West Provinces, were ruled by an officer of the imperial court, the Nawab-Wazir, who had made himself independent. The present province of Bengal was in the possession of another lieutenant of the emperor, who had established himself permanently there. The principality of the Dekhan was another recently established modern government, which had peeled off as a fragment from the empire; it is still represented by the Nizam and state of Hyderabad. The Carnatic, the part of Southern India between the Bay of Bengal and the table-land to the westward, was ruled over by a Mahomedan noble, styled the Nawab of Arcot, who was originally subordinate to the Nizam, but who had in turn made himself independent. The state of Mysore, to the west of the Carnatic, was held by Haidar Ali, a Mahomedan soldier of fortune, who had dispossessed the descendants of a long line of Hindu rulers from the government.

Rajputana.

Lastly, there were the various Hindu states of Rajputana. The chief of these were alone among the rulers of India legitimate, in the sense that they had inherited their dignities from long lines of ancestors; all the other ruling houses (save that of the emperor, whose rule had virtually come to an end) were of recent origin.

Toleration of Indian Mahomedanism.

India presents a remarkable contrast to all other countries which have come under Mahomedan rule, in that whereas everywhere else the whole population

CHAP. II.

was forcibly converted to the faith of the conquerors, the conservative force of Hinduism exerted a passive resistance which was never overcome, and Islam, elsewhere so intolerant, here adopted an entirely different policy; and although many instances occurred of religious persecution, the attitude of the Mahomedan conquerors to Hinduism was almost uniformly that of religious and political toleration. The imperial armies were composed in large part of Hindu troops; Hindu officials were largely employed in the civil departments of the state, and the emperors on many occasions married the daughters of Rajput princely houses. The Mahomedan population scattered throughout India, who now make up about one-fifth of the whole, are probably for the most part the descendants of the hordes which accompanied the Pathan and Mogul invaders, or followed in their footsteps, and they still live among the Hindu communities on terms of mutual forbearance and toleration. One exception occurs in the case of Eastern Bengal, where alone are over twenty millions out of the fifty-five millions of the Mahomedans in India, and where they constitute one-half of the total population of that tract, implying a comparatively large process of conversion. Possibly the Hinduism in this part of the country was of a different type from that obtaining elsewhere. It may be added that under the influence of Hinduism the Mahomedans of India have acquired many caste practices of a quasi Hindu kind which are unknown to the votaries of Islam elsewhere.

Village communities.

India also remains the only country where the system of village communities, which probably once obtained among all Aryan peoples, has never been overthrown. Under that system the practice of building isolated cottages or houses is unknown; the agricultural community, who form the great mass of the population, all dwell in villages, usually walled in, each within its own land, the boundaries of which have been fixed from time immemorial. The village land may be parcelled out into shares among different holders, or it may be held in commonalty, but the record of the village possessions is always preserved intact. The ruler of the state is recognised to be the owner of the land, and to him the rent is paid; but subject to this claim, the right of the villagers to occupy the land is indefeasible, and has been uniformly recognised by rulers of all times and classes. Race has succeeded race, dynasties have been created and swept away, but the village system has in the main been left undisturbed. The agricultural classes necessarily suffered greatly from the invasions and intestine commotions which make up the record of Indian history, and of which the ravages wrought by the Maratha hordes are the most recent instances. Even so late as the beginning of the present century the wide tracts of devastated country still lying waste testify to the misery inflicted by these ruthless marauders. But, in the main, Indian wars were carried on by means of mercenary soldiers, gathered together by the prospects of pay and plunder. The village communities, as such, took no part in the quarrel; the village system remained intact, and its inhabitants, if driven away for a time, on the restoration of some semblance of order returned to resume their wonted husbandry. And if there was great suffering and loss of life, the survivors, in their diminished numbers, could soon make good the ravages of war and produce a sufficiency of food for themselves, until war renewed or famine brought a renewal of suffering. The problem presented by an increase of population, ever pressing on the means of subsistence, now arises for the first time in India, as the state of chronic war and disturbance has been succeeded by peace and security on British rule becoming established throughout the land.

CHAP. II.

Summary.

Such, briefly told, have been the circumstances which brought about the condition presented by India when the British appeared on the scene as a new political power. The country peopled in the north and south by two great races of different origin, but connected by the tie of a common religion exercising extraordinary influence, and which governs their conduct and feelings in every action and relation of life. The aboriginal races either absorbed among their conquerors or occupying the less accessible regions of the country. Intermingled with these, and spread over the country, many millions of Mahomedans, the descendants of those who had followed the banners of the foreign invaders—Arabs, Persians, Pathans, Moguls, Turks—but whose original characteristics have become merged in the peculiar status of Indian Mahomedans, as contrasted both with Hindus and with Mahomedans elsewhere. The political condition that of a number of independent states of strength and extent varying almost from day to day according to the changing fortunes of perpetual war, built up on the fragments of the ruined Mogul empire; all absolute monarchies, whether great or small; some ruled by the ancient Hindu princes who had achieved independence in the general turmoil, but for the most part the creation of different rebellious viceroys or successful soldiers of fortune, Hindu and Mahomedan. The principal power was the confederation of the Maratha chiefs, who held the descendant of the Great Mogul a prisoner in his capital, whose bands carried their ravages through almost the whole peninsula, but who were also constantly at war with each other, and united only by the aim of plunder. The disordered and precarious condition into which the people of India had fallen, and the unbridled military rule so long dominant, amongst other results had reduced Hinduism to a very dilapidated and disorganised state, while Mahomedanism had lost its political ascendency; the social state was one of general turbulence, lawlessness, confusion, and suffering. Such was the condition of modern India when the British appeared on the scene as a political and military power.[1]

[1] Sir Alfred Lyall's *Asiatic Studies* (p. 295), a work to which the writer brings an intimate knowledge of the subject, dealt with in an eminently acute and philosophic spirit, and which may be particularly recommended to those who would desire to gain an accurate perception of the religious and social condition of modern India.

CHAPTER III

RISE AND DEVELOPMENT OF BRITISH RULE IN INDIA

CHAP. III.

First settlement of English in India.

The first possession acquired by the British in India was the little island of Bombay, which was ceded to King Charles the Second in 1661, as part of the marriage-dowry of the Infanta of Portugal. Eight years later the island was presented by him to the East India Company, which also owned at this time some other trading depots, or (as they were styled) factories, on the west coast of India. Similar depots were subsequently established at Madras and other places on the east coast, and still later in Bengal. In course of time the factories at Bombay, Madras, and Calcutta became the three principal settlements, to which the others were placed in subordination.

Political state of India at the time.

These factories or settlements comprised, in the first instance, merely a few acres of ground occupied by the Company's warehouses and the residences of their officers; and they were held only under favour of the native sovereign of the territories in which they were situated. At the time of the first occupation of Surat, on the west coast, and of the acquisition of Bombay, the Mogul dynasty was still in its full vigour, and shortly afterwards the Emperor of Delhi completed the conquest of the Mahomedan kingdoms of the Dekhan. This effected, he held a sway over all the states of India, more or less distinctly acknowledged at different times, as the tide of fortune ebbed and flowed, during the interminable wars subsequently waged between the emperor or his lieutenants, and his refractory vassals. But, as has been described in the preceding chapter, on the death of Aurangzib, in 1707, the Mogul empire rapidly fell to pieces; and at the time when the English first began to take a share in Indian politics, it had become broken up into a number of separate kingdoms, possessed, some by provincial viceroys of the Mogul emperor, who had established their own independence and an hereditary monarchy; others by the descendants of the ancient Hindu dynasties, which had never been thoroughly subdued, and rose to independence as soon as the strong hand of the early Mogul emperors was withdrawn; while in other quarters adventurers had raised themselves from obscurity to a foremost place among the rulers of the country. In the state of constant war, of which almost all parts of India were now the scene, it is almost impossible to distinguish with precision the exact limits at that time of the different kingdoms and provinces throughout the country. These limits, as has been explained, varied almost from day to day, and the vassal became the equal or the master of his lord, as circumstances or the fortune of war favoured his ambition. But about the year 1744, the following was the general political state of the country:—I. The Mogul emperor still held, nominally, the direct government of the greater part of Hindustan, or Upper India, as well as Punjab, a territory extending from the Indus to Behar; but the weakness of this remnant of the empire had been shown by the successful invasion of the Persian monarch, Nadir Shah, and the capture and sack of Delhi, five years before this date; by the conqueror's favour alone the emperor had been restored to his throne. In succeeding years Punjab was more than once invaded by the Afghans, under Abdali Shah, then rapidly extending his newly created empire, and was finally severed from the Mogul dominions in

The Emperor.

CHAP. III.

Rohilcund. 1751.—II. Rohilcund, the country between the Upper Ganges and the Himalayas, had been converted into an independency under Ali Mahomed, an Afghan soldier of fortune.—

Oudh. III. The viceroy of Oudh had become the independent ruler of a country which included, with Oudh, a large part of the present North West Provinces, and was at this time the principal support of the tottering Mogul throne. Four years later he was created Wazir of the Empire, and the title became hereditary in his family.—

Bengal. IV. The Viceroy or Subahdar of the three provinces of Behar, Bengal, and Orissa, although nominally appointed to his government by the emperor, had obtained possession of it only by force of arms, and had virtually converted it into an independent kingdom.—

The Marathas. V. The Marathas, although their empire had not yet reached its furthest limits, and the course of its extension was about to sustain more than one severe check, had already spread themselves nearly across the peninsula, reaching from the west coast to the borders of Bengal, and from the source of the Tumbuddra to the neighbourhood of Agra. The Marathas were in fact at this time by much the foremost power in India, and continued to occupy this position until their empire was broken up by Lord Wellesley, more than fifty years afterwards. The different military leaders of this nation had already converted the governments of the provinces confided to them into independencies, so that they virtually constituted a federation of states, bound to each other by ties of interest and nationality, rather than one kingdom. The principal of these states were in Berar, Guzerat, and the territories in Central India subject to Holkar and Sindhia. The descendants of the founder of the Maratha empire had sunk into the position of the holder of mere titular rank, and the post of minister and virtual head of the empire had become hereditary in the succession of Peshwas.—

The Dekhan. VI. The Dekhan, or south country, is the name generally given to the part of India south of the Vindhya Mountains. The Subahdar of this great tract had also become independent; the court title of Nizam-ul-Mulk, conferred on him by the emperor, had become hereditary, and is the name by which the descendant of the first independent Subahdar is still generally known.—VII. Subordinate to the Viceroy of the Dekhan, but soon to become independent of him, was the Nawab or Deputy Governor of the Carnatic, the tract of country on the east coast which now forms the principal part of the Madras Presidency.—VIII. Various principalities in the south of the peninsula, nominally subject to the Subahdar of the Dekhan, but over which his authority had at no time been strongly exercised. Of these, the chief were: Mysore, at that time governed by a Hindu prince of ancient family, but soon to fall into the power of the Mahomedan adventurer, Haidar Ali; Tanjore, governed by a Maratha prince of the house of Sevaji, the founder of the Maratha Empire; and the Hindu kingdom of Travancore, in the extreme south of the peninsula.—IX. The cluster of Rajput states, which make up the country known as Rajputana. The emperor had now quite lost his hold of this part of India, which had fallen under the domination of the Maratha chiefs; but the government had not been directly assumed by the latter, who were usually satisfied with levying contributions from the various states, leaving their princes more or less independent as regards their internal government, but devoid of political influence.

Carnatic.

Southern India.

Rajputana.

The affairs of the East India Company at the three settlements subordinate to them were administered at this time in each case by a President and Council, consisting of the senior agents (or, as they were called, merchants) of the Company, who received their instructions from the Court of Directors established in London. From this form of administration was derived the name of Presidency, applied to the territories of

Form of government of early British settlements.

CHAP. III.

which the President and Council in course of time obtained the government.

Hostilities between English and French settlers on Coromandel Coast.

At first, however, as has been stated, the British, as represented by the East India Company, held no Indian territory in their own right, with the exception of the island of Bombay; they occupied their factories merely as tenants holding at pleasure of the native powers, and these settlements consisted of only a few acres of ground covered by their warehouses and residences. This status continued until the year 1746, up to which time the British were of no political importance in India. In this year the war which had broken out between England and France extended to India, and the French settlers on the coast of the Carnatic raising forces with a view to drive the English out of the country, the latter, in self-defence, were obliged to enlist troops and engage in active hostilities. The result of the conflict was, on the whole, very unfavourable to the English arms, and the settlement of Madras was captured almost at the outset; but it was restored in 1749, on the news arriving in India of the Peace of Aix-la-Chapelle. The cessation of hostilities was however of but short duration. The death of the first Nizam, the Subahdar of the Dekhan, about this time, was the occasion for one of those struggles for the sovereignty of a vacant throne which were an ordinary condition of Indian politics, while simultaneously the subordinate kingdom of the Carnatic was also contended for by rival claimants. The English and French, espousing opposite sides, thereon entered actively into Indian politics, and at this period interest in the history of British India centres in the Madras Presidency, where these two nations, gradually ousting the native powers from the first rank in influence and importance, struggled against each other with varying success, and little intermission of hostilities, until the year 1756. Up to this time the two nations were ostensibly at peace in the East as well

They engage in politics of Dekhan.

as in the West; but on the breaking out of the Seven Years' War the directing influence of Pitt was extended to the contest on the Coromandel Coast, and the English, whose efforts were now directed by Lawrence and Clive, rapidly gained the ascendency. The power of the French in the Carnatic was finally broken, and their capital Pondicherry captured in 1761.

Overthrow of the French.

In 1756 occurred the tragedy of the Black Hole at Calcutta. This event led to the despatch of troops from Madras—where a considerable military establishment was now maintained—to succour the remnant of the Company's settlers in Bengal, who were hiding from the fury of the Nawab-Nazim, or Viceroy of that province, in the pestiferous swamps at the mouth of the Hugli. The reinforcements were commanded by Clive, who had already attained a high military reputation. Clive landed in Bengal in February 1757, and on the 23rd June was fought the Battle of Plassey, which drove the Nawab from his throne, and made the English virtually masters of his dominions.

Conquest of Bengal.

Thus, at one step, the English establishments in Bengal attained to a greater importance than had been as yet acquired by those of the Madras Presidency after many years of military operations on a considerable scale, while the political situation in the former country was already stronger and more secure. The territories garrisoned by the army which Clive hastened to construct in Bengal were also greatly more valuable than those occupied by the British in the South of India. The Nawab, whom they elevated to the throne in the place of Siraj-ud-daula, was a mere creature of the British; while, on the only quarter from which invasion was practicable—the north-west frontier—the emperor was too busily engaged in an attempt to regain his authority in his own provinces, to concern himself with affairs in Bengal. In Madras, on the other hand, although the English army was the most powerful military body afoot,

Comparative results of operations in Bengal and Carnatic.

CHAP. III.

the British ascendency was never unquestioned, and was at times hotly contested. The Nawab of the Carnatic was indeed little more than a puppet in their hands; but the Nizam, though generally friendly, was up to this time entirely independent; and on the west, the rising power of Haidar Ali, who had now almost become master of Mysore, foreboded the coming struggle which brought disaster to the British arms under the walls of Madras, and wellnigh extinguished their footing in Southern India.

Political status of English.

The political situation was however very similar in both places. The British, as the allies of the Nawab of the Carnatic, garrisoned his territories, the expenses of their troops being defrayed by him; the emoluments of the leading officials at the Presidency were mainly derived from the same source. In Bengal, also, the Company's troops occupied the Nawab-Nazim's territories, and fought his battles, funds being obtained in a similar way, donations granted by him as the price of sovereignty. In neither case did the Company, in the first instance, themselves govern the country, or draw its revenues directly. Their income was nominally derived from trade; the emoluments of their servants in India proceeded mainly from the same source, but were eked out by presents and bribes. The first territorial possession obtained in Bengal was the district lying south of Calcutta, termed the 24-Pergunnahs (or sub-districts), comprising about 1,200 square miles, which was assigned as an estate to the British in 1757 by the Nawab-Nazim whom they had placed on the throne of Bengal. The rent paid for the estate was presented by the Nawab to Clive, and by him eventually transferred to the Company, who thus became virtually proprietors as well as renters of the district. In the year 1760, the Nawab being in arrears in payment of the annual stipend due to the Company—the price of their support—was compelled to cede the revenues of the three

First acquisition of territory: the 24-Pergunnahs,

followed by Burdwan, Midnapur, and Chittagong.

rich districts of Burdwan, Midnapur, and Chittagong, situated in Lower Bengal, the collection of which was undertaken by English officials. The Nawab-Nazim was, however, still recognised as sovereign in these districts, as well as in the rest of the province, the Company holding their lands under him, and the civil jurisdiction of the country being exercised by his officers.

The Government of the Nawab-Nazim of Bengal overthrown.

This state of things lasted for eight years after the Battle of Plassey, when an important change took place in the state of affairs. In 1760 the English had fallen out with Mir Jafar, the Nawab whom they had set up after Plassey, and had deposed him, and placed his son-in-law, Mir Kasim, on the throne. Three years afterwards the disputes which had arisen between Mir Kasim and his supporters, almost from the date of his elevation, culminated in war, and the English replaced Mir Jafar in the government. Mir Kasim invoked the aid of the emperor, whose deputy he nominally was, and of the Nawab-Wazir of Oudh; but their united forces were finally completely overthrown by the English, and driven out of the province. On this the Emperor and the Nawab-Wazir abandoned the cause of Mir Kasim, and sued for peace. While negotiations were pending Clive returned to Bengal to assume the government a second time, and took charge of the negotiations, which ended in the grant (by the emperor) to the English of the revenues of Bengal, Behar, and Orissa,[1] the provinces which together make up the country known as Bengal. Thus, at one stride, the English stepped into the position of a sovereign power in India; for although they nominally held the country as deputy of the emperor, and in consideration of payment of an annual tribute, the emperor was, in fact, a suppliant for mercy. A few

The Emperor confers the government of Bengal on the English.

[1] The province here referred to as Orissa comprehended at this time only a small part of the country properly known by that name. Cuttack and the hilly country to the north and west of it had passed into the hands of the Marathas some years before, and the Orissa of which the dewani was now transferred to the English comprised little more than the present district of Midnapur.

CHAP. III.

years later, the provinces remaining under his direct administration were taken possession of by the Nawab-Wazir of Oudh, and he himself became a prisoner in the hands of the Marathas, when the English ceased payment of the tribute. In 1765 Mir Jafar died, and the English placed another son-in-law on the throne of Bengal, who agreed as the price of his elevation to surrender all share of the government, receiving merely the rank of Nawab and a fixed annual stipend. The English had already undertaken the military defence of the country; they were therefore now its entire masters; but the government was not openly assumed and undertaken in their name until 1772, when the provincial treasury was removed from Murshedabad to Calcutta, and British officials were established throughout the different districts, to undertake the collection of the revenue, and to superintend the native officials in the business of administration. It may be added that this, the first, was also the most valuable acquisition ever made in India.

Importance of the acquisition.

The territory ceded in 1765 not only exceeds greatly, both in extent and population, each of the Presidencies of Madras and Bombay, as at present constituted: it contains the most industrious and peaceful races in India, and the most fruitful soil; while the network of navigable rivers with which it is intersected supplies the means for conducting an extensive commerce, which has only been provided a century later, in a partial and imperfect way, in other parts.

Territorial acquisitions in Carnatic:

While this great development of British power in Bengal was taking place, the Presidency of Madras was also acquiring territorial possessions. In 1758, Clive detached a brigade of the newly raised Bengal army to the east coast, to aid the Madras Government in its struggles with the French; and in the following year, the fort of Masulipatam was captured from that nation, when the district immediately adjacent to it was conferred by the Nizam-ul-Mulk on the English, in consideration of the aid given in maintaining his claim to the sovereignty of the Dekhan. In 1765, the Nawab of the Carnatic granted to the Company the revenues of the country surrounding Madras, now known as the district of Chingleput, in return for services rendered; but the Madras Council farmed the estate on lease to the Nawab himself, and did not enter on the direct management of it until fifteen years later.

Masulipatam, district of Madras,

Northern Circars.

In the same year when Clive obtained the grant of Bengal from the emperor, he also secured the gift of the maritime province known as the Northern Circars—comprising the present five districts of Guntur, Masulipatam, Rajahmundry, Vizagapatam, and Ganjam—which he made over to the President and Council of Madras to take possession of. The latter, however, about this time, disregarding the gift of the emperor, applied for and obtained the same grant from the Nizam. The first Nizam having been the emperor's lieutenant, and nominally holding his subahdari at the emperor's pleasure, the assent of his descendant might in strictness have been deemed unnecessary; but all allegiance to the emperor on the part of the ruler of the Dekhan had been now cast off, and the confused state of Indian politics at this period rendered it impossible to determine the conditions which constituted a sound title. Practically, the conveyance of territory depended solely on power and convenience, and the Madras authorities naturally looked to the ruler with whom they came directly in contact, and who possessed the means of active interference, for establishment of their claim. Treaties such as that made with the emperor carried with them a certain degree of moral force; but it was more convenient for the President and Council to found their claim to these Northern Circars on the gift of the Nizam than on that of the emperor. In effect, the result of their proceeding was a delay of a few months in the establishment of their title to this territory; the Guntur Circar, which

CHAP. III.

had been granted by the Nizam to his brother for life, did not lapse to the English until some years later.

Change in the form of Indian government.

The next important change which bears on the subject of this work occurred in 1773. Up to this time, the administration of each settlement or Presidency had been of the same form, and was vested in a Council of the senior civil servants of the Company, varying in number, but usually from twelve to sixteen. The senior presided, and the proceedings were decided by a majority of votes, but as many of the councillors held also offices which required them to reside in the interior, the whole number was seldom present. So long as the ostensible business to be conducted consisted of trading operations, a Board composed of the traders—or merchants as they were termed—in the service of the Company, was a suitable agency for conducting that business; while, as the requirements needed were, mainly, probity and zeal in the interests of their masters—qualities which however were not always exhibited—seniority was as good a basis for selection as any other. But now that the Company had become a sovereign power, wielding a considerable army, and exercising extensive administrative functions, a Board of twelve or sixteen, the members of which were constantly changing, became an altogether unsuitable instrument for performing the functions of government. As, however, has usually happened throughout the history of the East India Company, the reform was not initiated by that body, or carried out by its own desires, but was forced on it by pressure from without. The enormous fortunes suddenly amassed by the Company's officers; the mutual recriminations between masters and servants, and between the members of the service themselves, as to the shares to be respectively taken in the nefarious practices on which this wealth was based, extending from the region of pamphleteers to the walls of Parliament; the conspicuous position occupied, from their wealth, by the Company's

Defects of the then existing form.

civil and military officers on their return to England, and the parliamentary influence they were able to exert; the public excitement occasioned by Clive's astonishing career, and by the renown attending British conquests in the East:—all these circumstances combined to create an interest in Indian affairs, perhaps even greater than has ever been since exhibited, if we except the episode of Warren Hastings's trial. The result was that a laborious investigation into them was undertaken by a Select Committee of the House of Commons, whose report was speedily followed up by legislation.

Act of 1773.

Heretofore the legal status of the Company had been based on a Royal Charter granted in the year 1698, which gave them authority to exercise civil and criminal jurisdiction at their settlements, and to maintain troops for their defence. By an Act of Parliament passed in 1767, the teritorial acquisitions lately obtained in India were vested in the Company for two years, and an Act of 1769 confirmed them in these possessions for a further space of five years, but neither Act altered in any way the mode of administration in force. The Act of 1773,[1] which may be regarded as the basis of all subsequent legislation for determining the form of Indian government, is the first statute which distinctly recognises the Company as fulfilling other functions than those of trade. It was, however, directed principally to the administration of Bengal. In lieu of the numerous Board, with its frequently changing President, a Governor General of Bengal was appointed, with a Council of four members, all of whom were named in the Act, which provided that they should not be liable to displacement for a term of five years. All future appointments of Governor Generals and Councillors were vested in the Court of Directors, and were to be made for a similar term—the Court however being allowed a power of recall. The Presidency of Bengal

Governor General and Council appointed for Bengal;

[1] 13 Geo. III., Cap. lxiii.

CHAP. III.

was defined in the Act to be 'all the territorial Acquisitions and Revenues [of the Company] in the kingdoms of Bengal, Behar, and Orissa,' and the powers of government in these were 'vested in the Governor General and Council of the said Presidency, in like manner as the same now are, or at any time heretofore might have been exercised by the President and Council or Select Committee in the said kingdoms.' Here, then, we have the first definition of a Presidency, in the new sense which now came to be applied to the name, while the fact is also for the first time distinctly recognised, that the British, as represented by the Company, were holding possession of 'kingdoms' in the East. The right of the Company to wage war had been previously so far admitted that they had been empowered by the Charter of 1698 to raise troops for the defence of their settlements, a power which was renewed by a Charter granted in 1753; while a King's regiment (the 39th Foot) had been sent to India in 1756. But this regiment, although it was an active agent, by its share in the Battle of Plassey, in the Company's conquest of Bengal, was despatched to India in order to oppose the French troops; and the 79th Foot, which shortly followed it, was sent out with the same object. That the Company should itself be competent to wage war, even with the French, was up to this time not specifically recognised by either Charter or Act of Parliament.

and vested with control over other Presidencies.

The Act of 1773 refers to the two other Presidencies only obliquely. It provided that the Governor General and Council of Bengal, or the major part of them, should have the power of superintending and controlling the management and government of the Presidencies of Madras, Bombay [and Bencoolen [1]], so far that the President and Council of those Presidencies were not to make war or negotiate treaties 'without consent and approbation of the said Governor General

[1] A settlement in the island of Sumatra, ceded to the Dutch in 1825.

and Council first had and obtained,' except in case of imminent necessity, or of their having received special orders from the Court of Directors. They are also required 'constantly and diligently to transmit advice and intelligence to the Governor General and Council of Bengal,' of 'all transactions and matters whatsoever relating to the government, revenues, or interest of the said United Company.' In other respects the administration of the two other Presidencies was not interfered with. They continued to be governed by a President and Council, usually composed of the senior civil servants, but the practice arose about this time for the Court to nominate and send the President out from England. The Governor General appointed to Bengal under the Act of 1773 was Warren Hastings, a civil servant of the Company, and at the time President of the Council.

Events of Hastings's administration.

Under the rule of Hastings and his Council, the Bengal Presidency was extended by the addition of the zemindari (or estate), as it was termed, of Benares, comprising the present large and populous districts of Mirzapur, Benares, and Ghazipur. The Raja of Benares, whose father had obtained that title from the emperor, was a vassal (if the term may be appropriately employed) of the Nawab-Wazir of Oudh, whose dominions at this time extended far beyond the province now known under that name, and who, having become independent of the emperor, had converted his vice-royalty into an hereditary monarchy. The Raja held his territories on condition of furnishing an annual tribute to the Nawab-Wazir, and exercised full criminal and civil powers within them, but had no independent relations with other states. A similar arrangement was established by Clive in 1765, and maintained until 1774, when, in connection with engagements entered into between the Nawab and the British, the allegiance and tribute of the Raja were transferred to the latter. In 1781, the Raja having been driven into rebellion by the

Annexation of Benares.

CHAP. III.

hard treatment to which he was exposed by the Governor General, his territory was confiscated to the British Government. This was the only annexation made to the Bengal Presidency during Hastings's administration, but that period was distinguished by a great advance in the military and political position of the British. In virtue of an agreement made with the Nawab-Wazir of Oudh, they undertook the protection of his territories against the Marathas; and the cantonments of the Bengal army were advanced from Benares to Cawnpur and Fatehghar, where a strong brigade was now permanently stationed. The year 1779 was made memorable by the despatch of a military force from the Bengal army across the peninsula, to aid the Bombay Presidency in its struggle with the Marathas—a remarkable feat when the circumstances of the times are considered. It was during Hastings's presidentship, but before his appointment as Governor General, that the direct government of Bengal was assumed by the English.

Advance of British garrisons.

Bengal Army co-operates in Maratha war.

Defects in Act of 1773.

The events of Hastings's stormy administration brought prominently into view the defects in the form of the Indian Government, as constituted by the Act of 1773. A government by a majority of a council, the members of which were constantly changing; in which the Governor General was supreme one day, and outvoted the next, and his most important measures thwarted and upset—such a system could only work at all under an able and strong-willed President; with what difficulty it was carried on even under those conditions, the well-known history of that period plainly showed. Another very grave defect consisted in the ill-defined character of the relations subsisting between the Governments of the different Presidencies. The Act did indeed confer a controlling authority on the Governor General and his Council in matters of peace and war, and it required the authorities of the other Presidencies to report to the Bengal Government all proceedings requiring to be made known. But it was left to them to determine what proceedings came under these conditions. So long as each Presidency was an isolated settlement, occupied only with local politics, the necessity for some central authority to control all diplomatic and military operations might not arise; but the Maratha empire, which had by this time reached its zenith, was now in direct contact with the territories possessed or defended by the Bombay and Bengal Governments, while it was in a position to assert a potent influence over the politics of Southern India. And in the Maratha War of 1775–82, already referred to, the evils of divided counsels became glaringly apparent. The Bombay Government first made a treaty, which the Bengal Government disallowed, and superseded by a separate agreement directly between themselves and the Marathas. Hardly had this been signed, when it was upset by the arrival of despatches from the Court of Directors approving of the arrangements made by the Bombay Government; whereon the latter re-entered at once upon negotiations directly with the Maratha chiefs, in disregard of the instructions received from Bengal And during the subsequent operations, the commander of the Bengal column employed at Bombay acted throughout in almost entire independence of the Government of that Presidency. Not the worst feature in the complications arising out of this conflict of authority was the appearance of bad faith thus cast over the dealings of the English with the native powers. This, combined with the actual political immorality too often exhibited by the British at this time, placed their conduct on some occasions in hardly a more favourable light than was presented by the contemporary native states.

Act of 1784.

But notwithstanding that, during the previous ten years, the vices inherent in the constitution of the Indian Government had been thus brought prominently

CHAP. III.

to notice, the next parliamentary legislation on the subject was far from supplying an adequate remedy. Pitt's India Bill,[1] passed in 1784, was principally directed to the provision of a machinery which should enable the Ministry to control the proceedings of the Company. Up to this time the Government of the Crown had but imperfect means of access to the records of the Company's transactions. Investigation into their affairs could in practice only be conducted by appointing special commissions or parliamentary committees from time to time, and control would be necessarily limited to impeachment, or the negativing of their proceedings by special Acts of Parliament—measures, however, which the Government had not ever employed. The Bill of 1784 accordingly provided a remedy for these inconveniences by establishing a Board of Commissioners, who formed a part of the Ministry, and who, besides being furnished with access to the whole records of the Company, were vested with a power of veto over all the proceedings of the Directors, and of framing orders to the authorities in India, which the Directors were bound to adopt unaltered, and to transmit as if emanating from themselves. By the establishment of this Board of Control, the Home Government of India nominally passed from the Company to the Crown. But the establishment of the Board was framed on a limited scale, while that of the Court of Directors continued undiminished. The Directors were still vested with the management of the Company's trade, with the patronage of first appointments to the civil and military services, and the nomination of, and power of recalling, the different Governors and Commanders-in-Chief, while the initiation of all business virtually remained with them. And since in every department of affairs a large part of the authority must necessarily rest with the party which

Changes in form of Home Government.

[1] 24 Geo. III., Cap. xxv.

initiates proposals, because the mere power of veto and control cannot in practice be constantly applied, the change virtually effected by the Act was by no means so great as would appear to have been intended; at any rate, the amount of power which the Court continued to exercise was sufficient to justify in great measure the popular opinion, which always continued to identify them with the Home Government of India.

and of Indian Governments.

With respect to the executive administration in India, the Act of 1784 created statutory governments of a Governor and Council for the 'Presidencies and Settlements' of Fort St. George (Madras) and Bombay. The nomination to all these appointments was vested in the Court of Directors. By the same Act the powers of the Bengal Government over the other Presidencies were somewhat extended. The Governor General and Council of Fort William were 'to control and direct the several Presidencies now or hereafter to be established in the East Indies, in all such points as relate to any transactions with the country powers, or to war or peace, or to the application of the revenues or forces of such Presidencies in time of war, or any such other points as shall from time to time be specially referred by the Court of Directors of the said Company to their superintendence and control;' whereas the Act of 1773 confined their power of interference to matters of war and negotiation with native states, and gave no authority to control the war expenditure of the other Presidencies. Further, the Bengal Government were vested with power to suspend presidents and councillors of the other Presidencies disobeying them, and the Governments of the latter were required to send them all needful information on matters of import, and were prohibited from making war or treaties independently.

This power of suspension apparently gave the Bengal Government the complete control contemplated

CHAP. III.

over the two other and now subordinate Presidencies, but an obstacle remained which legislation could not overcome. So long as communication between the different capital towns continued to be tardy and infrequent—carried on by means either of a difficult and often dangerous journey, through roadless and robber-haunted tracts, or of a tedious and uncertain voyage—great independence of action necessarily remained with the different local authorities in every part of India. The Court of Directors possessed, by law, complete power of control over the proceedings of the Governor General, yet they were practically quite powerless to enforce their own views on his policy; and almost every war and conquest made in India were carried out in opposition to, and often in direct defiance of, the orders from England.

Insufficiency of change.

Mr. Pitt's celebrated Bill further left unremedied the grave defect that the executive control of the Bengal Government was vested in the majority of a constantly changing Council. Hastings, who left India in the beginning of 1785, had succeeded by force of character and ability in eventually obtaining the supremacy, but not before the passions evoked in the council-chamber had vibrated throughout all parts of his administration; and under the feeble rule of his successor, Mr. Macpherson (who owed his appointment to the accident of seniority), the evils of divided counsels became again apparent in the vacillating measures of the Government. On the appointment, however, of Lord Cornwallis to the Governor-Generalship, in 1786, he made it a condition of accepting the post, that the Governor General should be vested with the power of overriding his Council. This provision was accordingly established by an Act of Parliament[1] passed for the purpose, which declares that this power may be exercised in extraordinary cases, making certain provisions

Appointment of Lord Cornwallis.

Act of 1786.

[1] 26 George III. Cap. xvi.

for the previous interchange of written explanations between the different members of the Council. But it was left to the Governor General to determine what matters should be deemed to be extraordinary, and the practical result of the measure was to render the power of the Governor General supreme. The councillors subsided from the position of active members of an executive board into the subordinate one of witnessing and occasionally advising on the proceedings of their president, a state of things which remained in force until within the last few years. The same Act conferred similar powers on the presidents or governors at Madras and Bombay. It also provided that no persons should be appointed to the Councils, other than the Commander-in-Chief, who had not been twelve years resident in India in the civil service.

War with Mysore.

Heretofore each Presidency had maintained diplomatic relations with the neighbouring native states—the authorities at Bombay negotiating with the Maratha ministers at Poona, and those of Madras with the Nizam and the states of Southern India; but from the date of Lord Cornwallis's arrival in the country the management of all important diplomatic relations passed into the hands of the Governor General, as was contemplated by the Acts of 1784 and 1786, and the British agents stationed at the Courts of Poona and Hyderabad henceforward received their instructions direct from the Bengal Government. The direction of military affairs soon followed the same course. The war with Tipu, the ruler of Mysore, son of Haidar Ali, broke out in 1790, and was conducted in the first instance by the Government of Madras; but the Governor General—who also held the commission of Commander-in-Chief in India, under the authority of the Act of Parliament of 1786—being dissatisfied with the manner in which the operations were carried on, and perceiving that it was impossible to control affairs

CHAP. III.

properly from Calcutta, went to Madras, and assumed charge himself of the military and diplomatic operations in that quarter. He landed at Madras at the end of the year, and the war, although chequered with some reverses at first, was brought to a successful conclusion in the early part of 1792, when Tipu was compelled to sue for peace under the walls of Seringapatam. The territory which he was required to cede on this occasion comprised the present collectorates or districts of Malabar and Salem, and part of the district of Madura. Malabar was placed under the Bombay Presidency in the first instance, but was transferred to Madras in 1800; the other cessions were at once placed under the jurisdiction of the latter. A civil administration was organised for them, composed of British officials.

The treaty with Tipu was made in person by Lord Cornwallis. But although the Act of Parliament of 1786 gave him power to overrule his Council, it did not empower him to act without it. The Act throughout defines the Governor General *and* Council to constitute the Government; consequently the proceedings conducted by Lord Cornwallis alone were, strictly speaking, invalid. An Act of Parliament was accordingly passed, in 1791, confirming the special powers the Council had provisionally conferred on him to act without them, until three months after termination of the war. Later Acts have made this power general.

Administrative reforms of Lord Cornwallis.

Still more important than territorial acquisitions and political changes were the administrative reforms which signalised the rule of Lord Cornwallis. The authority of the Nawab-Nazim of Bengal had been avowedly replaced by that of the English in the year 1772; but the duties of the English district officials had as yet been mainly directed to the collection of the revenue; the administration of civil and criminal justice continued to be conducted by native agency, imperfectly supervised by European officers. This native agency was at the time notoriously inefficient and corrupt, and Lord Cornwallis substituted for it a system of administration directly by European officers, of a kind which has ever since been maintained. The establishment of definite laws and procedure for the guidance of the courts of justice and the information of the people; the creation of those courts, with their defined graduated powers, and provisions for the conduct of appeals; the hierarchy of district and controlling officers—the magistrate, collector, and judge, and the superior boards for the general management of the revenues; all these were his creation; while the new organisation of the army, although not actually carried out until he had left the country, was the effect of his recommendations. Up to this time the military officers of the Company's army, besides being ineligible for promotion to high rank, and liable to constant supersession by those of the royal service, were otherwise on a most unsatisfactory footing, promotion running in one unwieldy list for the whole of each army; while the effect of the extreme disproportion between the number of the junior and senior grades was only mitigated by the high rate of mortality caused by the unhealthy climate, and aggravated by the dissipated habits of the period. The best commentary on the measures introduced by Lord Cornwallis is to be found in their stability. The army organisation of 1796 lasted, without material change, until the abolition of the Company's system in 1861; while, as regards civil affairs, one country after another has been annexed, until the British territories in India comprise a vast empire; but the administrative system throughout the country, introduced in turn into each conquered province, has been based on the Cornwallis type, and until the time of Lord Canning every branch of the administration bore the impress of his policy.

But the greatest of his reforms was that effected in

CHAP. III. the character of the Indian public service, which, when Lord Cornwallis left India, was already well advanced on the road to that reputation for integrity which it has ever since maintained, standing henceforward second to none in the world. This great and rapid reform was effected partly by the example of his own pure character, but mainly by the establishment of a highly liberal system of remuneration, in lieu of the pittances in the way of pay heretofore allowed to all classes, and which afforded the recipients no alternative between poverty and dishonesty. This great measure, without which decent government of India was impossible, was carried out in the space of a few months. When we bear in mind the difficulty that is generally experienced in making not only any organic change in a public service, but in effecting even the slight modifications of practice called for by the progress of time, we may estimate properly the force of character possessed by Lord Cornwallis, which enabled him to carry out his great measures against the traditionary prejudices of his masters. The fact seems to be that, in view of his simple-mindedness and unaffected manners, his great capacity and high administrative powers have not been always sufficiently appreciated. The revenue settlement of Bengal established by him may have been faulty, viewed by present lights, but, considered with reference to the loose and crude system which it replaced, it bears a very different aspect. And if the Bengal Regulations of 1793 err on the side of over-complexity, in prescribing too tedious and refined a procedure of the courts of law, their introduction constituted an improvement of exceeding value on the chaotic state of confusion, and the total absence of method and defined responsibility, which marked the course of Indian administration before his advent.

The weakest point of the polity established by Lord Cornwallis is to be found in the systematic exclusion which it enforced of the natives of the country from all share in the administration. Whether he considered it hopeless to attempt a purification of the native service, cannot be said; but while the hitherto insufficient emoluments of the European officials were enormously raised, in order (to use his own words) 'to put them beyond the reach of temptation,' the remedy adopted as regards the inefficiency of the natives was, as far as possible, to dispense with their services altogether in offices of importance; nor was any attempt made to elevate the condition of the classes retained for subordinate posts, either by improved pay or prospects of preferment.

This part of his measures was, unfortunately, only too steadily persisted in; and it is not until within the last few years that the impolicy and injustice of thus excluding the natives of the country from all but the humblest share in the administration have at last been recognised and in part remedied. But it is easy to be wise after the event; nor is it reasonable to suppose that Cornwallis would have left this blot permanently to deface his measures, had he continued to preside over them. On the contrary, from the freedom he displayed in building up, it may fairly be presumed that he would have been the first to alter what further experience showed to be defective.

Renewal of Company's Charter.

Act of 1793.

To resume our narrative. The Charter granted to the Company by the Act of 1773, expired in 1793, when it was renewed for another term of twenty years. The principal new provisions of the Act of renewal[1] will be referred to later on.

Administration of Lord Wellesley.

The administration of Sir John Shore (afterwards Lord Teignmouth), who succeeded Lord Cornwallis, the last member of the Indian Service appointed to be Governor General until the time of Sir John Lawrence in 1863, was marked by no change of importance; and

[1] 33 George III., Cap. lii.

CHAP. III.

we may pass on to the eventful period of the Marquis Wellesley, under whose rule the political state of India underwent a complete change. The Act of Parliament of 1784 forbade the Indian Government from making war or even treaties with native powers, except for absolutely defensive purposes, without the sanction of the Home Government. It also forbade further annexations of territory, and the prohibition was repeated in the Act of 1793. With these conditions Lord Cornwallis, so far as was practicable, had complied. The war with Tipu was forced upon him by the aggressive conduct of that prince; hostilities having become necessary, they were pushed on with a degree of vigour new to Southern India, and the cessions of territory obtained from Tipu at the peace seemed necessary as a means of reducing his power for the future within safe limits. But except in this case Lord Cornwallis strove to maintain the balance of power, and always treated the Nizam and the Marathas as friendly allies, on a footing of equality with the English. The policy pursued by Lord Wellesley had, on the contrary, the distinct object of making British authority paramount throughout the country, and reducing the different native states to a position of complete dependence on it. The first war undertaken was indeed forced on him by the hostile attitude assumed by Tipu, whose power, though weakened by the previous contest, was not broken.

Conquest and partition of Mysore.

This war, which took place in 1799, ended in the conquest of the kingdom of Mysore. Of this a part was made over to our ally, the Nizam; the province of Mysore, as defined at the present day, was restored to the family of the former Hindu princes; the remainder was annexed to the British dominions. The territory so obtained comprised the present collectorates of Canara, on the west coast, Coimbatur, and the Wynaad and Nilgiri Hills; while, a few months later, the Nizam made over a part of his share, the present districts of

CHAP. III.

Bellary and Cuddapa, in payment for the subsidiary force, which ever since that time has maintained the authority of the Nizam in his kingdom.[1] The same year saw the annexation of the Hindu principality of Tanjore, the most fertile tract in Southern India. Finally, in 1801, the Nawab of the Carnatic—the nominal rulers of which had been for many years in a position of entire dependence on the British, and whose revenues were mortgaged beyond redemption to pay their military expenses—was required, as a condition of succeeding to the titular rank of Nawab, to resign his kingdom formally. This acquisition gave us the districts: of Nellore, in the north; North and South Arcot, in the centre; Trichinopoly and Tinnevelly, in the south of the peninsula. Thus, in a few months, the Madras Presidency was developed from a few scattered districts into the great province now known by that name, comprising the whole of Southern India with the exception of the province of Mysore and the small district of Coorg, which occupy the centre of the peninsula, and the Hindu principalities of Travancore and Cochin at the extreme south. Since that time the only territorial changes in this presidency have been the addition of the district of Karnul, in the north of the Presidency, annexed in 1841 on account of the treason of the ruling Nawab; and the transfer of the district of North Canara to the Bombay Presidency in 1862. The extent of the Madras Presidency was, therefore, nearly the same in the time of Lord Wellesley that it is now. The military establishment quartered in it was very much larger. It may be added that the Cornwallis system of Regulations was everywhere introduced, although a different settlement of the land revenue was made from that adopted in Bengal.

Annexation of Tanjore.

Cession of Carnatic,

and extension of Madras Presidency.

[1] This part of the country is still sometimes styled, by Madras officials, 'The Ceded Districts,' a term which might, with equal propriety, be applied to the greater part of India.

CHAP. III.

Cession of part of Nawab of Oudh's dominions.

The changes effected in the Bengal Presidency, in consequence of Lord Wellesley's successful wars, although relatively not so great, since the acquisitions of Clive still remained the largest and most important ever effected, were even more extensive and valuable than those in the Madras Presidency. In 1801 the Nawab-Wazir of Oudh—whose engagements with the British, entered into for the purpose of obtaining protection from the Marathas, had resulted in the establishment of embarrassing and complicated relations with his protectors—was compelled to cede the greater part of his kingdom, consisting of the lower part of the Gangetic Doab, comprising the present districts of Allahabad, Fatehpur, and Cawnpur; the country north of the Ganges, now divided into the Azimghar and Goruckpur districts; and the greater part of Rohilkhand, consisting of the districts of Bareilly, Moradabad, Bijnour, Budaon, and Shahjehanpur; a small portion of the province, less than an ordinary British district, being left to the Nawab of Rampur. The district of Farukhabad, held by a chieftain subordinate to the Nawab-Wazir of Oudh, was obtained shortly afterwards by cession of its ruler. The British territory in Northern India was thus bounded by the states of the great Maratha Confederation, which at this time reached its greatest limits, the territory subject to it extending from Malabar to the Himalaya. Sindhia, who was now the most powerful chief of the confederation, occupied the northern part of the empire, his territories bordering on the British frontier stations of Fatehghar and Moradabad He had possession of Delhi and the emperor's person, and a considerable tract of country to the west of that city was also under his authority.

Conquests from Marathas.

The great Maratha War broke out in 1803. In the war with Tipu of 1799, the operations had been dictated direct by Lord Wellesley, who proceeded to Madras for the purpose of being in immediate communication with the local Commander-in-Chief, and assumed charge for the time of the government of that presidency, in virtue of the authority conferred by the Act of 1793. On this occasion the Governor General remained at Calcutta, but the operations of the armies of the three Presidencies which took a share in the war, were all controlled from that place, the commanding generals receiving their instructions direct from the Governor General.

Of these armies, the two principal ones were—that under General Lake, the Commander-in-Chief in Bengal, which advanced from Cawnpur and Fatehghar; and the other under General Wellesley, composed of Madras and Bombay troops, which operated from Poona as a base. The first of these armies drove the Marathas out of the Gangetic Doab, captured Delhi and Agra, and finally compelled Sindhia to sue for peace, and to cede the whole of the territory occupied by him between the Ganges and Jumna, comprising the present districts of Etawa, Mynpuri, Allyghar, Bulandshahr, Meerut, Mazaffarnagar, and Saharanpur; the districts of Agra and Muttra, on the right bank of the Jumna; and the tract west of that river, known at that time as the Delhi territory, comprising the collectorates of Goorgaon, Delhi, Rohtak, Hansi, Sirsa, and Paniput. To these acquisitions must be added the collectorate of Banda, west of the Jumna, near its junction with the Ganges, and certain tracts in Bandelkhand, ceded by the Peshwa, as will be noticed presently. These conquests, with the districts ceded by the Nawab-Wazir of Oudh in 1801, and the province of Benares, acquired in 1781, make up the great territory known by the now inappropriate title of the North West Provinces, the most important and, next after Bengal, the most populous of the great provinces of British India. This newly acquired country was attached to the Presidency of Fort William, and administered by the Governor General and Council of

Formation of N.W. Provinces.

CHAP. III.

Bengal; but some years later, a separate Board of Revenue and Courts of Civil and Criminal Appeal were established for it, and located at Allahabad. The Bengal Regulations were applied to these territories, which were organised in districts, to the administration whereof the usual staff of covenanted civil servants was eventually appointed.

Conquest of Cuttack.

Simultaneously with the operations under General Lake, an expedition was despatched from Lower Bengal into the province of Cuttack, then belonging to the Raja of Berar, another chief of the Maratha confederacy, who was finally obliged to cede it. This province also was added to the Bengal Presidency. It is in fact a district of the country known as Orissa, inhabited by the Oriya-speaking race, of which the other part had become a British possession in the time of Clive. By this conquest the Madras and Bengal Presidencies were brought into contact with each other on the seacoast. But practically they continued to be, and still are, quite unconnected. Even in the present day no direct road connects Calcutta with Madras. The post is conveyed by a circuitous route which approaches Bombay, and the journeys of travellers between the two places are still mostly made by sea. Portions of what will eventually be a direct line of railway between Calcutta and Madras are now in course of slow construction.

Acquisitions in Western India.

The cession of Cuttack, and the terms generally obtained from the Marathas, were due, as is well known, as much to the victories obtained by the army under General Wellesley in Kandesh and Berar, as to the operations of the force under General Lake. The war in that quarter was ostensibly undertaken on behalf of the Peshwa, the nominal head of the Marathas, in view to relieve him from the oppression of the chief of the confederacy. The result of the war in this quarter was to transfer the charge of the Peshwa from Sindhia and Holkar to the British Government. His territories were occupied by the Bombay army, and a British resident or controlling minister was appointed to his capital, Poona. But the districts ceded by him in Western India, in return for these benefits, were shortly afterwards exchanged, in greater part, for the territory in Bandelkhand already referred to; and, with the exception of some lands in Gujarat, the Bombay Presidency still possessed no territorial possessions, the province of Malabar having been transferred to Madras.

These wars and the occupation of these territories involved a large addition to the military forces of the Company, and the native troops, even when reduced to a peace establishment at the conclusion of the war, were considerably in excess of their present strength. The Madras army especially, even including the increase of British troops maintained since the Mutiny, was then much larger than it is now. The civil service was also at this period largely extended, and the establishment of English covenanted servants of the Company now for the first time approached to its present strength. The large establishments of English officials serving in the various special departments of the Government are of a later growth.

Result of Lord Wellesley's administration.

The administration of Lord Wellesley may be regarded as the third great epoch in the formation of the British Indian Empire. The acquisition of Bengal, Behar, and Orissa was in a great measure accidental. The managers of the Company's affairs at that time, both in England and India, would have been quite satisfied with maintaining the state of things under which the Nawab-Nazim had the appearance, and they the reality, of power. That he should be driven to try conclusions with them was quite unexpected, and Clive, opportunely returning to India, discerned the advantage of the acquisition offered. The era of Lord Cornwallis was marked chiefly by administrative reforms, the terri-

CHAP. III.

torial extension effected by him having been comparatively small; while, as has been already observed, his foreign policy was directed to maintain the political status he found existing in India, and especially to cultivate friendly relations with the Marathas. Lord Wellesley was the first to perceive that in India a political equilibrium was impossible; that peace was only to be ensured by establishing the preponderance of British power; and that the task of breaking down the Maratha Confederacy, whose ravages had desolated some of the fairest tracts of the land, was as practicable as, sooner or later, it must have been necessary to be undertaken. The result of the contest, although it was signalised by some hard fighting, was never for a moment doubtful, and from this time the Company became beyond all question the paramount power in India, even the states which remained independent submitting to receive a supervising British agent at their courts, and a subsidiary garrison of British troops. Henceforward the only country which could measure swords against it with any chance of success lay beyond the Sutlej; and from this time it may be said that the duties of territorial government took the place of buying and selling as the leading pursuit of the Company's servants in India.

His policy reversed by successors.

This policy was worked out by Lord Wellesley, not under the guidance of, but in direct opposition to, the wishes of his masters in England. The Directors, although they had from the first carried on their trade at a loss, still clung to trade as the only means of squaring their balance-sheet, and regarded with distrust every addition of territory, as productive of debt and financial embarrassment. Very much the same view appears to have been held by the English ministry; while the question has been much debated, whether Lord Wellesley's measures were not so far voluntary, rather than forced upon him by circumstances, as to constitute an infraction of the Acts of Parliament of 1784 and 1793, which enjoined a defensive and neutral policy, and distinctly prohibited territorial aggrandisement. However that may have been, the course pursued by Lord Wellesley, once entered on, could not be retraced; but the Court notwithstanding vainly desired to return to the former state of non-intervention and political equality with the Maratha powers; and the influence of their sentiments so far affected the policy of Lord Wellesley's immediate successors, that the complete pacification of Central India contemplated by him, was suspended on the eve of its accomplishment, and deferred till twelve years later. The Maratha war of 1817–18 was the fruit of the timid policy of non-intervention pursued from 1805 until that time, and was forced on Lord Hastings's administration by the state of lawlessness which had grown up in Central India. The war resulted in the complete pacification of India. The Bombay Presidency as a territorial expression may be held to date from this time, the countries on the western side of India, then acquired from the Peshwa, Sindhia, and Holkar, being eventually placed under the Government of Bombay, which province thus became one of the great territorial divisions of the country. The formal procedure of the law-courts prescribed by the Bombay Regulations, which closely resembled those of Bengal, was introduced gradually into these provinces; but a large tract of country in the centre of India, near the source of the Narbada, ceded after the war by the Maratha government of Nagpur, was taken under the direct control of the Governor General in Council, and styled the 'Saugor and Nerbudda Territories.' It was at first placed in executive charge of a Political Agent with a staff of assistants, subsequently of a Commissioner, with a Deputy Commissioner and Assistants to each district, chiefly military officers. This province was not brought

Maratha war of 1817–18.

Extension of Bombay Presidency.

Territory acquired in Central India,

CHAP. III.

under the Bengal Regulations, but the officials were enjoined to conduct their procedure in accordance with the spirit of the Regulations, so far as they might be found suitable to the circumstances of the country and its backward state of civilisation. Other districts situated in Bengal had previously been exempted (by a special regulation) from the operation of regulation law, but this is the first case of what afterwards was frequently repeated, the deliberate formation of what became known as a 'non-regulation' province.

and in Himalaya.

In addition to these acquisitions, Lord Hastings's administration was also signalised by the gain of a tract of country in the Himalaya from the Nepalese, ceded in 1815, at the termination of the war with that people —a country more extensive than productive, but precious to the English in India from its beauty and healthfulness—that portion of the Himalaya which reaches from the mountain watershed of the Jumna to the present frontiers of Nepal, on the east extremity of Rohilkhand. This territory was also placed under a special Commissioner, and was not brought under the operation of the Regulations.

Company's Charter renewed. Act of 1813.

An Act of Parliament passed in 1813 [1] renewed the Company's Charter for a further term of twenty years.

Burmese war of 1824: conquest of Assam, Arracan, and Tenasserim.

The next event to be recorded is the Burmese war of 1824, which resulted in the acquisition of the country called Assam—the valley of the great river Brahmaputra on the north-east of Bengal; the maritime province of Arracan, at the head of the Bay of Bengal; and the province of Tenasserim, a narrow strip of land on the lower shore of that bay. Assam and Arracan were attached to the Bengal Presidency, so far that they were administered by the Governor General in Council, and that the local officers were placed under the supervision of the Board of Revenue and Appellate Court at Calcutta; but since the people of these sparsely

[1] 53 George III., Cap. clv.

inhabited tracts differ in language and customs from the Bengalese, and those of Arracan in religion also, and the countries were not rich enough to bear the expense of the ordinary system of administration, they were not brought under the Regulations, but they were provided each with a special staff, mainly of military officers.[1] The Tenasserim province was dealt with in a similar way, but the garrison for it was furnished from the Madras army.

Further renewal of Charter. Act of 1833.

In 1833 the Charter of the Company again expired, and another Act of Parliament was passed, renewing it for a further term of twenty years.[2] By this Act the Company's functions as traders were abolished, and several changes were made in the form of government, of which the following are the most important:—

Subdivision of Bengal Presidency.

I. The fact that the Presidency of Fort William had far outgrown manageable dimensions was then for the first time recognised; and the Act provided for its division into two separate presidencies—one to be styled the Presidency of Fort William in Bengal, the other the Presidency of Agra. A separate Governor was to be appointed for the latter, on the same footing as the Governors of Madras and Bombay.

Governor General of Bengal becomes Governor General of India.

II. Instead of, as heretofore, vesting the Governor General in Council *of Bengal* with a power of general control over the Governments of the other Presidencies, the new Act provided, that 'The superintendence, direction, and control of the whole civil and military government of all the said territories and revenues in India shall be, and is hereby vested in a Governor General and Councillors, to be styled the Governor General *of India* in Council.'

III. The power of making laws and regulations for their Presidencies was withdrawn from the Govern-

[1] The administrative staff of the 'non-regulation' territories was furnished by the army in the absence of a sufficient supply of civil servants. The salaries were fixed on a lower scale than obtained in the regulation districts.

[2] 3 & 4 William IV., Cap. lxxxv.

CHAP. III.

ments of Madras and Bombay, and the duty of legislating for all India was placed on the Governor General in Council, subject to the usual power of veto exercised by the Court of Directors.

Increased control vested in Supreme Government.

IV. The control of the supreme government was asserted much more distinctly than in previous Acts. No Governor was to have power to create offices, or grant money, without the previous sanction of the Governor General of India in Council, who was invested 'with full power and authority to superintend and control the Governors and Governors in Council of Fort William in Bengal, Fort St. George, Bombay, and Agra, in all points relating to the civil and military administration of the said Presidencies respectively.' The latter were bound to obey all orders received from this authority, and to furnish periodically copies of all their orders and proceedings, and all other information called for. It is by means of the returns thus periodically supplied from this time forward, that the Supreme Government is now able to exert an efficient control over all Indian affairs.

Governor General empowered to act without Council.

V. The Governor General in Council could pass a law, from time to time, authorising the Governor General, when visiting any part of India, to exercise all the powers possessed by the Council collectively, except that of making laws and regulations; the Governor General, in such cases, was to nominate a member of the Council to be President of it during his absence, who would exercise his powers.

Special arrangement for Bengal Army and Civil Service.

VI. Although the Bengal Presidency was to be divided into two, the Bengal Army and Civil Service were not to be divided; and the Act recited that, for the purposes of the Mutiny Act, 'the Presidency of Fort William in Bengal shall be taken and deemed to comprise under and within it all the territories which, by or in virtue of this Act, shall be divided between the Presidencies of Fort William in Bengal and Agra respectively.'

CHAP. III.

Modifications proposed in Bill.

These and other important provisions of the Act of 1833 will be referred to again in the chapters which deal with the Governments of India and the different Provinces. The passage of the Bill through Parliament was vigorously opposed by the Court of Directors, mainly because it abolished the Company's power to trade, the idea being still tenaciously clung to that trade was a source of benefit to the Company, and some of the most experienced members of the Court being strongly of opinion, that to throw it open to public enterprise would be injurious to the people of India—an opinion which carried more weight before than after the event. But, as regards the change in the form of Indian Governments, there were many who thought that the Bill of 1833 did not go far enough. The Governor General of that period, Lord William Bentinck, recorded his opinion that 'the local details pressing upon the time of the Supreme Government utterly preclude the performance of the higher and more important functions of its office,' and that the Governor General and his Council should be relieved from the executive administration of any one presidency—also that the Commander-in-Chief should be relieved from the direct charge of any particulur army. Sir Charles (afterwards Lord) Metcalfe, then a member of the Supreme Council, expressed the same opinion. Mr. Charles Grant (Lord Glenelg), the President of the Board of Control, drafted the scheme of his Bill very much according to Lord W. Bentinck's views, except that the Governor General was still to be Governor of Bengal. It was also intended that Councils should be abolished at the minor Presidencies; but at the recommendation of the Court their retention was left optional. Whilst the Bill was passing through Committee in the House of Commons, it was proposed that the Governor General should have two Lieutenant Governors under him for the Bengal Presidency, and another amendment was

CHAP. III.

moved that the Governor General should be relieved from the charge of any particular Presidency. But these amendments were lost.

Modifications carried out afterwards.

The creation of the fourth, or Presidency of Agra provided by the Act of 1833 was never carried out, the proposal of the Court of Directors, that a Lieutenant Governor should be appointed to the Agra[1] division of the Bengal Presidency, being accepted by the Board of Control, and legalised by an Act passed in 1835.[2] The country placed under the new Lieutenant Governor was styled the North West Provinces, an infelicitous term, always geographically incorrect, and rendered still more inappropriate by the subsequent conquest of Punjab. The government of Bengal, the remaining part of the Presidency of Fort William after the North West Provinces had thus been partially separated, was henceforward conducted by the Governor General alone, with an entirely separate establishment from that attached to the Government of India.

Considering the state of India at this time—that the three Presidencies were practically quite isolated, the means of communication with each other being very tardy and imperfect—it will probably be considered that the plan suggested by Lord William Bentinck and Sir Charles Metcalfe, that the supreme government in India should be concerned only in supervising the other governments, to be four in number, would have been premature. The state of Central India at that time did not admit of a central Government being placed there; while to have conducted the whole business arising between India and England by means of a supreme government, situated at Calcutta or anywhere else, would have been productive of extreme delay. Under

[1] The Appellate Courts and Board of Revenue of the Upper Provinces were moved from Allahabad to Agra about this time. The mutiny brought to light the political disadvantages of making Agra the capital, and Allahabad was again made the seat of government of the North West Provinces.

[2] 5 & 6 William IV. Cap. lii.

the state of things then obtaining it was far simpler and more convenient for the Governments of Madras and Bombay in regard to the greater part of their affairs to correspond directly with England; while, on the other hand, the amount of business coming up in those days from the four subordinate governments, would probably not have been sufficient fully to employ the central authority. But, as will be seen hereafter, the conditions of the case are now entirely altered. The difficulty of communication has disappeared; the number of separate administrations under the Supreme Government has risen from four to ten; the business of government in every department has enormously increased; the control of all the Indian armies is now exercised directly by the Government of India; while various causes, to be stated hereafter, combine to remove the differences of regulation and system which at that time militated against a general fusion of Indian administration under one head.

Further additions to British possessions.

The further additions made to the British Empire in India, from 1833 to the present time, may now be briefly stated.

Coorg;

In 1834 the small mountainous principality of Coorg, in Southern India, was annexed. The Commissioner who administered the affairs of the Raja of Mysore, the western part of which province adjoins it, was made Commissioner of Coorg also.

territory on the Sutlej;

So early as 1809 the British Government, under the administration of Lord Minto, had assumed the protection of the numerous petty Sikh states lying between the Jumna and the Sutlej, and brigades had been quartered at Ludiana and Ferozepur, on the left bank of the latter river, to protect them against the incursions of Runjit Singh, the ruler of Punjab. On the failure of heirs to some of these chieftains, their possessions, on their death, were deemed to have lapsed to the British Government, which thus became possessed, between the years 1836 and 1843, of part of the country now known as the

CHAP. III.

Cis-Sutlej States, comprising the districts of Thanesar, Amballa, Ludiana, and Ferozepur. This territory not attached to any presidency, but was placed under the Governor General's Agent who had charge of the diplomatic relations on this frontier, and the superintendence of the remaining protected chiefs.

Karnul;

In 1841 the Nawab of Karnul, in the north of the Madras Presidency, was discovered to be engaged in a plot for the subversion of our power. He was accordingly deposed, and Karnul now forms one of the districts of the Madras Presidency.

Sind.

In 1843 Sind was annexed. The non-regulation system was adopted for this province, which was eventually placed under the Government of Bombay.

Sikh war.

In 1845 the war with the Sikhs broke out. At its conclusion the British Government occupied Punjab, and appointed a Council of Regency, with a British officer, styled Resident, at the head, to conduct the government of the country on behalf of the Raja, a minor. That part of Punjab between the Sutlej and Beas, a tract of very fine country called the Jalandhar Doab, or Trans-Sutlej States, was however annexed, and placed in charge of a Commissioner, under the orders of the Resident at Lahore. In 1848 Punjab broke out into insurrection; the result of the war which followed was the annexation of the whole country. The province was not attached to any Presidency, but the direct control was assumed by the Governor General in Council, the executive government being vested at first in a Board of Administration of three members, and afterwards in a Chief Commissioner. The non-regulation system was adopted, with a mixed administrative staff of civilians and military officers.

Annexation of Trans-Sutlej territory.

Annexation of Punjab.

Second Burmese war. Cession of Pegu.

In 1852 occurred the second Burmese war, which was terminated by the cession of Pegu. Here also the non-regulation system was adopted, the province being put in charge of a Commissioner, who was placed directly under

CHAP. III.

the orders of the Government of India: the garrison of the province was supplied by the Madras army.

Further renewal of Charter. Act of 1853.

In 1853 the Charter of the Company was again renewed.[1] In anticipation of this event, Select Committees of Inquiry were appointed, in the previous year, from both Houses of Parliament, who examined a great number of witnesses, and collected an immense amount of evidence on the state of India. No detailed reports were drawn up by the Committees, but the evidence taken sufficiently indicated the nature of some of the changes which were desirable. Strong testimony was borne to the inconvenience and injustice to the people of Bengal, of the arrangement which placed that province directly under the Governor General. It was pointed out that not only did the vastly greater labour imposed on that personage of late years, in his capacity as head of the Supreme Government—arising out of the large additions of territory acquired, and the increase of business in every department of the administration—necessarily engross his whole time, or at any rate leave no leisure for adequate supervision of the separate affairs of this province; a still greater defect was the constant change of Bengal administrations. The necessity for their presence near the army and the frontier, during the wars which had prevailed almost without intermission since 1838, had made the Governor Generals, from the time of Lord Auckland, almost strangers to their capital; at most they had paid brief and unfrequent visits to it. During their absence the senior Member of Council acted as Governor of Bengal, under the provision of the Act of Parliament; and as the same person seldom remained senior Member of Council for many months, and the acting Governor was moreover displaced whenever the Governor General returned to Calcutta, the province of Bengal was thus constantly subject to a change of rulers; and the

Lieutenant Governor appointed for Bengal.

[1] 16 & 17 Vict., Cap. xcv.

CHAP. III.

government virtually fell into the hands of the Secretary, who might be an officer of small experience and at any rate was wholly irresponsible. The notoriously backward and neglected state of Bengal, particularly in regard to public works, and the inefficient state of the police, evidenced by the prevalence of gang robberies and other crimes, were pointed out as being a necessary consequence of this defective saperintendence. As to the form of government to be given to Bengal, the progress and vigorous administration apparent in the North West Provinces were cited as proof of the superiority of a system of undivided responsibility over government by a Council or Board, and a similar plan was recommended for the Lower Provinces. Whether this superiority was due to the particular form of government adopted for the North West Provinces, or to its being equipped with a responsible government of any form, will be discussed hereafter: it will suffice to observe here, that the case for a change of some sort was clearly made out, and the Act of 1853 provided that the Court of Directors might either appoint a Governor to Bengal, or authorise the Governor General in Council to appoint any servant of the Company of ten years' service in India to be Lieutenant Governor 'of such part of the territories under the Presidency of Fort William, in Bengal, as may not be under the Lieutenant Governor of the North West Provinces.' A Lieutenant Governor was accordingly appointed, whose seat of government was fixed at Calcutta.

Annexation of Nagpur.

In 1854 the Rajah of Nagpur died, without heirs, and his kingdom was deemed to have lapsed to the dominant power. The non-regulation system was introduced here also, under a Commissioner and staff of civilians and military men chosen from the three Presidencies. Nagpur had been already for many years garrisoned by Madras troops.

In 1856 the kingdom of Oudh was annexed to the

British dominions. The Punjab system of administration was introduced into this province, with a Chief Commissioner at the head, and a staff of officials taken from the civil service and army.

Annexation of Oudh.

Recent changes.

The following important territorial changes and additions have taken place since the great events of 1857:—

Transfer of Delhi Territory to Punjab.

I. The country formerly known as the Delhi Territory, up to the right bank of the Jumna, and including the city of Delhi and adjacent districts, was transferred from the North West Provinces to Punjab, and the Chief Commissioner of that province thus enlarged was made a Lieutenant Governor.[1]

Formation of Central Provinces;

II. A new territorial division, the Central Provinces, was created in 1861, by detaching the country known as the Saugor and Nerbudda Territories from the Government of the North West Provinces, and uniting it to the province of Nagpur; the amalgamated provinces were placed under a Chief Commissioner.

of British Burma.

III. In the same year the territories which had been ceded by the Court of Ava in 1825 and 1853, viz., Arracan, attached to the Government of Bengal; the province of Pegu, and the long maritime tract, on the east coast of the Bay of Bengal, called the Tenasserim and Martaban Provinces—heretofore under separate Commissioners, directly subordinate to the Government of India—inhabited by races of the Buddhist faith, speaking the Burmese language, were amalgamated into one province, styled British Burma, and placed under the administration of a Chief Commissioner.

Administration formed for Berar.

IV. In 1853 the Nizam ceded the province of Berar in perpetuity, in payment for the expense of the force maintained for his support, known as the Hyderabad Contingent, the contributions due to the British Govern-

[1] The first Chief Commissioner and first Lieutenant Governor of Punjab was Sir John (afterwards Lord) Lawrence, subsequently Governor General of India.

CHAP. III.

ment for keeping up which had fallen greatly into arrears. Berar is administered directly by a Commissioner, with the usual mixed staff of civil and military officers. This country, however, is held only in trust for the Nizam. The revenues and expenditure are accounted for separately from those of British India, and any surplus, after defraying all expenditure, including the cost of the contingent, is paid over to the Nizam. The Commissioner is under the immediate orders of the Resident at Hyderabad, who exercises a general superintendence over the affairs of the province.

Straits Settlements transferred to Colonial Office.

V. The settlements of Penang, Malacca, and Singapur, in the Malayan Archipelago—which, since their acquisition in the last century, had been deemed to be a part of British India, and garrisoned by Madras troops, with a Governor appointed by and reporting to the Governor General in Council—were transferred, in 1866, to the Colonial Office, the Indian officials and troops being withdrawn.

Assam constituted a separate Province.

VI. In 1874 the province of Assam was removed from the control of the Bengal Government and constituted a separate administration under a Chief Commissioner.

Mysore restored to native rule.

VII. The province of Mysore, on the overthrow of the usurping dynasty in 1799, had been restored by Lord Wellesley to the representative of the ancient line of Hindu princes; but in 1831 the continued misgovernment of that country led to the British authority assuming the direct administration. In 1881 the administration was again transferred to native rule, on the attainment of his majority by an adopted son of the late Maharaja. The Agent to the Governor General, who has replaced the Chief Commissioner in Mysore, continues to administer the adjacent small British province of Coorg.

Annexation of Upper Burma

VIII. In 1886 took place the annexation of Upper Burma. The amalgamated provinces of Upper and

Lower Burma, with the provinces of Arracan and Tenasserim, already united with the latter under the name of British Burma, now form the Chief Commissionership of Burma. CHAP. III.

IX. A new administration has been formed in recent years, extending for the most part over the table-land beyond the mountain range which forms the north-western boundary of India, west of the Indus and south of Punjab. The nucleus of this was the district of Quetta, first occupied in 1876 and purchased from the Khan of Khelat. To this were added certain districts acquired from Afghanistan in 1879 by the treaty of Gandamuck, while still later an adjacent extensive, but thinly peopled, country, owning no definite allegiance to any ruler, and the prey of robber tribes, has been brought under British rule. The administration was placed on the footing of a Chief Commissionership in 1887. Baluchistan.

In 1858 the government of India was transferred from the Company to the Crown.[1] In place of the Court of Directors and the Board of Control, the supervision of Indian affairs was vested in a Secretary of State, with a Council of fifteen members. Upon the creation of this body, the title of the Supreme Council of India was changed to that of Council of the Governor General. The subsequent changes made in the constitution of this Home Council of India and of the different governments in that country will be referred to more particularly in later chapters of this work. Transfer of government from Company to Crown. Act of 1858.

Having thus followed the course of the development of English rule throughout the country, it may now be useful to recapitulate the territorial divisions into which British India has for administrative purposes been divided. Provinces of British India recapitulated.

I. The Presidency of Fort William in Bengal has, Bengal.

[1] Act 21 & 22 Vict., Cap. cvi.

CHAP. III.

since 1833, been separated into two divisions. Of these the lower or south-eastern portion, comprising the original conquest of Clive with subsequent additions in the same quarter, is under the administration of an officer styled Lieutenant Governor of Bengal. This great country, which is about three-fourths the size of France, but has a population nearly twice as numerous, comprises four distinct elements:—(1) Bengal proper, the fertile and thickly populated deltas of the Lower Ganges and Brahmaputra, inhabited by the Bengali-speaking race. (2) Behar, the basin of the Upper Ganges, also fertile and thickly populated, the people of which speak Hindi. (3) The maritime district of Orissa, resembling Bengal in physical aspects, but inhabited by Oriyas. All of these are subject to the uniform legal and administrative system obtaining in what are known as the Regulation Districts of India. (4) Various outlying tracts, of which may be especially mentioned the extensive territory south of Behar, still inappropriately termed the South-West Frontier. This tract, which has an area not far short of that of England, forms the eastern shoulder of the great table-land of Central India, and is for the most part a wild and mountainous country, clothed with forests, and inhabited, like the other similar regions included in this class, by aboriginal races, speaking different tongues.

The total population of the country under the Government of Bengal exceeds seventy-one millions; but the non-regulation portion of the country contains but a small proportion of this total, and contributes scarcely any appreciable share of the general revenue. Nevertheless, the average population for the whole province, although almost wholly agricultural, is nearly 500 to the square mile, more than the average for the United Kingdom, with its crowded manufactures, and parts of it are much more densely inhabited, the rate approaching in some districts to one thousand persons per mile. Bengal is divided into nine commissionerships or divisions, comprising forty-seven districts.

N. W. Provinces and Oudh.

II. The other portion of the Presidency of Fort William, known as the North West Provinces, has been administered for nearly sixty years by a Lieutenant Governor. The province of Oudh has recently been amalgamated with it, and the land revenue of the united province is considerably larger than that of any other province. It has an area not much less than that of the United Kingdom, and ten millions more inhabitants, having an average population of over 440 to the square mile, a density exceeding that of every European country except Belgium. The government comprises forty-nine districts grouped in nine commissionerships.

Madras.

III. The territory under the Governor and Council of Madras is in extent somewhat smaller than that under the Lieutenant Governor of Bengal, with about one-half the population, giving an average density of about 250 to the square mile, considerably more than that of France. The province comprises twenty-one districts. The intermediate administrative link of a Commissioner between the government and the district officer which obtains in other provinces has never been introduced into Madras.

Bombay.

IV. The Bombay Presidency covers an area of 125,000 miles, but this includes a large extent of desert on the borders of Sind. The population of the province is nineteen millions, or little more than one-fourth of that in Bengal; the province comes second in the amount of land revenue contributed. The British territories of this government are very much mixed up with those of the various native States which are superintended by the government of Bombay. The province is divided into twenty-three districts, of which five are in Sind, under five commissioners.

Punjab.

V. Punjab, under a Lieutenant Governor, is of

CHAP. III.

about the same extent, and contains a population about two-thirds as great as that of the kingdom of Italy. The upper part is well cultivated and thickly peopled; towards the south, where it joins Sind and the great Indian desert, the soil, barren from the want of rain, supports only a scanty population. The Punjab is divided into thirty-one districts, grouped under six commissioners.

Central Provinces.

VI. The Central Provinces, under a Chief Commissioner. This province is as large as Great Britain. While several districts of it are highly fertile and productive, it contains also a large proportion of uncultivated and forest land, sparsely inhabited by aboriginal tribes, and the total population is only about eleven millions. It is organised in four divisions, with eighteen districts.

Assam.

VII. Assam. Also under a Chief Commissioner. Nearly as large as England. The province is the principal seat of the flourishing tea industry, but it comprises a large extent of primeval forest, and the population is less than five millions. It is organised in thirteen districts under three commissioners.

Berar.

VIII. Berar, administered by a Commissioner in subordination to the British Resident at the capital of Hyderabad. Somewhat larger than Denmark, and with a population of three millions, or about one-half as large again, organised in six districts. It has been explained that although Berar is directly under British rule, and administered under the same regulations as obtain in other provinces, it is held in trust for the Nizam.

Burma.

IX. Burma. With the additions made in 1886, this is now the largest province of British India, and is nearly as large as France. Burma presents great varieties of physical aspect. The delta of the Irawadi is an expanse of low-lying land unsurpassed in fertility, but Upper Burma comprises extensive tracts of virgin forests, precipitous mountains, and elevated table-lands as yet but little cultivated, and the total population is estimated at less than eight millions. The pacification of Burma has now been completed, but a considerable extent of the mountainous country which separates the valley of the Irawadi from the Bay of Bengal, occupied by scattered aboriginal races having no racial affinity to the people of Burma, and which have never before been subjected to any form of control, has still to be brought under settled government. Control over the tracts bordering on China and Siam is exercised at present through the tribal authorities with little direct interference.

The ruler of this great country is a Chief Commissioner. It is administered through the agency of eight commissioners, and is organised in thirty-five districts.

Baluchistan.

X. Baluchistan. This great country has not yet been completely surveyed, nor has a census been made of its scanty population. The British portion of this part of Asia is larger than the United Kingdom. Sterile for the most part, cultivation is rapidly springing up wherever water can be brought to the land, on which people are settling now that it has come under a regular government. Baluchistan is administered by a Chief Commissioner with a small staff of officers.

Coorg, Ajmir, Andamans.

To complete the list of separate administrations of British territory there must be added to the foregoing: IX, the little province of Coorg in Southern India; XII, the British district of Ajmir in Rajputana; and XIII, the Andaman Islands in the Bay of Bengal, the officials respectively in charge of which are directly under the Government of India.

Native States.

It remains to mention the different native States which still comprise a large proportion of the whole peninsula of India. All these are subject to the control of the paramount power, which is exercised in a greater or less degree, according to the nature of the treaty subsisting with each State. Generally speaking, they have unrestricted civil and criminal jurisdiction, raise

CHAP. III. their own revenues, some of them levy customs on the frontier of their territories, and all of them maintain a military force, more or less disciplined and equipped, and in some cases of considerable strength. But they have no political relations with other States, and in the larger of them garrisons are furnished from the Indian army. Their position is therefore somewhat analogous to that of the mediatised principalities of Germany. Of these States the most important is the dominion of the Nizam, the successor of the Mahomedan viceroy of the Dekhan at the breaking up of the Mogul empire. A British garrison is stationed at Hyderabad, the capital of the country, termed a subsidiary force, in consideration of which certain territory was permanently ceded by the Nizam in 1801 [1]; this force, it may be explained, being additional to that known as the Hyderabad Contingent, a local force under the orders of the Resident, and to the Nizam's own army. The Nizam's territory is not much less in extent than Great Britain, but a considerable part of it is waste or forest land, and it contains a population of only eleven and a half millions. The Resident at Hyderabad, who is also Chief Commissioner of the province of Berar, is one of the high officials directly under the Government of India.

Hyderabad.

Rajputana.

Another administrative unit is formed by the group of States, principally Rajput, which under the name of Rajputana occupies such a conspicuous place on the map of India, and in its earlier history. This great tract, which extends about 450 miles from north to south, and has an extreme breadth of more than 500 miles, comprises twenty-one separate States, which since the final overthrow of the Maratha power in 1817 have been under the protection of the British Government. The smallest of these States is smaller than an English county; the largest, Marwar, has a greater extent than Ireland, but bordering on the Indian desert contains a

[1] See page 51.

large proportion of sterile land. The total population of Rajputana is about twelve millions. An officer, styled Agent to the Governor General, is in general charge of Rajputana with his headquarters at Ajmir, a small British district situated in the centre of the country. A staff of six principal officers has charge each of a cluster of States. Rajputana is garrisoned by two weak brigades of the Indian army stationed at Nasirabad and Nimuch.

States in Central India.

Another important group of native States is that supervised by the Agent to the Governor General for Central India, which includes a large portion of the great table-land of Malwa, or Central India, and a number of States in Bandelkhand. Some of these are petty chieftainships of a few square miles, the owners of which are however independent of all authority save the British Government; but the Agency also includes the Maratha principalities of Holkar and Sindhia, once the most powerful chiefs in India; the dominions still in the possession of the latter form a country as large as Ireland. The table-land of Central India contains some of the finest parts of the peninsula, but it has been the scene of war and rapine from the first decline of the Mahomedan empire, a hundred and fifty years ago, until comparatively recent times; and the territories under the Central India Agency, nearly 80,000 square miles, contain only about ten millions of persons. One brigade of the Indian army is stationed in Central India, at Mhow.

The Maratha State of Baroda, which lies outside the Central India Agency, is supervised by a Resident and Agent to the Governor General. It is somewhat larger than Wales and considerably more populous.

Mysore, in Southern India, an elevated table-land of from three to six thousand feet above sea-level, is about as large and populous as Bavaria. The administration of this province, restored a few years ago to the repre-

CHAP. III. sentative of the old Hindu dynasty which had been dispossessed by a Mahomedan adventurer about one hundred years before, is closely modelled on the system obtaining in British provinces, and is administratively the most advanced of any native state. The Government of India is represented by a Resident, residing at Bangalore, the headquarters of the British force stationed in the province. This official is also Chief Commissioner of Coorg.

Kashmir. The State of Kashmir, besides the small valley of that name includes a great part of the Western Himalaya, including some of the highest mountains in that range. As large as Great Britain, the total population is estimated not to exceed two and a half millions. The Government of India is represented by a Resident.

Administrative Divisions. From the foregoing enumeration it will be seen that for administrative purposes India is divided into sixteen separate governments or administrations, the heads of which are directly under the Governor General in Council :—

Two Governors in Council, Madras and Bombay; three Lieutenant Governors, Bengal, North West Provinces, and Punjab; four Chief Commissioners, Central Provinces, Assam, Burma, and Baluchistan; Resident at Hyderabad and Chief Commissioner of Berar; five Agents to the Governor General for Rajputana, Central India, Baroda, Mysore (also Chief Commissioner of Coorg), and Kashmir; the Superintendent of the Andaman Islands, styled Chief Commissioner.

To the foregoing may be added for affairs beyond India the Residents in Nepal, which is practically an independent state, and in the Persian Gulf.

It may be useful to note also the native states whose affairs are supervised by one or other of the subordinate governments.

The ancient Hindu principality of Travancore, in the extreme south of the peninsula, which is in size about as large as an average district, and the still smaller State of Cochin, have both survived all the revolutions brought about by successive invasions of India, and the anarchy which followed on the dissolution of Mahomedan power. They are supervised by the Government of Madras, which also controls the chiefs of some wild tracts bordering on the northern districts of the Presidency. States under governments of Madras,

A great number of native States are interspersed among the Bombay districts, and supervised by the Government of that Presidency. Of these the principal are the possessions of the numerous petty chiefs in the Kathiawar peninsula and Gujarat. Altogether the part of India generally known as the Bombay Presidency consists of British and native districts in nearly equal parts. Bombay,

The native States supervised by the Government of Bengal consist mainly of wild and sparsely inhabited tracts on the borders of Behar and Orissa, inhabited for the most part by aboriginal tribes. Bengal.

The native States under the superintendence of the Punjab Government comprise an area of about forty thousand square miles. Of this nearly one half belongs to the Mahomedan principality of Bahawalpur, a great part of which, however, is little better than desert. There are several small Sikh States between the Sutlej and Jumna, and there are numerous petty chieftainships in the Himalayas—among which is situated the well known Sanatarium, Simla—whose allegiance was transferred from the Nepalese to the British, after the war of 1814. Punjab,

The southern parts of the Central Provinces contain some extensive tracts, almost uninhabited and uninhabitable, which are under the rule of native chiefs. and Central Provinces.

The following table exhibits the principal political divisions of India, as above described. The whole country in extent and population exceeds the continent of Europe without Russia. Area and population of India.

CHAP. III.

Area and Population, British India, 1891.

Provinces	Districts	Area in square miles	Population
BRITISH PROVINCES			
Under Government of India:—			
Ajmir . . .	2	3,000	540,000
Berar . . .	6	18,000	2,900,000
Coorg . . .	1	2,000	170,000
Andaman Islands .	1	2,000	20,000
		25,000	3,630,000
Madras	21	141,000	35,630,000
Bombay	23	125,000	18,900,000
Bengal	47	152,000	71,350,000
N. W. Provinces and Oudh .	49	106,000	46,900,000
Punjab	31	111,000	20,870,000
Central Provinces . . .	18	87,000	10,780,000
Assam	13	49,000	5,480,000
Burma	35	186,000	7,610,000
Beluchistan		33,000	250,000
Total British Provinces .		1,015,000	221,400,000
NATIVE STATES			
Under Government of India:—			
Rajputana States . . .	—	130,000	12,020,000
States in Central India . .	—	78,000	10,320,000
Baroda	—	8,000	2,420,000
Hyderabad	—	83,000	11,540,000
Mysore	—	28,000	4,940,000
Kashmir	—	81,000	2,540,000
Total	—	408,000	43,780,000
Under Provincial Governments:			
Madras	—	10,000	3,700,000
Bombay	—	69,000	8,060,000
Bengal	—	36,000	3,300,000
N. W. Provinces	—	5,000	790,000
Punjab	—	38,000	4,260,000
Central Provinces	—	29,000	2,160,000
Burma	—	110,000	unknown
Beluchistan	—	100,000	300,000
Total Native States . .	—	805,000	66,350,000
Total all India . . .	—	1,820,000	287,750,000

[1] For a more complete view of the subject dealt with in this chapter, the reader is invited to study the work bearing a similar title by Sir Alfred Lyall, a great book lately republished in form more adequate to its importance than that of the first modest edition.

CHAPTER IV

THE PRESIDENCIES

CHAP. IV.

Popular view that India consists of three Presidencies erroneous.

From the foregoing account of the conditions under which the government of British India is now administered, it will be readily perceived that the idea often popularly entertained, and still countenanced more or less by official usage, that British India is divided into three Presidencies, is entirely opposed to the actual state of things. This form of division, which was correct at one time, has long ceased to be in accordance with the facts. British India is now divided into ten great provinces, each under its own civil government. These governments are differently constituted, and are vested with different degrees of executive power; but they are quite independent of each other; and all of them, both in law and practice, exercise their functions subject to the direct authority and control of the Governor General of India in Council. It will also have been gathered from the last chapter that the titles popularly given to the three Presidencies, when they constituted the whole of British India, are not their correct names. The territorial division known as Madras is properly the Presidency of Fort George, and no such place as the Bengal Presidency has ever existed. The term 'Presidency' itself is commonly used in an ambiguous sense. Originally it was applied to the governing body at each of the three principal settlements, the Commission namely of President and Council,

Ambiguity of the term 'Presidency;

CHAP. IV.

to which the powers of the Company were delegated. From this meaning the term came to be extended to the territories of which those bodies in course of time obtained the possession; but even in this sense it has not been used with precision. The Acts of Parliament determining the form of government for India to which we have referred, all speak of 'the Presidency of Fort William in Bengal,' as if the Presidency were less than, and contained within, the country called Bengal; whereas, from the year 1813, it has been declared lawful to add various ceded territories beyond that country to the Presidency of Fort William. Further, the term 'Presidency' is frequently used, both popularly and in official language, to signify the capital town as distinguished from the interior of the country. Thus a person going to Calcutta or Madras is said to be going 'to the Presidency;' officials residing at those towns are entitled in consequence to certain extra or 'presidency allowances;' and the divisions of the army, of which the commanding general's headquarters are placed at the capital, are styled the 'presidency districts.'[1] It may be added that the name of each presidency has been somewhat differently derived. The Bombay Presidency takes its name, both officially and in common parlance, from the seat of government; that on the eastern coast, usually known by the name of the capital town, is styled in official documents by the name of the fort which overlooks the town; the third presidency derives the name popularly given to it from the most important of the different countries comprised within it.

and of name 'Bengal.'

Further the name 'Bengal' itself is also commonly used in three different senses. First, to denote the country, sometimes styled 'Bengal proper,' inhabited by

[1] This ambiguity is very conspicuous in the Army Act, one section of which employs the term 'presidency' in the sense of a territorial division, while the following one uses it to denote a capital town.

the people who speak the Bengali language. Secondly, it is applied to the territories formerly comprised in the subahdari or viceroyalty of Bengal during the Mahomedan era, namely, the three great provinces of 'Bengal proper,' Behar, and Orissa, which with the province of Cuttack, subsequently added, are now under the jurisdiction of the 'Lieutenant Governor of Bengal.' Thirdly, it is applied to the great plain of Upper India, extending from the mouths of the Brahmaputra to the borders of Afghanistan, which is garrisoned by the Bengal army, and administered by the agency of what, until lately, was styled the Bengal Civil Service, and which, speaking roughly, is comprised in the three Lieutenant Governorships and the Province of Oudh. This third application of the title 'Bengal Presidency,' which is the one most familiar to English readers, has no doubt arisen from the circumstance that the Bengal army has been administered directly by the Governor General in Council, who until 1833 was styled the General Governor in Council of *Fort William in Bengal*; and also because the official body, termed the 'Bengal Civil Service,' constituted the principal administrative agency throughout the countries garrisoned by the Bengal army. But, as we have seen, such a territorial division is not recognised by the law, and is quite inaccurate as a representation of facts. The Presidency of Fort William, as defined by the Act of 1833, comprises only the territories now under the jurisdiction of the Lieutenant Governors of Bengal and the North-Western Provinces;[1] while the so-called 'Bengal' Government—as that term is sometimes erroneously applied, not to the Lieutenant Governor of Bengal, whom it properly denotes, but to the Government which controls the Bengal army, viz., the Governor General of India in Council—is not more directly concerned with

[1] It is however a moot point between the Indian constitutional lawyers whether Punjab is within or without the Statutory Bengal Presidency.

CHAP. IV.

the administration of the provinces garrisoned by the Bengal army, than with that of any other part of India. It is even less concerned with such of these provinces as are ruled by Lieutenant Governors, than with the provinces like Burma and Berar, the administrators of which possess less independent authority than do the Lieutenant Governors.

Origin of the mistaken ideas on the subject.

As regards Madras and Bombay, the idea of a territorial division by presidential limits has until lately been so far appropriate that there were distinct armies and civil services employed in the territories under the jurisdiction of the Governments of Madras [Fort St. George] and Bombay respectively; and this fact has no doubt helped to foster the idea that there existed a third great territorial division, coextensive with the area covered by the third army and civil service. But even in the case of Madras and Bombay the assumed presidential organisation has long ceased to obtain. The troops employed in the Madras Presidency have certainly been none but Madras troops; but these are also extensively employed beyond the limits of that presidency. Nearly one half of the Madras army is serving in the transmarine province of Burma, a country the administration of which has no sort of connection with or subordination to the Government of Madras. That army also furnishes the garrisons of the States of Mysore and Hyderabad, and a great part of the Central Provinces, countries the administrations of which are under the direct control of the Governor General in Council, and even of a part of the Bombay Presidency, as well as for a part of Bengal. The portion of the Madras army remaining at the disposal of the Madras Government, and stationed within the Madras Presidency, has long been in fact a mere fraction of the whole. In the same way, the Bombay army, besides garrisoning the Bombay Presidency, also furnishes garrisons for the large stations of Mhow,

CHAP. IV.

Nussirabad, and Nimuch, situated in foreign states supervised by agents of the Supreme Government, as well as for the distant territory of Baluchistan.[1]

Connection between Bengal Presidency and Bengal army.

The common notion, moreover, that the Bengal Presidency—using the term in its popular sense, *i.e.* to mean the country garrisoned by the Bengal army—consists of the three Lieutenant-Governorships and the province of Oudh, expresses the facts only very roughly. The Bengal army garrisons these territories, but it also shares with the Madras army the duty of supplying troops for the Central Provinces and Burma, and with the Bombay army of garrisoning the native States of Central India and Rajputana.

Bengal Civil Service practically divided into two services,

Further, the body of officials heretofore comprising the Bengal Civil Service, though bearing one name, has for long been divided into two distinct parts, one of which is employed under the Bengal Government,

[1] How completely the separate presidential system has been extinguished by the force of circumstances is shown by the figures below :—

Distribution of Madras and Bombay armies, including British forces nominally borne on their establishments :—

—	Batteries Artillery	Regiments Cavalry		Battalions Infantry	
		British	Native	British	Native
Madras Army					
Stationed within limits of Madras Presidency . . .	4	0	1	2	10
Stationed in other Provinces and Territories . . .	10	2	2	9	22
Total . . .	14	2	3	11	32
Bombay Army					
Stationed within limits of Bombay Presidency . . .	16	0	3	6	14
Stationed in other Provinces and Territories . . .	9	1	4	5	12
Total . . .	25	1	7	11	26

CHAP. IV.

the other in the northern provinces of India. The candidates for the Civil Service have had to make their choice between these two divisions on first appointment, and shaped their studies in the Indian languages accordingly, during their period of probation in England. Henceforward the two divisions of the service were almost as completely separated from each other as they are from the Bombay and Madras Civil Services. The young civilians nominated to Bengal were at once on arrival placed at the disposal of the Lieutenant Governor of that province, while the first distribution of those who formed the second division, among the three northern provinces (the North West Provinces, Punjab, and Oudh), was made by the Government of India; but henceforward the employment and promotion of all were determined by the respective Lieutenant Governors. The only bond of union between these two divisions, beyond their common name, was in fact that the members of both subscribed to one common fund for retiring annuities and family pensions. This tie was obviously quite unimportant. The two divisions might at any time have been formed into two separate civil services for Bengal and Upper India without the smallest difficulty or infringement of vested rights.

for east and north of India,

Thus there have been in effect four and not three civil services. It may be added that the two divisions of the Bengal Civil Service are each much larger than either the Madras or Bombay Service. So far, however, from any further subdivision being desirable, the presumption appears to be quite the other way. The original division of the Civil Service into separate bodies, although suitable enough in former years, has long been unmeaning and useless. The popular notion that it secures that the officials shall be conversant with the languages of the people whom they are set over, is quite fallacious. The diversity of languages

each larger than Madras or Bombay Civil Service.

Separation of civil services maintained after it ceased to be necessary or suitable.

in different districts of the Madras Presidency is much greater than the diversity between the languages of adjoining districts of the different provinces and presidencies. The same remark applies to the enormous territory ruled over by the Lieutenant Governor of Bengal. A Bengal civilian may be sent from Behar, where the people are Hindustanis speaking Hindi and Urdu, to the extreme east of Bengal, where only Bengali is spoken, or to Orissa, where another distinct language is found; and a Madras officer may be transferred from the south of the peninsula where the language is Tamil, to the extremity of the Northern Circars, where the language is derived from a different stock, or to the Canarese district of Bellary. All that the presidential system secured was, that under no circumstances should a civilian step across the border from one regulation province to another, although the line of demarcation might be a purely arbitrary one, such as that which divides the Bombay and Madras Presidencies on the west coast, or the Northern Circars and Cuttack on the east. This condition, however, does not hold with respect to the so-called non-regulation provinces, which are officered by members of all the services, who are equally eligible for employment in the various imperial departments (political, finance, post-office, &c.), administered directly by the Government of India. In these cases the artificial division of the services fulfils no useful purpose, while it tends to perpetuate needless class prejudices and jealousies, and has certainly operated to deprive the Madras and Bombay services of their proportionate share of the higher appointments under the Supreme Government, which now almost always fall to their more fortunate brethren in the Bengal service. As a natural consequence the candidates who head the list at the annual competition for admission to the Indian Civil Service have usually chosen Bengal to the extent of the available

CHAP. IV.

vacancies; the rest were perforce appointed to Madras and Bombay.

Fusion of the three civil services into one.

The conclusion was therefore long ago warranted, that as regards the civil service, these presidential distinctions might with great advantage be abolished, and all Indian civilians be incorporated in one imperial establishment. This change recommended itself as one step further towards dispelling the notion still sometimes entertained, even in India, and partly justified by the present state of things, that the Supreme Government is not the Government of India, but the Government of Bengal, a belief productive of constant friction in the wheels of Indian administration.

The necessity for this change, first advocated in the earlier editions of this work, has at last come to be recognised, and has lately been carried out. From 1889 the obsolete presidential divisions have been abolished in this respect, and the members of the different services have been brought together in one 'Indian Civil Service.' The change was made as part of a comprehensive reorganisation of the whole system of civil administration throughout the country, so far as regards the personal agency employed, which will be referred to later on at some length.

Misconception caused by system of presidential armies.

If the preservation of presidential distinctions in the civil service for so long after they had ceased to be applicable, was at the worst rather stupid than harmful, the continued maintenance of the system of presidential armies up to nearly the present time has been extraordinarily mischievous. From 1860, when the old local establishments of European troops, which were separate small armies, were absorbed into the British service, all reason ceased for keeping up this divided administration which henceforward was quite without justification, and would have been wholly absurd if it had not been also very costly and inefficient. If the Governments of Madras and Bombay had been financially responsible for the armies nominally under their control, there might have been some show of reason for maintaining a system necessarily cumbrous and complicated. But the money for military expenditure is found by the Supreme Government, and from the time when it first undertook the responsibility, any real control of the Local Governments over their armies came to an end.

The presidential system had further ceased to be reasonable from the circumstance already explained, that the Madras and Bombay armies had long ceased to be employed wholly, or even mainly, in the provinces to which they nominally belonged, but were distributed also throughout various parts of India in the affairs of which the Madras and Bombay Governments had no concern. The necessity for abolishing this cumbrous and obsolete system was first pressed on public attention nearly twenty-five years ago, in the early editions of this work. That its maintenance has so long been persisted in is an illustration of the strong natural conservatism of the ordinary official mind. However, the reform first definitely taken in hand by the Government of Lord Ripon and followed up persistently by his successors has at last been carried through. One by one the different presidential departments have been amalgamated, and while the separation of the native armies has been carefully preserved, the unification of the military administration has been gradually accomplished. The Act of Parliament passed in 1893, abolishing the connection between the general officers commanding the Madras and Bombay armies and the Councils of those Presidencies, gave the finishing touch to the work. The Madras and Bombay Governments have now ceased to have any connection with army administration, and are placed on the same footing as all the other provincial governments in India in being concerned only with affairs of civil administration. At

CHAP. IV.

this point, therefore, the title 'Presidency,' applied to Madras and Bombay, ceases to have any force or meaning; they should be styled provinces like the other parts of British India. It has been explained that a 'Bengal' Presidency has no existence. When these conditions come to be generally understood it may be hoped that this obsolete and misleading term 'Presidency,' still a fertile cause of administrative embarrassment and confusion, will be dropped altogether from both official and popular use.

Misconception underlying parliamentary legislation on subject.

It should be added that the misconceptions here noticed were by no means confined to the public. The Acts of Parliament dealing with India have been defective not only from the ambiguities above referred to, the authorities who drafted them usually appear to have assumed that all the territories in India possessed by the Company necessarily belonged to one or other of the three presidencies; but no statutory definition of a presidency was ever laid down, and as a matter of fact various accessions of territories have taken place at different times which had never been declared to belong to any presidency. The governments established in these countries had therefore no statutory sanction. This omission is especially noticeable in the Act of 1853 renewing the Company's Charter, in which, while provision is made for the formation of a separate government of Bengal, no allusion is made to the existence of the province of Tenasserim, acquired in 1826, or of Pegu acquired in 1852, or of Punjab, annexed in 1849. In all these countries, therefore, the only legal sanction for the proceedings of the Indian governments and of the law courts set up therein rested on the right of conquest. The incongruity of the situation created by this statutory silence is obvious. In some parts of India the powers of the Company to exercise jurisdiction rested on the specific delegation of authority conferred by successive Acts of Parliament, while in regard to other and extensive territories, the law of England was altogether silent, and these territories were not recognised as having any statutory existence. This singular omission was rectified by an Act passed in 1854,[1] which provides that the Governor General in Council may take under his immediate authority and management any parts 'of the territories for the time being in the possession of or under the government of the said Company, and thereupon give all necessary orders and directions respecting the administration of such part or parts of the said territories, or otherwise to provide for the administration thereof.' The Act goes on to complete the statement by declaring that all powers not exercised by the Governor in Council of a Presidency or a Lieutenant Governor, 'shall be vested in and may be exercised by the Governor General in Council.' In other words, statutory recognition was thus for the first time accorded to the existence of territories in India not comprised within any one of the presidencies.

This Act had no retrospective effect, and did not therefore give statutory validity to the previous actions of the Indian Government in regard to their extra-presidential territories. The omission was rectified by a clause in the Act of 1861,[2] which conferred the necessary legal sanction on the proceedings of the Government of India therein up to date.

[1] 17 & 18 Victoria, Cap. lxxvii. Even so, the change is smuggled into being under the title, 'An Act to provide for the mode of passing Letters Patent and other Acts of the Crown relating to India, and for vesting certain powers in the Governor General of India in Council.' The general reader would possibly not discover from this that a statute which sets out by prescribing that the counter-signature of the President of the Board of Control to the Royal Sign Manual shall constitute valid authority for appointments to offices in India made under the Great Seal, brings also for the first time several millions of people formally within the British Empire and the government of the Company.

[2] 24 and 25 Victoria, Cap. lxvii., clause 25. An Act to make better Provisions for the Constitution of the Council of the Governor General of India, and for the Local Government of the several Presidencies and Provinces of India, &c.

CHAPTER V

THE PROVINCIAL GOVERNMENTS

CHAP. V.

Anomalous organisation of the provincial governments.

In the foregoing chapter the incorrectness has been pointed out of the popular notion—which, however, is not confined to the English public—that British India is constituted in three presidencies, and it has been explained that the country is actually divided into a large number of provinces, each with its own separate administration. And this being understood, the enquirer will at once be struck with the singular state of things under which, while the two most populous provinces, Bengal and the North West Provinces, are administered by Lieutenant Governors, two other provinces, much less populous and in many respects less important politically, Madras and Bombay, are provided with Governors and Executive Councils.[1] The cause of this anomaly has already been explained. The government originally created for Bengal was equipped with the same administrative machinery as was supplied to Madras and Bombay; but there was gradually imposed on it the government of all India in addition to its original jurisdiction; and the present provision made by the Act of 1853 for the wants of Bengal was in fact a makeshift arrangement, introduced when the want of a government of some sort for that province had

[1] Population of Bengal . . . . 71 millions.
" " North-West Provinces . 47 "
" " Madras . . . . 35 "
" " Bombay . . . . 19 "

been so thoroughly exposed in the previous Parliamentary enquiry, that a change could not with propriety be resisted any longer. The Act of 1833, which converted the Governor General in Council of Bengal into the Government of India, contemplated the creation of a fourth Presidency for the North West Provinces, and empowered the Court of Directors to carry out the change, leaving the Governor in Council to administer Bengal; but inasmuch as the Bengal army was not to be divided, and the Government of the new Presidency would have no army under its order, and would be concerned only with civil administration, the cheaper plan was adopted of appointing a Lieutenant Governor to the upper portion of the Bengal Presidency, an arrangement which received statutory sanction by an Act of Parliament passed in 1835. Similarly the Act of 1853 legalised the appointment of a Governor for the Bengal division of the Presidency of Fort William, but left it optional with the Court of Directors, instead of themselves appointing a Governor, to authorise the Governor General in Council to appoint a member of the Indian service to be Lieutenant Governor of that province. The latter plan was adopted, partly perhaps under the idea that it would leave the Governor General a greater share of authority in that province, and partly in view to economy. There is no doubt a saving: a Governor receives 120,000 rupees a year, a Lieutenant General 20,000 rupees less, and the latter has a smaller and much more economical household. But although the one holds a higher official position than the other, and is nominated by the Crown, while the Lieutenant Governor is appointed by the Governor General in Council with the approval of the Crown, and in popular estimation the former occupies a more powerful and important position, the office of the Lieutenant Governor of Bengal has really much more substantial authority and responsibility attached to it than that of

CHAP. V.

Governor of Madras or Bombay, and is inferior only in emolument and dignity.[1]

It is indeed generally supposed that the Government of India interposes more directly in the provincial administrations under Lieutenant Governors than with those under a Governor in Council, and that the latter have in some way or other a greater degree of authority and independence than the former. And the supposition is not unnatural; why otherwise should there be this difference of emolument and dignity? But in reality there is no difference whatever in this respect. Until lately, indeed, the Government of Madras, as well as that of Bombay, was charged with the administration of an army. The charge, which for many years has been little more than nominal, has now however altogether ceased, and all the provincial governments are now on the same footing, in that they have to deal only with the business of civil administration. On the other hand the Lieutenant Governors have gradually been invested with all the authority in civil business which at one time was retained by the Supreme Government, so that the two Governors in Council and the three Lieutenant Governors of Bengal, the North West Provinces, and Punjab exercise equal administrative authority and relative independence in financial and all other matters.

Bengal Government the most important of all.

With this equality of power the position of the Lieutenant Governor of Bengal has become by much the most important of any under the Supreme Government, by reason of the greater extent of that province, still more of its greater population and wealth, and the larger interests as compared with other parts of the country arising out of these conditions. The portion of the Indian Civil Service serving in Bengal is the largest official body in India.[2] The same thing holds good, not only in the Civil Service proper,

[1] The Governor is styled 'His Excellency,' like the Governor General, and takes precedence over the 'Honourable' Lieutenant Governor.

[2] The distribution of the Indian Civil Service, which fills the greatest part of the higher administrative appointments throughout the country,

but in all branches of the civil administration—police, education, law, public works, &c. Bengal is divided into forty-seven districts, exclusive of extensive non-regulation territories attached to it, against twenty-one in Madras and twenty-three in Bombay; and there are more law-courts, schools, jails, and public establishments of all kinds under the Lieutenant Governor of Bengal than in any other province. In fact he has the largest patronage of any person in India, and while the responsibilities of the Governments of Madras and Bombay are shared between the Governor and his Council, the Bengal Lieutenant Governor is absolutely uncontrolled in this respect by anyone. From every point of view the Government of Bengal is by far the most important in India, after the Supreme Government; and there appears not even a show of reason for maintaining the appearance of nominal inferiority to any of the other provincial governments. Next to the Bengal Government in importance ranks that of the North West Provinces, of which the same thing may be said.

And should be made a Governorship.

This anomalous condition has naturally not escaped the attention of those connected with Indian administration, and it has often been proposed that on the unification of the military administration being com-

affords a good index of the relative administrative importance of the different provinces. It is as follows:—

Directly under Government of India:		
Central Department	32	
Political Employ	43	75
Madras		143
Bombay		140
Bengal		186
North West Provinces		182
Punjab [1]		95
Central Provinces [1]		63
Burma [1]		43
Assam [1]		32
		927

[1] In these four provinces the administrative posts are filled only in part by civilians.

pleted, and the Madras and Bombay Governments relieved of the charge of the armies designated by those names, the provincial administration in Madras and Bombay should be reduced to Lieutenant Governorships. The process of equalisation ought undoubtedly to be carried out, but I venture to think it should be effected rather by levelling up, and raising the Lieutenant Governorships to the higher rank. In the case of Bengal especially there is an incongruity almost grotesque in styling the head of the administration of a country with seventy millions of people—a population exceeding that of the United States—a Lieutenant Governor. The change of status is called for by every consideration of fitness and propriety.

One consequence of this change might be that, whereas the Bengal Government is now filled, under the provisions of the law, by a member of the Indian service, it would become possible to appoint as Governor a stranger to the country, when the special knowledge and administrative training which have produced the signal results displayed in the North West Provinces and Punjab in past years, as well as in Bengal itself, would no longer be available. With a certain class of politicians, indeed, ignorance of his business on the part of a person in such a position is deemed to be in itself a qualification. Yet there is no precedent for such an arrangement. Colonial Governors are certainly often appointed without experience of their duties, but then they do not administer the government of which they are the nominal heads; their functions are for the most part of a ceremonial kind. In the Crown Colonies where the Governor does exercise authority, the duties are on a trifling scale. In India only does the ruler of a large and populous country actually administer the government. There the welfare of the province entrusted to his charge depends on his efficiency; the business is of a technical kind demanding for the proper discharge of it long and special experience, while the duties are heavy beyond comparison with those to be discharged by an administrator in any other part of the world. It may be said that affairs at Madras and Bombay have got on fairly well under some Governors who have had neither experience nor ability; but then the business and responsibility have been shared with experienced colleagues in their Councils. One advantage, indeed, so far as it goes, may be found in selecting a Governor from the peerage or lower ranks of a Ministry, that it brings Indian official life to that extent in touch with the English political world, and creates a certain amount of interest in Indian affairs among persons who might otherwise be without it. Further, the possession of personal experience is not always without disadvantage in one respect. It is scarcely possible that a man should be raised from the ranks of a service in which his life has been passed without taking with him more or less of bias for or against some of his old associates, which may be displayed in the subsequent distribution of patronage. But when all this is said, the fact remains that for the effective administration of an Indian province, a knowledge of the people of India, of their religions and some at least of their languages, and of the complicated system of law, usage, and land tenure with which the business of civil administration is mainly concerned, is an essential qualification. An untrained man from England, or a successful Colonial Governor, who has earned his popularity by a dignified and courteous performance of the ceremonial duties of office, but who has perforce left all business to his responsible advisers, must on first arriving in India be ignorant of the very elements of the business coming before him, and form his judgment at second hand on the advice of those about him, nor will the brief tour of office suffice to make good his deficiencies. The case

CHAP. V.

of the Governor General is not apposite. That high personage is not, or should not be, engaged on details; moreover the Supreme Government is better provided with advisers than the subordinate governments; while in statesmen of the class usually appointed to this high office, genius may supply the place of experience. On the whole, the conclusion would appear to be that while the Government of Bengal should certainly be placed on the same footing as regards emoluments and standing as that of Madras and Bombay, the number of governorships open to persons not belonging to the Indian service should not be extended. But should Bengal be made an open appointment, it may be remembered that the Governments of Madras and Bombay have always been freely conferred on distinguished members of the Indian service, and so no doubt would be that of Bengal.

With a Council.

Whether Bengal be administered by a Governor or a Lieutenant Governor, the head of the government of the province should be aided by a Council. That great country is altogether too large a charge for a single ruler. Government by one man has indeed produced remarkable results in the North West Provinces under a Thomason and in Punjab under a Lawrence, as well as during later years in Bengal under its successive Lieutenant Governors; but the great and complicated interests in this last province involve an amount of business beyond the capacity of any one man to deal with, and the progress of administration there has reached a point when continuity of policy is even more required than individual energy. This would be secured by a Council the members of which do not vacate office simultaneously, while the addition of a Council would be a salutary check on the exhibition of personal eccentricity.

The means for creating such a body without sensible expense are to be found in the existing Board of Revenue.

This comprises two members, who are the highest officers in the administrative branch of the service. Although styled a board, practically they exercise distinct and separate functions, one being at the head of the great department of land revenue, and the other of the departments of opium, assessed taxes, and excise, and they meet together as a board only for the hearing of certain classes of appeals. They would take these duties with them into the Council, thereby saving a great deal of correspondence which now goes on between the Board and the Government, and would administer such other departments of business as the Governor might allot to them on a redistribution of duties between himself and his Council. A fourth member should be added for public works, which in Bengal are now on a scale of importance to call for the superintendence of a responsible minister. Power should be given to the Governor to overrule his Council, a power possessed by the Governor General and the other Governors, his reasons for doing so being formally placed on record. This power would seldom if ever have to be exercised, but such a statutory provision is a necessary condition for establishing the responsibility of the Governor in case of emergency.

Calcutta High Court should be placed under Bengal Government.

It has been explained that the Lieutenant Governor of Bengal has already precisely the same degree of independence and authority as the Governor in Council of Madras and Bombay. One exception, however, must here be mentioned. The High Court of Calcutta continues to be under the orders of the Governor General in Council in all matters where the authority of a government comes into action, and such of the judges as are appointed by the Queen from the Indian service are in form nominated by the Governor General, although in fact the nomination is made by that authority on the recommendation of the Lieutenant Governor. This connection between the local High Court and the

CHAP. V.

Supreme Government is no longer appropriate, a separate High Court having many years ago been established in the North West Provinces, while Punjab and the other more recently created provinces have each their own Appellate Court. The jurisdiction of the Calcutta Court is thus now limited to Bengal,[1] and it should undoubtedly be placed in the same relations towards the Government of that province as the High Courts of Madras and Bombay hold in regard to the governments of those provinces, when the connection of the Supreme Government with the former would cease. This change would no doubt have been already carried out but for the tendency of administrative reform in India to lag behind the requirements apparent.

The Councils at Madras and Bombay have until lately consisted of three members, two chosen from the Civil Service, and the local Commander-in-Chief. On the latter being placed with the army he commands under the direct orders of the Commander-in-Chief in India, it was no longer appropriate that he should be directly connected with the civil administration of one in particular of the many provinces over which his army is distributed, and by the Act of Parliament passed in 1893[2] he has ceased to be a member of that Council. A possible inconvenience from the change may be that whereas the Governor might usually count on the vote of the Commander-in-Chief in cases where his two civilian colleagues were opposed to him, when the Council being equally divided he had the casting vote, he is now liable to be outvoted. In the case of many of the past Governors the presumption would have been that in such a conflict of opinion the Governor was in the wrong and his more experienced colleagues in the right. The law, however, has already established the principle that responsibility should rest ultimately with

[1] It also hears appeals from Assam and in certain cases from the Recorder of Rangoon, but this is a matter of detail.

[2] 56 & 57 Vict., Cap. lviii.

some one person, and this the highest, by conferring the same power on the Governor of a Province as is already possessed by the Governor General of overruling his Council, the reasons for doing so being formally placed on record. Further, in Bombay and Madras, as in Bengal, a fourth member of Council might advantageously be added for public works, the interests of which do not receive at present the systematic attention they require.

CHAP. V.

Bengal Council should be executive and not consultative only.

It will have been gathered from what has been said on the subject, that in proposing a council for Bengal, a purely consultative body is not contemplated, in which three men would do the work now done by one man, but a Council the members of which should divide between them the ordinary administrative business of the Government. This change in constitution from consultative to executive has been fully carried out in the Council of the Governor General, as will be explained in the following chapter, and also to some extent in the Councils at Bombay and Madras, although in the latter a great deal of business which elsewhere would be deemed too petty for such procedure, appears to be still dealt with collectively. This is probably because there would otherwise not be enough for the Council to do. Madras is cut off by other provinces from the north and so is without a foreign frontier. It is inhabited by a docile and orderly people; and having enjoyed a long period of settled government free from wars and intestine disorders, the administrative machine there is much less heavily weighted than in the other great provinces, the interests to be dealt with are simpler and easier to deal with, while a great deal of business which might appropriately be dealt with by a Government so circumstanced, is intercepted by the intermediate agency of the Board of Revenue. A Council at Madras is absolutely necessary so long as the Governor is appointed direct from England, but a Council and a Board of Revenue

CHAP. V.

are not both wanted, and the latter in the interests of economy might with advantage be abolished.

Direct correspondence between India Office and Madras and Bombay Governments should cease.

While thus bringing the administrative organisation of the greater provinces into accordance with present needs and conditions, the opportunity should be taken to discontinue the direct correspondence still maintained between the Madras and Bombay Governments and the India Office. This is now little more than a matter of form, and limited for the most part to trivial details, while it is carried on under the cognisance of the Supreme Government, which is supplied with copies of all the letters which pass. It is a mere survival from the time when the three presidencies were isolated countries and when three separate military establishments were maintained by the Company, recruited and administered directly by the Court of Directors. But, maintained in any form, the practice is objectionable, as tending to create unnecessary friction between the head and subordinate governments. There should be only one authority in India directly responsible to the home government.

North West Provinces.

The territory inappropriately called the North West Provinces, with which Oudh is now incorporated, may in a general way be defined as the basin of the Upper Ganges and its tributaries. This, like Bengal, is an immense plain, watered by that river and the Jumna, both navigable in an imperfect fashion for vessels of small burden almost throughout their course. Of less extent than the other large provinces, it comes next after Bengal in population, and is almost as densely inhabited. It is more uniformly cultivated, and contains a smaller quantity of waste land than any other part of the country, its land revenue being the largest in India. This part of the country has, from time immemorial, given a government to the rest of India.[1] Here

Their magnitude and importance.

[1] The country known as the Delhi territory, west of the Jumna, with the great city of that name, was, however, transferred after the Mutiny from this to the Punjab Province.

first settled the Aryan race, which supplanted the aboriginal possessors of the country. Here, too, was established the great Hindu monarchy which was overcome by the first Mahomedan invaders. Here was fixed the seat of government of the different dynasties of Mahomedan emperors, who retained a partial hold of the Gangetic plain for some time after the rest of their empire had crumbled away. And here are to be found some of the most exquisite of the memorials, which, having escaped the ravages of Maratha barbarism and English indifference, still attest the taste and magnificence of the Pathan and Mogul rulers.

The people of these parts are, if we except Punjab, which, until modern times has been regarded as beyond Indian limits, the physically finest and most warlike people of India, and until recently have furnished the greater part of the armies both of the British and their predecessors. If Bengal be the most fertile, this province and Punjab are politically the most important. Although for the most part a vast plain, with but a small elevation above sea level, it is sufficiently raised above the rivers which water it to be secure from inundation, and is usually free from the visitation of either excessive rain or drought, while the extensive irrigation works carried out over a large portion of its surface have lessened the danger from the latter calamity. To these advantages may be added the possession throughout the breadth of the country of what is entirely wanting in the greater part of Bengal and many other parts of the country, an excellent material for road-making; to which is chiefly due the fact that the province is better supplied with good communications than any other part of India. This is the only province in India throughout which only one language is spoken.

The North West Provinces with Oudh form the most compact territory in India, if the term can be properly applied to so extensive a country. In regard

CHAP. V.

to administration, the charge is as important as Bengal; it comprises forty-nine districts as against forty-seven in the latter, nearly twice as many as in Bombay, and more than twice the number of districts in Madras, and every consideration which makes for styling the head of the Bengal Government a Governor, applies equally to this great province. Here also, as in Bengal, the Governor should be aided by a Council. The circumstances, indeed, are not quite the same. The North West Provinces have no maritime cities or great centres of European trade, with large communities of non-official Europeans; the number of English settlers is small, and thus it is not subject to the conflicts of class interests which have to be dealt with in Bengal, and in respect to which the position of a single ruler is necessarily more difficult and delicate than that of a collective government. But the amount of business to be transacted here is beyond the capacity of a single administrator to deal with properly, while the province has arrived at a condition when the vigour and impulse to progress which the rule of one man can impart, may be fitly replaced by the greater continuity of policy which would be secured under the administration of a Governor aided by a Council. So far from the head of the administration losing by the change—not to mention the relief from the pressure of work now imposed on a single man, and that a great deal of business which has now to be disposed of in his name by irresponsible secretaries would then fall to be dealt with by members of the Government with recognised authority—it would be of great advantage to the Governor if all appointments and promotions in the public service of this province, a much larger body than that in Madras and Bombay, were made in consultation with and on the joint responsibilities of colleagues, instead of at his sole pleasure. Far from detracting from his authority, such a change should increase it, while the popularity

Should have a Governor and Council.

of the Governor with the great services under his orders should undoubtedly gain. The feeling often entertained among its members, that preferment is determined too much by personal bias, is one of the weak points in the system of administration by a single man, whose decisions are not subjected to the advice and criticism of any colleagues.

The material for the formation of a Council for the North West Provinces with little or no additional expense is available, as in Bengal, in the absorption of the Board of Revenue, the two officials at the head of it being advanced to the higher position, taking up with them their present duties. But whether or not the Governor be aided by a Council, the administration of this province being concerned almost wholly with the native population, an intimate acquaintance with the language and customs of the people, the Indian regulations, and the diverse and complicated tenures of land, are essential qualifications in the Governor, and are to be gained only by the experience of an official lifetime. The government of this province is as distinctly an Indian official post as any appointment in the service. A stranger to the country, whether connected with an English political party or coming with colonial experience, would be perfectly inefficient for the place. But, indeed, the idea of making such an appointment has never been mooted.

Designation of these provinces should be changed.

It needs hardly be added that a legislative effort should be made without further loss of time, sufficient to procure that the present designation of this province be altered to one more rational. The Act of 1833 which provided for the creation of a fourth presidency out of this part of the country, called it the 'Presidency of Agra.' The capital of the province having been moved to Allahabad, the latter city would furnish a better name for it, but 'Hindustan' would be still more appropriate.

CHAP. V.

Punjab should also be made a Governorship.

Punjab, which as well as the North West Provinces is situated beyond the tropics, and is in great part, like the latter, a vast plain, enjoys from its northerly situation a colder winter climate than the rest of India, although subject to extreme heat in summer; and being watered by rivers which although barely navigable in their upper part afford great facilities for an extensive system of artificial irrigation, now in course of being gradually carried out, it promises to become eventually a great corn-producing country. It derives great political importance in the scale of Indian provinces from its frontier position, and the warlike character of its inhabitants, who proved to be the most stubborn opponents ever encountered by British arms in the East, and who now supply the most valued element in our native army. Of smaller extent than Madras and Bombay, it contains more administrative districts than they, and a somewhat larger population than the latter. The Punjab government being charged with the diplomatic relations with the independent or quasi-independent tribes on its frontiers to the west and north, extending over more than a thousand miles, is not less important than any other, and the head of it should certainly be raised to the status of a Governor, of equal dignity with the other heads of provinces. Here, however, the personal element comes into play in a special degree; the system of administration also is of a simpler, or as it is often styled more patriarchal, form than in the older provinces—although under the universal application of our codes of law this simplicity is rapidly disappearing; and while the disadvantages attending government by a single person, uncontrolled by responsible colleagues, have not always been absent here, the case for change is by no means so strong as in Bengal and the North West Provinces, and the introduction of a Council might be deferred for the present.

Central Provinces.

The Central Provinces are a collection of territories

obtained at various times from different Maratha states. They include a great portion of the table-land of Central India, in which rise the Narbada and Tapti flowing into the Indian Ocean on the west coast, the Sone and other tributaries of the Ganges, and the Mahanadi and several branches of the Godavari which fall into the Bay of Bengal. This country has suffered more than any other part from the ravages and intestine feuds of the Marathas. It was the stronghold of the Pindari freebooters of 1817, and has only of comparatively late years possessed a settled government. In extent it nearly equals Great Britain, and falls not far short of the larger provinces of India; but a great part consists of forests, waste land, and barren hills, sparsely inhabited by aboriginal tribes, and the revenue is at present comparatively small. There are, however, some very fertile portions. The wide plain of Nagpur is one of the most productive cotton fields of India; the Raipur district and the valley of the Narbada are rich in grain; and the whole country, being naturally fertile, bids fair to become under settled government a very valuable portion of the Indian empire. The administration of the Central Provinces is under a Chief Commissioner.

Assam.

Assam, upon its acquisition from the Burmese in 1824, was attached to the province of Bengal, and so remained until a few years ago, when that overgrown, unwieldy government was lightened by the separation of Assam, which was formed into a separate administration under a Chief Commissioner. Assam, whose people are distinct in race and language from the Bengalis, is the smallest of the great provinces, but nearly as large as England. A great part of it is still covered with primitive forest, and the population is at present less than five millions, about the same as that of England in the reign of James I. But the soil is rich; Assam is the principal seat of the rapidly expanding Indian tea industry, in which a large number of English settlers

CHAP. V.

are engaged; rich coal deposits have been found in the north, and when opened up by railways and its wastes peopled by immigrants from overcrowded Bengal, the province will probably advance to a prominent commercial position.

Smaller provinces.

The smaller British provinces directly under the Supreme Government; Berar under the jurisdiction of the Resident of Hyderabad with a commissioner in immediate executive charge; the little province of Coorg in Southern India administered by the Governor General's Agent at Mysore; and the Andaman Islands in the Bay of Bengal, a convict settlement, the head of which is styled a chief commissioner, call for no special notice here.

Burma.

Lastly comes Burma, now, with the addition made in 1886, the largest province of all. The country inhabited by the Burmese themselves is nearly as large as France, but there are in addition many thousand square miles, sparsely occupied by aboriginal tribes. Most of these lie beyond the borders of Burma proper, to the north and east; but there is a great tract of very mountainous country, clothed in dense forests and jungles, which separates the maritime districts of the province on the Bay of Bengal from the basin of the Irawadi, inhabited by barbarous races. On the side of Burma no attempt was ever made by its native government to subdue these savages, and nothing was known or heard of them except when they sallied down from their mountain fastnesses to harry and plunder, carrying away into slavery such of their Burman captives as they spared from slaughter. And, for so long as the country at the back of these mountains was occupied by a foreign power, our intercourse with these tribes was limited to punitive expeditions on the occasions of their raiding into our maritime districts, and our troops did not penetrate beyond the fringe of the British border. But after the occupation of Upper

Burma, when British territory embraced both sides of these tracts, it became necessary to bring it into order. The operations undertaken in this view have been attended with great difficulty from the nature of the country, range after range of precipitous mountains with knife-edged summits, separated by narrow ravines clothed in pestiferous and almost impenetrable jungle, and the beds of rapid torrents, while from spring to autumn the vapour-laden winds from the sea pour down a deluge of continuous rain. Systematic operations were first undertaken in 1889, when columns sent in from the west and east succeeded under extreme difficulties in working their way through these obstacles, and effected a junction in the centre of the country. This accomplished, exploration was extended, and post after post established, and the pacification of the country—the occupants of which are known under the general name of the Chin tribes—is being surely if slowly accomplished. The work undertaken to the north of Burma has been much of the same kind. The tribes—Kachins and others—which occupy these tracts had been a source of constant trouble to the Burmese Government, of which they were practically independent; they harboured all the malcontent refugees from Burman misgovernment and levied blackmail on the peaceable dwellers in the open country. The fastnesses to be penetrated in this direction are less difficult than those above referred to, but the country is very extensive, and can be approached only from one side, and the people are brave and skilful in their mode of warfare. The work of pacification is, however, being gradually pushed forward until the whole country shall be reduced to peace and good order up to the Chinese frontier, although it is not in contemplation to occupy all of it permanently, and the administration of a great part of the country will be left to the tribal chiefs. It is these operations of which so much has been heard during

CHAP. V. the last few years—for the pacification of Upper Burma itself was effected in the first three years after annexation; operations carried out as much in the interest of the Burmese themselves, who can now live in security on the frontier, as for establishing the *pax Britannica* throughout the country; operations in which captains and lieutenants have led independent commands and made reputations, and which have illustrated once more the admirable qualities of the gallant native troops an dmilitary police, mostly Gurkhas and Punjabis, by whom the work has been carried out.

The Shans and other tribes on the eastern frontier of Burma, formerly under the nominal jurisdiction of the Burman Government, are more peaceful in character, and in their case it has only been necessary that an exhibition should be made of British power to establish a complete pacification of these extensive territories, which have now become an integral part of the province. These upland tracts, but partially inhabited at present from long absence of any regular government and the security it offers for peace and property, are for the most part healthy and naturally fertile, and will hereafter become a valuable possession. In addition to this outlying portion of the province which has come to us as an inheritance from the Burman Government, there are further extensive tracts beyond the Salween River as far as the left bank of the Mekong, as to which it cannot be said that any specific sovereignty has ever been established, and over which we have not assumed the direct rule; but which have now necessarily come under our political influence in the same degree as other frontier tribes on the borders of the empire.

With regard to all the wild tribes with whom we have come in intimate contact for the first time in Burma, the experience of similar cases on the frontier of Assam indicates that, although absolute savages and

CHAP. V.

ferocious in habit at the outset, when once subdued they become soon converted into peaceful, law-abiding subjects; and it is in this direction, dealing with people whose religion does not go higher than a rude fetish worship, untrammelled by the insuperable barriers of the Hindu caste system or the faith of Islam, that the Christian missionary may hope to find one of the most promising grounds in the East for the exercise of his beneficent influence.

Head of this administration should be a Governor,

The province of Burma, which is thus the largest in the Indian empire, and the political and commercial importance of which will certainly become more prominent from year to year, should be constituted into a governorship without loss of time. The administration has altogether outgrown the original character indicated by its present form, and the title of the head of the administration is absurdly inappropriate for the position he holds.

as well as head of Central Provinces, and of Assam.

A similar change is called for in the administrative constitution of the Central Provinces and Assam. In earlier days, when these administrations were first created, the Chief Commissioner of the Province was merely the local representative of the Governor General in Council, which body reserved to itself all nominations to the various administrative posts in the province, as well as complete financial control. These limitations have been gradually withdrawn, and the Chief Commissioner now virtually exercises the entire patronage within his province, and possesses the same degree of financial independence as the Governors in Council and the Lieutenant Governors of the larger provinces. The time has certainly come when this expansion of his authority should be distinctly recognised, and the head of the administration be called—what he is already in everything but the name—a Governor. The notion commonly obtains among those who have to deal with these matters that the head of an Indian province should

CHAP. V.

properly be called a Lieutenant Governor, and (as has been mentioned above) it has been proposed at various times that, for the present Governors in Council of Madras and Bombay, a Lieutenant Governor should be substituted. But clearly the next place in the official hierarchy below the Governor General is not a Lieutenant Governor, but a Governor. The former title would be appropriate only in the case of a province being subdivided into Lieutenant Governorships under the Governor. It has, indeed, been objected that, whereas a Lieutenant Governor is a person nominated by the Government of India, a Governor must necessarily be appointed by the Queen, that is by the Secretary of State of the day. This idea, however, is not based on the natural condition of things, but merely on the fact that while the Lieutenant Governors are selected from the Indian service, and nominated by the head of the Government there, the two Governors of Madras and Bombay are appointed from home. But there is no innate necessity for this distinction being maintained. When the Straits Settlements were under the Indian Government the officer in charge was a 'Governor,' but the office carried smaller emoluments than attach to many comparatively subordinate appointments. The nominating authority, in each case, is a point to be settled by the Act of Parliament which makes the change of title, and would, no doubt, be determined by the fact that for all these Governorships, except Madras and Bombay and perhaps Bengal, local experience is an absolutely necessary condition for an effective administration. The change here advocated is called for if only to bring home to the people of England the magnitude and importance of the great provincial appointments of the Indian empire. For so long as the present nomenclature is maintained, people who are well informed on other subjects will continue to be possessed with the notion that India is still divided into three Presidencies, that the Governments of Madras and Bombay are next in importance to the Government of India, and that the other great provinces are merely outlying tracts which are administered in some sort of way imperfectly understood by the direct agency of the Supreme Government. With a more appropriate classification the actual organisation of the Indian empire in eight great provinces[1] under Governors having all equal independence and authority, and all occupying the same relative position to the Supreme Government, would then come to be understood, and questions of Indian administration might receive more rational treatment than they now get. If, however, it would facilitate the change here advocated, Lieutenant Governors might be assigned to the two less important provinces—the Central Provinces and Assam. The ruler of Burma should certainly be a Governor, but the administration of that province has not yet reached the stage of development to need the establishment of an Executive Council.

Statutory authority for nearly the whole of these changes already exists. The Act of 1833 provides for the appointment of a Governor in Council to the 'Presidency of Bengal and of Agra (North West Provinces),' and the same Act empowers the Home Government of India to alter the limits from time to time of the several Presidencies. An Act of 1835 gave power to the Court of Directors to suspend the creation of separate Presidencies of Bengal and Agra, and to appoint a Lieutenant-Governor to that part of the then existing Bengal Presidency which was to have formed the Agra Presidency. But the first Act appears to be still in force, and Section 57 gives power to the Court (now to the Secretary of State) to determine the number of Councillors to be appointed to any Presidency, or to

[1] Eight provinces, excluding the great tract of Baluchistan, and the smaller administrations—Berar, Ajmir, Coorg, and the Andamans.

CHAP. V.

suspend the appointment of Councils therein. Further, the Act of 1861 empowers the Governor General to appoint a Lieutenant Governor to any province. To this authority, however, is attached the condition that a Legislative Council shall thereon be established in the province, and the Acts as they stand, while apparently still giving authority to convert the Lieutenant Governors of Bengal and North West Provinces into Governors, and to advance any Chief Commissionership to a Lieutenant Governorship, does not provide for the case of Punjab and Burma if these are to be made Governorships, while the law as regards Bengal and the North West Provinces introduces the obsolete term 'Presidency,' which ought, under any circumstances, to be got rid of. And on every consideration it will no doubt be desirable, if not absolutely necessary, to obtain fresh statutory powers from Parliament for all the matters to be embraced in this important and much-needed reform.

Economical scale of Indian government establishments.

In connection with this subject of the Provincial Governments, a noteworthy point is the simplicity and economical scale on which they are organised, a characteristic of Indian administration generally, which is entirely opposed to the superficial view commonly held on the subject, and which is in striking contrast to what obtains in other parts of the British possessions. The Governors of Madras and Bombay indeed have establishments adequate to their position.[1] The three Lieutenant Governors have each a private secretary and one aide-de-camp. A Chief Commissioner has no per-

[1] Perhaps more than adequate in one respect. In addition to a private secretary and a couple of aides-de-camp, these Governors have each a military secretary on their staff. The title is a misnomer; the officer in question has nothing to do with military business, which, so far as it has not already come to an end, is conducted by the military secretary to the Government—an officer at the head of the military department, and not on the personal staff of the Governor. The former is, in fact, merely a superior aide-de-camp, the head of the Governor's household, and his duties are wholly of a ceremonial kind.

sonal staff, but he is allowed the services of a junior member of the civil service as a personal assistant to help him in his private correspondence. Thus an officer governing a territory as large as a European kingdom, with a population of many millions, and living among a people who attach an almost excessive degree of importance to the outward trappings of rank, lives like a private gentleman, and, it may be added, on a smaller salary than the governors of some petty islands in the West Indies and outlying settlements.

Some territorial redistribution desirable.

It will have been gathered from the historical summary in Chapter III., that the present distribution of territory among the provinces of India has come about in a more or less haphazard way, governed by the circumstances of the times, and in many cases without regard to distinctions of race and language. A redistribution, based on those distinctions, is indeed impracticable, short of subdividing India into a very much greater number of provinces; but there are some strong reasons in favour of a certain amount of redistribution, indicated by the practical inconvenience which attends the maintenance of the present administrative divisions.

After a brief term of a separate government for Sind, that province was attached to Bombay, but the amalgamation has been from the first distinctly inconvenient and inappropriate. The people of Sind differ entirely in race and language from the people inhabiting the rest of the Bombay Presidency, and Sind being separated from the latter by the great Indian desert, communication is, and is likely for an indefinite time to be practicable only by sea. The port of Karachi, on the other hand, is the natural outlet for the commerce of Punjab, and the line of separation between the two provinces is purely artificial. The main line of railway through Sind is merely a continuation of the Punjab system of railways, and is administered from Lahore;

CHAP. V.

while the control of diplomatic relations on the mountain frontier of Sind was many years ago removed from the cognisance of the Bombay government. The propriety of transferring Sind from Bombay to Punjab has therefore long been recognised. The practical objection, beyond the temporary inconvenience which attends all such changes, is that with the loss of Sind and its three millions of people and fifty thousand square miles (a large part, however, consisting of desert), Bombay, already the smallest of the great provinces, would still further become disproportionately small. A rational compensation, however, might be given by adding to Bombay some of the western districts of the Central Provinces, inhabited by Marathi-speaking people in close affinity with those of the adjacent Bombay provinces, and for the trade of which Bombay is the natural outlet. In fact it may be said that if, when the province of Nagpur was annexed some forty years ago, the railway system had already been in existence, that province would certainly have been attached to Bombay in the first instance. If this change were now carried out, compensation might advantageously be given to the Central Province by attaching to it some, if not all, of the existing districts now known under the general name of Orissa. The parts of these ceded by the Marathas in the time of Lord Wellesley, were added to the Bengal Presidency as the only arrangement possible at the time, and they formed part of the Lieutenant Governorship created in 1854. But land communication between Bengal and Orissa has always been difficult and tedious, and although this difficulty may eventually be overcome by railways, the people of Orissa are not Bengalis; it would be advantageous to give the Central Provinces an outlet to the sea, and a great advantage to reduce the excessive size of the province of Bengal.

A further change in the same direction is indicated

by obvious political and geographical conditions. The maritime district of Chittagong has no natural affinity with Bengal, while land communication between the two can only be established in the distant future. Chittagong, indeed, has hitherto been cut off on the land side from every other part of the world by roadless tracts deemed impassable; but the railway now in course of construction from that port up to the north of Assam, will bring it into easy communication with that province, to which it would make an appropriate addition. All the districts south of Assam, indeed, might advantageously form part of the transfer, which would comprise an area of 12,000 square miles, with about four millions of people. Bengal would still have a population of sixty-three millions, and would remain the most populous, and commercially, the most important province of the empire, while in the future it is likely to prove the most difficult to govern, another reason for bringing it within more manageable dimensions.

CHAPTER VI

THE SUPREME GOVERNMENT

CHAP. VI.

Development of Government of India out of Government of Bengal.

SOME account has already been given (Chapter III.) of the gradual development of the Government of India from what was, in the first instance, the government of the Bengal Presidency only. The first statutory recognition of a definitive government for the territories of the East India Company in Bengal was accorded in 1773, when a Governor General and Council were appointed to that Presidency. In 1793 that body was given a position of limited authority over the Governments of the other two Presidencies, and the Governor-General, when visiting Madras or Bombay, was empowered to suspend the Government of that Presidency and to assume the administration of it. The Act of 1813, renewing the Company's Charter, made no change in the form of the Government, but by abolishing the right of the Company to trade in India, relieved the Government of the charge of all commercial business save that connected with the Company's monopoly of the China trade, abolished twenty years later. By the Act of 1833 the Governor General in Council of Bengal became the Governor General in Council of India, and was vested with the 'superintendence, direction, and control of the whole civil and military government of all the said territories and revenues in India,' but retained the direct Government of the Bengal Presidency. It has also been explained how, by degrees, the Governor

General in Council has withdrawn from the immediate administration of that or any part of the country, and is now concerned only with the general supervision of the various provincial administrations by the governments which have been constituted for them from time to time. The former presidential system has also come to an end, although the title presidency is still used without any definite meaning, and British India is now actually divided into eight great provinces, each with its own administration in direct subordination to the Supreme Government. Adding to these the smaller provinces and the different administrations through which the business of the various native states is carried out, there are altogether fifteen governments or administrative officers in direct communication with the Governor-General in Council.[1]

The Government of India, while thus gradually withdrawing from the direct government of any part of the country, has, on the other hand, assumed the administration of all the Indian armies; it has also taken immediate charge of the financial business of the country, conducted, as well as the post-office and telegraph departments, by establishments which throughout India are directly under the Supreme Government.[2]

[1] Two Governors in Council—Madras and Bombay.
Three Lieutenant Governors—Bengal, North West Provinces, and Punjab.
Three Chief Commissioners—Central Provinces, Assam, and Burma.
Agent to the Governor General in Rajputana (also Commissioner of Ajmir).
Agent to the Governor General in Central India.
Resident at Hyderabad (and Chief Commissioner of Berar).
Resident in Mysore (and Commissioner of Coorg).
Resident at Baroda.
Resident in Kashmir.
Governor of the Andamans.
To which may be added the Residents in Nepal and the Persian Gulf, territories beyond India.

[2] It has already been mentioned (page 97) that the High Court of Calcutta is still directly subordinate to the Governor General in Council, instead of being, like the other High Courts, under the government of the Province within which its jurisdiction is limited. This anomaly will no doubt before long be got rid of.

CHAP. VI.

Composition of Government of India.

The Government of Fort William, as constituted by the Act of 1773, consisted of the Governor General and four Councillors, who were named in the Act. By the Regulating Act of 1784 it was provided that the Councillors should be three in number, to be chosen from the Civil Service, the Commander-in-Chief being an additional member, and to have 'voice and precedence' next after the Governor General. The nomination of all the members of the Government was vested in the Court of Directors. The Act of 1793, renewing the Company's Charter for a further term of twenty years, confirmed this constitution, but made the appointment of the Commander-in-Chief as an additional member permissive and not obligatory; the power of so appointing him has always been acted on from that time. The Act of 1833 provides that one of the three ordinary Councillors, heretofore all appointed from the civil service, might be appointed from the army, a provision which has ever since been acted on.

Its legislative powers.

By the Act of 1773 the Government of Bengal, in addition to its executive functions, was given statutory powers to make laws (styled 'Regulations') for that presidency. Later Acts gave similar powers to the Madras and Bombay for their respective territories. By the Act of 1833 these powers were withdrawn from the two (now) subordinate governments, and the duty of making laws and regulations for the whole of India was placed on the Supreme Government, which was strengthened for the purpose by the addition of a fourth member, whose appointment was made on the nomination of the Court of Directors, approved by the Crown. This additional member, whose qualifications were not stated, but who it was contemplated should always be an English lawyer, had rank and precedence after the other members, and was not to take a part in the executive business of the Government, but could sit and vote only at meetings for making laws and regulations.[1]

In the same Act an important provision was introduced that the Supreme Council might meet in any part of India. Before this, proceedings held anywhere but at Fort William (Calcutta) would have been invalid. This provision, however, was not made use of until thirty years later.

Government of India relieved of administration of N.W. Provinces, and of Bengal.

It was under the Act of 1833, modified by an Act of 1835, that the civil administration of the North West Provinces was vested in a Lieutenant Governor as already described.

In 1853 an Act was passed renewing the Company's government of India, not for a further definite term as heretofore, but 'until Parliament shall otherwise provide.' The same Act authorised the appointment of a Lieutenant Governor for Bengal, and that thereon the Governor General should cease to be Governor of that province. By this change the Supreme Government was relieved of the direct administration of any part of the presidency of Fort William. The same Act restored to the Governments of Madras and Bombay the power of local legislation, and created the system of Legislative Councils, Supreme and Local, described in the next chapter.

Change of title.

In 1858, on the transfer of the Government of India from the Company to the Crown, and the creation of a Secretary of State and Council of India at London, the Supreme Council in India became the 'Council of the Governor General.'

Expansion of Council.

In 1861 was passed the Indian Councils Act, by which another or fifth member was added to the Governor General's Council. Until 1859, the fourth ordinary member had always been a barrister; but in that year the financial difficulties of the Indian Government led to a vacancy in that office being filled up by the ap-

[1] The first person appointed to this office was Mr. [Lord] Macaulay.

CHAP. VI.

pointment of an experienced financier (Mr. James Wilson, then Secretary to the Treasury); and on his death in the following year his successor at the English Treasury was appointed to his place. This arrangement had left the Council for the time without a legal member, and it was therefore provided by the Act of 1861 that the Council should consist of five ordinary members, of whom three only must belong to the Indian service, and that one member should be a barrister of five years' standing. At the same time all the ordinary members were placed on an equal footing, and henceforward held precedence in order of appointment, and took part in all the deliberations of the Council.

Provision for filling temporarily office of Governor General.

Heretofore the senior ordinary member of Council succeeded under statutory provision to the office of Governor General, should it be vacated, pending the arrival of a successor. Since, under the new arrangement as to seniority, the senior member might be a person appointed for legal or financial requirements, without experience of Indian administration, it was now provided that such vacancy should in future be filled temporarily by the Governor of Madras or of Bombay, whichever had been first appointed.

Mode of appointing Councillors.

Until 1869 the two members of the Governor General's Council above referred to were appointed by the Queen by warrant under Her Majesty's Sign Manual, while the other three members (belonging to the Indian service) were appointed by the Secretary of State in Council with the concurrence of a majority of members present at a meeting. By an Act passed in this year, it was provided that all the members of the Governor General's Council should be appointed in the same way, by Royal Warrant. In other words, the patronage of these appointments was transferred from the Secretary of State in Council to the Secretary of State.[1]

[1] All these appointments of Governor General, Governors, and Members of the different Councils in India, are held for five years. This

CHAP. VI.

Appointment created of Public Works Member of Council.

In 1874 an Act of Parliament was passed providing for the addition of a sixth member to the Governor General's Council for 'public works purposes.' The same Act makes it permissible to diminish the number of the other members, saving that the legal member be always maintained. This is the first instance of the law specifically assigning particular duties to a member of council. As a matter of fact, the Act is now in abeyance. On the first occurrence of a vacancy in the new office, in 1880, it was not filled up, and the Council has ever since remained at its former strength of five ordinary members, and the charge of public works business has been taken by one of these without any reference thereto in his warrant of appointment, under the general arrangements made for the transaction of business by the Government of India to be referred to presently.

Council formerly a consultative body,

The affairs of the Government of India are conducted like those of all other governments in various departments—foreign, finance, military, &c., each in charge of a secretary under whose signature, according to statutory provision, every order of the Government must issue.[1] But although its business is thus distributed among appropriate departments, until a comparatively recent period these were superintended and dealt with by the Government in its collective capacity. The law recognised only a Governor General in Council, and by the Governor General in Council all business was carried on. In earlier times, indeed, the Government was a board, whose proceedings, as is well known, the President with difficulty controlled, and whose conflicting decisions, swaying to and fro as the

however, is a practice determined only by usage and understanding; no limit of time is specified in the warrants of appointment.

[1] The Act of 1798 (sect. 39) prescribes that the signature shall be that of the Chief Secretary, and that 'all orders shall be expressed to be made by the Governor General in Council, and not otherwise.' By the Act of 1813 the signature may be that of the Secretary of the Department to which the proceedings relate.

CHAP. VI.

majority turned to one side or other, spread confusion, indecision, and disgrace over the land. This defect was remedied by the Act of 1786, which enabled the Governor General to override the decision of the majority of the Council after an interchange of minutes in which the opinions on both sides should be formally recorded. The power (renewed in subsequent statutes) thus held in reserve it has practically never been necessary to employ. With the introduction of the proviso a reaction took place, and from being uniformly obstructive the Council became perfectly subservient. In the time of the Marquis Wellesley its share in the business of the Government appears to have been merely formal. The 'board,' as he used to term it, was seldom consulted till after the event, and orders were more often issued in his sole name than on their joint authority. This practice appears to have been quite illegal, so long as the Governor General was with the Council at Calcutta; but appointment to the Council in those days was determined by seniority, and the dullest man had his turn. After Lord Wellesley left India, the procedure reverted to what the Acts of Parliament contemplated. Under this procedure the Council acted in the capacity of advisers only, offering opinions on the cases put before them, but exercising no individual responsibility. All papers requiring the orders of Government were circulated by the secretary of the department among all the members of the Government, in order of seniority, and therefore being first laid before the Governor General. Cases the opinions recorded on which were in accord with each other, were then usually disposed of by the secretary; those on which there appeared to be a difference of opinion were brought up to meetings of Council for personal discussion.

An obvious defect in this procedure was the order of circulation; the member of the Council best qualified from previous experience to deal with a case might be the junior, who would get the papers last, so that his colleagues might have no opportunity of learning his opinion on it before recording their own. Another defect lay in the burden thus placed on the Governor General, who had to lead off in every case, not only with an opinion, but by setting out the issues on which opinions must be recorded. In fact the procedure was appropriate for only a very limited amount of business. As the affairs of the Government became continually more weighty and complex, from the great extension of territory, the introduction of railways and other public works on a large scale, and the development of education and all branches of the civil administration, they became altogether beyond the power of one man or a council acting collectively to deal with. Lord Dalhousie, before resigning the office of Governor General, recorded an authoritative opinion to this effect. The enormous extension of territory which occurred during his term of office sufficiently accounts for the great increase of business which dates from that time; and to prevent an utter collapse, under the pressure of affairs in all departments—military, political, financial, &c.—caused by the Mutiny, Lord Canning abolished the practice of dealing with business by the Council collectively, and introduced a beginning of the present system, under which each member takes the management of one or more branches of the administration, and only important affairs are referred to the Governor General, or to the whole Council. This, however, was at first merely a matter of private understanding and arrangement within the Council; the first public announcement of the introduction of what is virtually a cabinet government, was in effect made when James Wilson was appointed a Member of Council, as has been mentioned above, in order to take specific charge of the financial business of the Government, the responsibility for which was distinctly accepted by him and his successors, and

CHAP. VI.

recognised by the Governor General and the rest of the Council. The arrangement was not however in the first instance legal, since the Act of 1853 and preceding Acts required that every order or proceeding of the Indian Government should be the order or proceeding of the Governor General acting in conjunction with his whole Council; but the Act of 1861 legalised it, a clause therein providing that the Governor General should be empowered to make any arrangements he may deem fitting for the more convenient disposal of the business of the Council, and that any act done under the orders so passed 'shall be deemed to be the act of the Governor General in Council.'

has now become a body of ministerial heads of departments.

The system thus introduced has since then been fully developed, and the Governor General and his Council now practically form a cabinet of administrative heads of departments, the premier in which, however, besides holding a much higher official and social position than the other members, takes a much more active share in the superintendence of the various departments than is the case in any European country. Perhaps the position might be more accurately likened to that of an absolute monarchy where the king rules through his responsible ministers, but yet rules himself.[1] The Governor General always himself takes charge of the Foreign Department, the most important and perhaps the most laborious of all, which comprises the affairs relating to all territories other than the British provinces, both within and beyond the frontier. The Home Department, under a member of the Civil Service, which deals with all business connected with the general internal administration of British India; the Department of Finance and Commerce, the minister in charge of which may or may not be a

[1] This simile, of course, puts out of sight the controlling power of the India Office, and regards the Indian Government merely in respect to its relations with India.

member of the Indian service; the Legislative Department under the legal member; the Military Department which administers the army and marine service under the military member; and the Public Works Department, make up the list of administrative bureaus.

This change of system, and the increasing pressure of public business which has brought it about, involved another important modification in procedure. The Governor General had been frequently called away for prolonged periods from the seat of Government, while the Council always remained there. This state of things first received statutory recognition in the Act of 1793, which provided that on the Governor General going to another Presidency (the only form of absence which appears to have been contemplated), the powers of the Governor in Council therein should be suspended, and that during such absence from his own government, a President of the Bengal Council should be appointed who should exercise the powers (not of the Governor General) but of a Governor in Council. During the absence of the Governor General, therefore, the Council while exercising specific functions, was reduced to a subordinate position, the Governor General still apparently retaining his authority over the Presidency of Fort William, although this is not expressly stated. The provision was defined more clearly and its terms modified in the Act of 1833, in which authority was given to the Governor General in Council from time to time to pass a law, authorising the Governor General, when visiting any part of India, to exercise all the powers possessed by the Governor General in Council collectively, except the power of making laws and regulations; the Governor General in such cases was to nominate a member of the Council to be President of it during his absence, who would exercise his powers. This provision was very largely made use of; many of the Governor Generals until 1863 were absent from

Calcutta and the Council during the greater part of their term of office. The Member of Council nominated to be President was always the senior of that body, an arrangement made statutory by the Act of 1861. During these absences the Governor General was accompanied by some of the Secretaries to Government, usually those of the Foreign, Military, and latterly the Public Works Departments, in whose places acting appointments were made to the charge of their respective departments at the capital. Thus there were for the time two distinct and separate governments of India, each having by law full powers as such. The degree to which the Governor General acted on his own responsibility naturally depended in great measure on the character of the person holding the office. For the disposal of ordinary current business it was usual to divide the country into two parts, the business coming up from Madras, Bengal and the countries to the south being dealt with by the President in Council at Calcutta, that from the northern province by the Governor General. This as regards ordinary business; in dealing with the larger questions with which Lord Dalhousie and Lord Canning were specially concerned, the distant Council had necessarily but little share. On the other hand, in proportion as the business of the government became more complicated and technical, especially in connection with finance, the Governor General became less able to act alone or to take an effective share in it while absent from the capital, with the result of a complete congestion of business on these occasions, the disposal of which was necessarily postponed till it could be taken in hand by the Government when re-united. When Sir John Lawrence became Governor General, the administrative delays from this cause had reached a point at which a remedy became absolutely necessary, by the Governor General either ceasing to absent himself from the capital, or taking the Government with him during his absence from it. The latter course, which the improvement in the means of moving about the country then for the first time made readily practicable, was adopted, and except for short winter tours, no Governor General has or will ever again absent himself from his Council.

Effect of the change.

Thus the form of the Government of India has undergone a great change, and from a consultative Council presided over by the Governor General, who initiated all business, and under whose direct orders the secretaries of the different departments carried on their duties, has now become in effect a Cabinet Government, under which the business is carried on as in all European states in separate departments. While, indeed, as has been said, the Governor General takes a much more particular and active share in departmental business than any European prime minister, the extent to which a Member of Council refers departmental business to the former instead of disposing of it himself, is a matter of private understanding between the two. Further, the secretary in charge of each department[1] attends at least once a week separately on the Governor General, who in this way keeps himself informed of the business of the different departments to any extent that he desires; and it rests with the Governor General to decide whether a case referred to him should, or should not go before the whole Council, although the member in charge may claim,[2] if he thinks fit, that such a reference should be made. As a matter of fact, and as would naturally follow under such a system, the great majority of cases in each department are disposed of by the Member of Council in charge on it, the more important being referred to the Governor General. When the two differ as to the mode of dealing with a case, or

[1] The position of the secretary of a department in India is similar to that of the permanent under-secretary of a department at home.

[2] Under statutory provision. 33 Geo. III. Cap. 52, sec. 38.

CHAP. VI.

when the latter thinks it is of sufficient importance for reference to their colleagues, the papers are first circulated among them, and then brought up and discussed at a meeting of the Council.

Position of Governor General in the Council.

In whatever way a decision may be arrived at, whether by the Member of Council in charge, of his own motion, or after reference to the Governor General, or after deliberation of the whole Council, every order issued from a department is signed by the secretary of it in the name of the Governor General in Council. This procedure is strictly in accordance with the law of 1861 already referred to, which provides that the Governor General should have power to make rules for the conduct of the business of the Council, and that every act done in accordance with those rules shall be deemed to be the act of the Governor General in Council. But the personality of the individual member being thus kept out of sight, the nature of the great change which has come over the actual working of the Government, and the degree to which the departmental system has been carried, is still imperfectly understood even in India; while in England the popular belief appears to be that the whole business of the government is conducted directly by the Governor General, acting to some extent with or by the advice of a Council, about whose functions and powers nothing definite is known.

This conception is probably strengthened by the practice of the Secretary of State, or his subordinate Under-Secretary if the former is a member of the House of Lords, when answering a question or in the course of debate, to speak of communications received from the Viceroy, or of instructions or enquiries which were about to be made to him. The minister, when he speaks of 'the Viceroy,' means of course the Government of India as constituted by law, for the Governor General of himself can neither receive nor issue any orders, save in the exceptional cases provided for by statute. The misconception is further strengthened by a practice, in itself unimportant, and in other respects harmless. In the telegraphic communication between the Indian Government and the Secretary of State which goes on daily—one might almost say hourly, in order that a message may get on to the wire as an official one, and so be charged to the proper head of service, it must carry the stereotyped official address 'From Viceroy to Secretary of State,' or *vice versâ*; and thus, as many of these in the case of military operations, famines, &c., are published in the English newspapers or in blue books in their original form, when the public see, for example, 'Viceroy to Secretary of State, send out the ten locomotives at once,' or, 'Men on famine relief works reduced to 2,450,' they naturally suppose that these telegrams have emanated directly from the Viceroy, whereas they are purely departmental messages, of which in all probability he knows nothing, and about which he certainly ought not to have been troubled.

Having regard, however, to the actual facts, apart from popular impressions, it might appear from the foregoing statement that relatively to each other the Council have gained and the Governor General has lost authority from this change of procedure. The Member of Council who now initiates all business in his own department, and disposes of the greater part of it on his own authority, in the name of the Governor General in Council, occupies a much more important position than he formerly did, while the law is still in force under which, upon all cases which come before it, the decision is determined by the votes of the majority; the Governor General has a casting vote, but this, in a council of seven, can seldom come into operation. In any despatch to the Secretary of State upon a case where the Council have not been unanimous, the opinion of the Government of India therein expressed is always

CHAP. VI.

the opinion of the majority, and cases are to be found in blue books where the Governor General has been among the minority which, according to the rules, has merely the right of recording a minute of dissent.[1] But, as so often happens in public affairs, the actual practice is very different from the theoretical and formal conditions. Not to press the familiar illustration of the English Privy Council, the functions of which have been superseded by the Cabinet, a body unknown to the law, there are not wanting indications that the Cabinet itself is undergoing the process of being superseded by a smaller informal body within it, and that before long the position of a Cabinet Minister will of itself carry little more significance than that of a Privy Councillor. And in the case of the Government of India there are various conditions which more than counterbalance the apparent and theoretical preponderance of a majority of the Council. The rapid postal service of modern times, and still more the telegraph, place the Viceroy in much more frequent and intimate communication with the Home Government than used to be the case. He has thus information of the opinions and sentiments of the Secretary of State and the Cabinet which may be, and often must be, unknown to his colleagues, and is therefore in a much better position to know whether any proposed action is or is not practicable than they can be. Moreover the Member of Council (his rights and responsibility under the law notwithstanding) must always feel that while perhaps even his name may be unknown out of India, and that, his brief term of office ended, he will retire into obscurity, the Governor General, *vis-à-vis* to the Home Government and Parliament, and in the view of the British public, is the one person responsible for the government of India; that

[1] That the decision in all cases should be governed by the votes of the majority is implied in previous Acts, but is explicitly laid down in the Act of 1833.

upon him will and must rest the credit for good results, and equally the odium for any mistakes or misfortunes, if not wholly, at any rate in a very much greater degree than upon his colleagues. These considerations must always be present before the Members of the Council as a check against any undue tendency to assert their own views and opinions against his. Further, the right of initiation lies practically with the Governor General; he can prevent, or at any rate retard a decision being arrived at against his own opinions. Except in the business of his own department the Councillor's action comes in only at the stage of criticism on proposals already formulated, while, as has been said, the Governor General, conducting the Foreign Department—the most critical of all—has naturally a greatly freer hand than a Member of Council would have in the same position. At any rate the system works very smoothly, with little or none of the friction which, under a strict interpretation of the law, it might be assumed would often arise. The Viceroy, usually a man of superior ability and experience gained in English public life; his Councillors, men who have made their way by force of ability to the head of a service composed of able men, who bring with them an experience gained in an official lifetime: when men so circumstanced meet round a table to discuss business, of which the fullest information is available to all of them, and where no party prejudices are called into play, they will usually arrive at a unanimous decision. And so, as a fact, differences and formal dissents are the exception; and while the Governor General has, under the law, the power of formally overriding the Council or a majority of it, no instance has ever occurred—at any rate none has occurred for many years—of this power being resorted to. Further, the Governor General, as the head of the State, the representative of the Queen, and the fountain of honour, stands apart from his Government; and, conducting as

CHAP. VI. he does himself the department which deals with native States, the Government in their eyes is embodied in his person, a conclusion warranted in their case by the fact that the British representative at the court of a native state is styled 'Agent to the Governor General,' and not Agent to the Government of India. On the whole it may be said that the authority of the Governor General has increased rather than diminished; that he is called upon now-a-days to intervene only in the more important class of business, instead of as in old taking the lead in everything, is because this is the only possible way of carrying on the government, with the enormous mass of business that has now to be dealt with, and of enabling the head of it to get through his share. As it is, the cases referred to the Governor General from other departments make together a formidable daily mass of papers. And this is only a part of his work. In constant and intimate communication with the different governments and administrative agents throughout the country, as well as with the Secretary of State at home; with the immediate charge of diplomatic business within and without the empire, from which some cause for anxiety is never absent; loaded, in addition, with the burden of ceremonial duties, especially in connection with the chiefs and princes of a country where ceremonial and etiquette possess an exaggerated degree of importance, duties ever increasing as the means of travel and communication improve; the Governor General of India has literally hardly ever an hour to call his own, and the office involves the carrying a sustained burden of business, high pressure, and anxiety which only great powers and public spirit can sustain unimpaired for even the few years of a Viceroy's reign.[1]

[1] It may be mentioned that the title of Viceroy has no statutory recognition. It was first used in the Queen's proclamation of 1858, announcing the assumption of the Government of India by the Crown. The only title employed in Acts of Pariament is that of Governor

Relative position of councillors and governors of provinces.

The administrative system of the Government of India above described, which is thus the outcome of long practical experience, offers little room for practical improvement. But it is inconsistent with the actual state of things that the position of a Member of the Governor General's Council should be inferior in precedence and emolument to that of a Governor or a Lieutenant Governor. It is unquestionably the more important. Not to say that the member is in fact the authority to whom the provincial government submits its references for orders, the one has a much greater influence on the progress and efficiency of the administration than the other, the great changes and reforms in it being usually initiated by and carried out through the influence and agency of one or other of the members of the Council. This greater importance ought to be properly recognised and the precedence of these different authorities to be modified accordingly. Further, it is not desirable that the Governor General should have, as Members of his Council, persons whose further advancement should be dependent on the pleasure of himself and his colleagues. They are appointed to the Council by the Queen and their position in that capacity is therefore thoroughly independent; and it is not appropriate that they should be eligible for subsequent advancement to a Lieutenant Governorship by a lower authority.[1] I am far from wishing to imply that these conditions exert any conscious influence in restraining the independence of a Councillor. The sense of duty, and a man's own temperament whether in the way of obstinacy or weakness, are usually more powerful incentives to conduct than the smaller impulse of self-interest; but from all the considerations advanced, it

General, and, what is singular also, the title of Viceroy has not been introduced into the Queen's Warrant of appointment of a Governor General.

[1] Lieutenant Governors are appointed by the Governor General in Council.

CHAP. VI.

does seem desirable that the position of a Member of the Governor General's Council should be recognised as and made the highest in India, under that of the Governor General, to which an Indian public servant can rise, and beyond which he should have no preferment in India to look forward to.

Commander-in-Chief also a member of Council.

It has been mentioned that the Commander-in-Chief is an extraordinary member of the Council. He has not charge of any department, for which indeed his own duties would leave him no sufficient leisure, but he takes part in all the deliberations of the Council. He thus acts in a twofold capacity, being a member of the Government, and also as Commander-in-Chief its servant. The position has sometimes been objected to on the ground that it is incongruous that an official should first of all submit proposals to the government, and then be able to come up and vote upon them as a member of that body. An objection of another kind has also been taken, that an officer, presumably the ablest and most experienced available, should be for administrative purposes subordinate to the Military Member of Council, usually a junior and presumably less experienced and distinguished officer. This last objection is only made by those who have lost sight of the constitutional principles which govern the relations between the State and the Army, and by assuming that the Commander-in-Chief in India is vested in some indefinite way with more independent authority than is possessed by the Commander-in-Chief in England, or indeed in any country, an assumption based on no foundation. The Commander-in-Chief is at the head of one department of the army, the command and discipline of the troops, the most important department, but still only one of many. In this respect he has full authority, subject to the regulations laid down by the Government, and as responsible for the discipline and efficiency of the troops he has the practically uncontrolled power of selection for appointments in all the combatant branches of the army, involving an enormous patronage which as regards the Indian army (the native troops) extends to every regimental post, as well as to every staff appointment in the country.[1] But besides this great department of discipline and command under the Commander-in-Chief, there are also the various administrative departments of the army, for the most part spending departments, the ordnance, commissariat, transport, clothing, fortifications and military buildings, and stud; these, which together with the business which comes up from the Commander-in-Chief, make up the whole business of the army, are administered in the military department of the government by the Military Member of Council. The objection that in this connection a senior officer ought not to be placed under a junior is obviously irrational. The functions of the Military Member of Council are exercised as a member of the Civil Government, in which capacity his military rank is so far in abeyance that he is ineligible to exercise any military command. In England the exigencies of party government seldom admit of the services of a military officer being available as Secretary of State for War, which is an enormous disadvantage to the military administration. In India, at any rate, the system in force is essentially the same as that which obtains in the great countries of Europe, where the spending departments of the army, as well as the Commander-in-Chief (when there is one), are directly under the civil government as represented by the Minister of War. As to the proposal sometimes put forward from perfectly irresponsible quarters that the spending departments—the commissariat, ordnance, and so forth, which deal with what is technically called supply, should be put directly under the Commander-in-

[1] The nominations to a very few of the highest commands are made by the Horse Guards.

CHAP. VI.

Chief, involving in fact the abolition of the Military Member of Council, it may perhaps be sufficient to say that there is no sort of precedent for such an arrangement. Nominally this has indeed been done lately in regard to the British army, but only nominally, for in fact the action of the Commander-in-Chief is controlled at every point by the civil departments at the War Office, and so far as the change has been carried, it has led to nothing but increased confusion and mal-administration, and would inevitably break down under the first stress of war. Even so in England the authority of the civil minister is still maintained over the Commander-in-Chief. If the office of Military War Minister in India were abolished, the financial and administrative responsibility now exercised by him would have to be transferred to one of the civilian councillors, thus introducing all the evils of the English system without the necessity arising from party and parliamentary government to bring it about. The Indian system, which in all essential respects corresponds exactly with what obtains in Germany and France, has always worked with perfect success, whereas that lately set up at home—in violation of all precedent and without any parliamentary sanction—has never been put to the test of trial; it has been unequivocally condemned by an authoritative royal commission, and those who are best acquainted with the subject predict disastrous failure whenever trial shall be made of it. Apart from these considerations there is the practical objection that the Commander-in-Chief in India has as much to do as one man can perform in the command of all the Indian armies, which involve his absence from the seat of government for many months in the year, and would render it impossible for him to give that personal attention to the details of the administrative departments which require continuous attention from day to day.

The other objection taken to the system, is that the

Commander-in-Chief, a servant of the Government, should be also a member of that Government. But in India military affairs are relatively of so much greater importance than in England, that it is of the highest advantage to the Government to be in immediate personal communication with the head of the army. So far from the position of the military member of Council being weakened by the arrangement, it is in reality greatly strengthened. When the Commander-in-Chief has personally to advocate and discuss with his colleagues in Council measures submitted by him in his executive capacity, the necessity for proposals involving expenditure which might seem reasonable and indeed unanswerable when framed in the Adjutant-General's office, may often be found to disappear under such criticism. In this way the financial position of the military member receives support rather than the reverse from the presence of his military colleague in the Council. On the other hand, the condition that the Commander-in-Chief as a member of Council can appeal to the Viceroy, and from him to the whole Council, against a decision of the military department, ensures that the proposals put forward by him shall be fully and fairly considered. He has access to all the papers in the case, and the opportunity of replying to the arguments advanced by the Military Department in opposition to his own, and in this way a decision satisfactory to all parties will usually be arrived at on a basis of reasonable compromise.

At first sight it might seem, indeed, that a system, under which one man is responsible for the efficiency as well as the discipline of troops, while another authority is responsible for supplying the equipments on which that efficiency is largely dependent, involves a dangerous division of responsibility. It is, however, as has been said, the system which obtains in every well-administered army. A discussion on this point cannot

CHAP. VI.

be pursued here, but it may be just mentioned that as regards the Indian military administration, the actual practice naturally diverges from what may appear to be the official order of procedure. As a matter of fact, the disposal of questions of equipment, armament, and defence is the result of joint deliberation. No change of equipment, no military work is carried out without the opinion of the Commander-in-Chief being formally obtained in writing. Almost all changes arise out of proposals initiated by the Commander-in-Chief himself; and apart from the formal correspondence there will always be, between reasonable men, a full and free personal discussion. And while the Commander-in-Chief, who has theoretically as well as practically the whole patronage of the army, and nominates to every command—the action of the Government being limited to confirming his nominations, these nominations, when good sense and good judgment obtain in high quarters (where these qualities are usually found) will commonly be the result of previous communications, and will further have obtained the approval of the Viceroy before they are made. Similarly, while the military member of Council nominates to all the administrative appointments, he will be unfit for his position if he does not take care that his nominations shall be in general accordance with the wishes of the Commander-in-Chief, so that these important posts may be filled by men who have the confidence of the latter.

Economical footing on which council is organised.

The Council of the Governor-General presents another illustration of the simplicity attending some aspects of Indian government which has been already referred to in connection with what are called the minor administrations. The contrast between the practice obtaining in England, where the utmost clerical assistance possible is afforded to those charged with administrative duties—not only the minister at the head of the department, but the under-secretary of it, and even the heads of the various sub-departments being each provided with a private secretary, or some corresponding aid under another name—and the state of things obtaining in India, where the Member of Council conducting a great department of the State, and one of the busiest persons in the country, is allowed no assistance of the kind whatever, and carries on his work as a country gentleman or a struggling author might do, is sufficiently striking. In consequence, the Member of Council is overloaded with a lot of petty personal business and semi-official correspondence as to which offence would be given were it to be conducted through his office, or otherwise than in his own hand, and if separated from his family has to begin the day with sending or answering his dinner invitations, a condition in the last degree extravagant, because wasteful of time that should be better employed. That he should not be allowed some assistance of the kind so plainly needed to save him from these vexatious interruptions, is probably due to a petty feeling of jealousy at the India Office, and incapacity to understand the change which the position of the Member of Council has undergone, from that of an adviser leisurely minuting in his own hand on papers referred to him, and the responsible and often overworked administrators of one of the great departments of the Indian Government.

Seat of Government of India.

The question, what is the most fitting place for the seat of the Government of India, is one which has been much discussed both publicly and privately. The establishment of that Government at Calcutta was in the first instance accidental, due to the circumstance that this Government had gradually grown out of the Government of Bengal. Not to say that the exhausting and unhealthy climate of Calcutta makes it singularly unfit for the transaction of business always carried on at high pressure, there are obvious disadvantages in placing the Government at a distance from all the more

CHAP. VI. powerful and warlike races on whose loyalty and contentment the peace of the country depends, and also in locating it permanently in a Europeanised city. It is not too much to say that a person who passes his official life in Lower Bengal may come away at the end of it knowing little more of India than if he had remained in Europe. The necessity imposed on the Governor General to make himself acquainted with other parts of India, has always taken him away from Calcutta for a considerable part of his time. Almost from the first British occupation of portions of the Himalaya Mountains, in the year 1818, Simla has been occupied as a summer quarter by the Governor General at the end of his cold-weather tours, as well as by the Commander-in-Chief and the Army Headquarter Staff. The Simla ridge was selected from the first for its greater height above the other accessible ranges which rise up from the plains of India, and the contrast it presents between the bare southern slopes of these ranges and the grateful shades of the forest which still covers its summit. The settlement has gradually expanded into a considerable town, but the numerous summer cottages scattered upon its slopes for long furnished the only available accommodation of any sort for the official establishments. For the last thirty years it has been the regular summer residence of the Supreme Government and a portion of the public offices, the remaining part being left at Calcutta, to which the Government returns for the five or six months of the cool season. Simla, besides its comparatively high elevation (8,000 feet above the sea) which gives it a temperate climate, has the further advantage over Darjiling and other Himalayan stations to the eastward of a comparatively moderate rainfall, although even at Simla the rainfall is excessive during the summer months, according to European ideas. It is nearly sixty miles by road from the foot of the moun-

Simla.

tains, up to which only, so far, a railway has been brought. The intervening distance presents however no special obstacles to the construction of a mountain railway, which might and should have been made before this, and the construction of which cannot be much longer delayed; and even with road communication, Simla is only a few hours' journey from what may be termed the military centre of the country. With a temperate but relaxing climate, and during the wet summer months, the absence of any distractions, it is well adapted for the continuous hard work which alone enables the business of the Government to be got through. The great practical difficulty, however, in the way of satisfactory work in this mountain capital was for many years the insufficient accommodation, the public offices, as they were called, being scattered over the mountain slopes in hired cottages—a single department requiring as many as a dozen of these—crazy, dark, and ill-ventilated—a curious contrast to the palace in Whitehall where the home business of India is conducted. For so long as the Government timidly professed to make the summer move to Simla each season for that season only, possibly never to return, this temporary arrangement had perforce to be put up with, and the Government competing with the public for the limited accommodation available drove up house-rent to an artificial rate. To the Marquis of Ripon's administration is due the praise that, in addition to other measures of great merit which have never received proper recognition, it put a stop to this extravagant and discreditable makeshift state of things. During his lordship's viceroyalty permanent buildings were constructed for all public departments, as well as for army headquarters, convenient and substantial, but simple and economical in design, to the great advantage of public business.[1] In this way has

[1] Some of these were not completed until after the arrival of his successor.

CHAP. VI.

Calcutta.

been settled the long-debated question where the seat of the Government of India should be. It was at the same time formally recognised that Calcutta also must continue to be occupied for one half of the year, and under Lord Ripon's Government permanent offices were constructed there for the many departments which during the previous uncertainty had been scattered over the city in hired houses, while various dilapidated government buildings were rebuilt. One want Lord Ripon left to be supplied by his successor. The Viceroy while at Simla, like everyone else occupied a cottage. For so long as he went there for a *villeggiatura*, spent with a small staff in retirement away from his Government, the arrangement was not unsuitable; but when, on being joined by the members of his Government, a small dining-room had to be turned weekly into the Council Chamber, while the rain-driven verandah did duty as a waiting-room for persons in attendance or visitors seeking admission at other times; and when with improved communications the rulers and chiefs of India began to come up to Simla in increasing numbers to pay their respects to the head of the Government, the insufficiency of this accommodation became as inconvenient as apparent. This defect was made good during the government of the Marquis of Dufferin and Ava. The Viceregal Lodge, erected on a high crest of the mountain, now forms the first prominent object seen by the approaching traveller as he winds his way round the spurs of the ascending road, a building handsome and commodious, but not more than appropriate for the purpose; it was finished only in time to be occupied by his successor.

Thus the seat of the Supreme Government has, at last, been finally fixed upon, but, as will have been understood, the decision was arrived at rather as a gradual outcome of circumstances than of deliberate purpose from the first, and it is probably far from being the best possible arrangement. If the thing had to be done over again, probably no one would propose to select Calcutta as a permanent seat of government for even a part of the year. A town set in a swamp out of which there is only a single carriage-road, or the top of a precipitous mountain buried in mists for a great part of the summer, has its obvious drawbacks, while the dislocation of work caused by a move every six months is inconvenient and expensive, but as things are, unavoidable. The west of India, in immediate communication with England by sea, is naturally indicated as the most appropriate position for the seat of government, while there are places on the lofty table-land above the Ghats, as Poona and Nassick, which can be occupied without inconvenience all the year round, and have the advantage of still higher mountain sanataria easily accessible. But it would certainly have involved great effort and much practical inconvenience for some years to have struck out an entirely new line; under the circumstances, Lord Ripon's Government undoubtedly took the best course practicable, and the question may now be regarded as finally disposed of.

CHAPTER VII

THE LEGISLATIVE COUNCILS

CHAP. VII.

Legislative powers of Indian Governments.

We have so far been dealing with the different Indian Governments in reference to their executive functions only. But, in addition to these, they are also charged with the office of framing and passing laws. In the first instance the two functions—executive and legislative—were exercised by the same body. The Governor in Council of Madras and Bombay, as well as the Governor General in Council of Bengal, had each powers to make 'Laws and Regulations' for the territories subject to them respectively, powers first imputed to them inferentially by the Act of 1773, and explicitly conferred by succeeding Acts. In 1833, as has been stated, these powers were withdrawn from the Madras and Bombay Governments, and the duty of legislating for all India was placed upon the Governor General in Council, at the same time created Governor General of India. In this year also there appeared the first germ of what has since expanded into a legislative council, in the appointment (referred to in the preceding chapter) of an additional member to the Supreme Council of India as it was then called, who was declared eligible to sit and vote only at meetings held for the purpose of making laws and regulations.

First Legislative Council.

By the Act of 1853 [1] a Legislative Council of India was formally established, consisting, in addition to the Executive Council, of four members nominated by the

[1] 16-17 Vict. Cap. 95.

Governors of Madras and Bombay and Lieutenant Governors of Bengal and the North West Provinces respectively, with the Chief Justice and one Puisne Judge of the Supreme Court of Calcutta. Two additional members chosen from the Indian service might be and were nominated by the Governor General, so that the Council thus consisted of twelve members, including the Commander-in-Chief. In the absence of the Governor General, who seldom took part in the proceedings, the Chief Justice presided as Vice President. The sittings of this Legislative Council were held in a building specially provided for the purpose, and the proceedings were conducted in public. The Council, as thus constituted, and especially the Vice President (who had been made Chief Justice on the completion of his tour of office as legal member of Council), soon began to manifest a spirit of would-be independence, which took the form of opposition to, or at any rate of criticism on, the proceedings of the Government; an attitude absurdly inappropriate, inasmuch as it was appointed for the purpose of making laws and regulations only, was in no sense representative of anything or anybody, and was obviously from its constitution unfitted to make provisions for the redress of grievances. Its proceedings in this capacity were quickly brought to a stop by an Act of Parliament passed in 1861,[1] reconstituting the legislative body on a new footing. By this Act the number of ordinary members of the Executive Council, now styled the Council of the Governor General (a Council of India having been established in England), was increased from four to five—one to be a barrister of five years' standing, with the Commander-in-Chief, as before, an extraordinary member. In addition the Governor General was to nominate not less than six or more than twelve additional members, one half of whom were to be persons not in the service of

Change made in 1861;

[1] The Indian Councils Act of 1861, 24-25 Vict., Cap. 67.

CHAP. VII.

the Government. All laws passed by the Council before coming into operation were to receive the assent of the Governor General, or to be reserved by him for the assent of the Queen. Power was also given to the Governor General to pass ordinances which would have the force of law—a power provided for cases of emergency. The same Act established Legislative Councils in Madras and Bombay on a similar basis, the Governor nominating the Advocate General and not less than four or more than eight additional Councillors in each case, of whom half must be non-officials. The legislative power of these Local Councils was limited to such local affairs as the Government of India might decide not to deal with in the higher council. The assent of the Governor General was made necessary to all Bills passed by them. The Act was also applied to Bengal, where a Council of the Lieutenant Governor was established, and authority was given to the Governor General to extend it to the North West Provinces and Punjab by proclamation. In these Councils the number of non-officials was not to be less than one-third the whole number. The Act was applied to the North West Provinces in 1875.

and creation of provincial Councils.

The rules for the conduct of the business of the Legislative Council in India—which may be taken as the type of all the similar local bodies—are framed under the Act by the Governor General. In regard to these, and to the constitution of the Council, it has to be considered that the official councillors must of necessity be in a majority, and that the non-official members are called up, not to initiate measures, which must be framed by the executive Government, but to give advice and counsel during the passage of measures through the Council. But, subject to this condition, the procedure aims at securing the greatest possible publicity to the measures brought forward, and also the fullest criticism; but the debates must be strictly

Procedure.

limited to the discussions of the measure in hand. The meetings are held weekly in the Council Chamber of Government House, the Governor General presiding. Members speak without rising; the public are admitted by orders to the sittings. The proposal to legislate on any subject being first approved in the Executive Council, the Bill is drawn in the Legislative Department with the aid of the member of the Council, executive or legislative, particularly concerned, who takes charge of the measure. If this specially affects some particular province or department, advantage will usually be taken of a vacancy to appoint some official serving in that province or department to the Legislative Council in order that he may take charge of the measure. To the Bill, when printed, is attached a statement of the objects and reasons for which it has been prepared, and the member in charge, when moving for leave to bring it in, further explains its nature in his opening speech. On leave being given to bring it in, the Bill is thereon published in English in the 'Gazette of India' and in the gazettes of all the provinces affected by it, also in the vernacular gazettes of the Local Governments concerned, who are called on to report on the measure. They, in their turn, refer it to the district and other officials concerned, whose reports and opinions are attached to their own when submitted. All these references being received, a select committee of the Legislative Council is appointed to deal with the Bill in the light of the information thus brought to bear upon it, and any further criticism available from officials or non-officials interested is invited. The Bill as amended in Select Committee, after being reported to the Council, is republished in the Gazette, and referred back to the authorities concerned for further consideration. On their final report being received, it is brought up again and ordered to be taken into consideration on a certain date. This

CHAP. VII. reconsideration is ordinarily the final stage, the Bill, after a debate continued for as many sittings as may be necessary, being thereon passed. The Bill, after passing through the Council, becomes law on receiving the assent of the Governor General, but it may be disallowed afterwards by order of the Queen, conveyed through the Secretary of State.

It will thus be seen that the legislative business is mainly done in the Select Committee, the proceedings of which in connection with a Bill of importance will usually extend over several months, and sometimes over several years. The proceedings of the Council are, in fact, the mode adopted of recording formal sanction publicly to the measure; but they afford opportunity to the members who are in a minority in the select committee on certain points to explain their views publicly, as well as to every member, whether he was on the committee or not, to record his opinion whether by way of approval or the reverse. The most prolonged discussions usually take place on questions which involve taxation. It must be remembered, however, that a majority of the Council consists of Government officials, and that from the nature of the case the Government must have means of carrying the measures through which it brings in. The Bills however being seldom of a contentious nature, but introduced in order to provide a recognised statutory want, the criticism arising is generally limited to points of detail, and the final debate is mainly useful as affording an opportunity to the Governor General and Members of the Executive Council to state publicly their reasons for having recourse to the measure of legislation in question.

The constitution of the Legislative Councils, the only part of the administration in which non-official persons take a part, obviously opens up the great question, how far the form of the government of India is susceptible of being further modified in the direction of extending the association of non-official persons in the work of legislation, and of introducing a representative element or otherwise, compatibly with the conditions under which that Government, at any rate for a very long time to come, must necessarily be carried on. Reserving the remarks to be offered upon this important subject for a later part of this work, I will here merely describe the further development which the Legislative Council has recently undergone. By the Indian Councils Act of 1892[1] the number of additional members of the Governor General's Council to be nominated by the Governor General, has been extended to a minimum of ten and a maximum of sixteen—making the whole number twenty-three; while the corresponding numbers for the Councils of Madras (Fort St. George) and Bombay are fixed at eight and twenty respectively, in addition to the Advocate General in each case. The Governor General in Council is authorised to increase by proclamation the number of councillors in Bengal and the North West Provinces to twenty and fifteen. Further, the Governor General in Council, with the approval of the Secretary of State in Council, may make regulations as to the conditions under which these nominations or any of them shall be made by the Governor General, Governors, and Lieutenant Governors respectively, and prescribe the manner in which such regulations shall be carried into effect.

Expansion of Legislative Councils Act of 1892.

Although the Act thus assumes the gradual expansion of these Councils, providing the minimum as well as the maximum number of members for each, this maximum has in each case been nominated at the outset. Further, the alteration made permissive in the mode of nomination, and under which, instead of this being made directly by the Governor General, or Governor or

[1] 55-56 Vict., Cap. 14.

CHAP. VII. Lieutenant Governor and confirmed by the Governor General, as the case may be, the Governor General in Council, subject to the approval of the Secretary of State, may delegate the right of nomination (or to be more accurate, the right of making recommendations of persons to be nominated) for a whole or part of the appointments to other bodies, has been at once availed of. Regulations for giving effect to this delegation have been laid down, as to which the procedure adopted for Bengal and Madras may be taken as illustrations of the arrangements everywhere introduced by them.

In Bengal, thirteen of the twenty members of the Legislative Council are to be nominated by the Lieutenant Governor, of whom not more than ten are to be officials of the government; the nomination of the remaining seven is delegated as follows:—The municipal corporations of the cities and towns in the province will recommend two members; the district (rural) boards of the province will nominate two; one nomination each has been given to the Corporation of Calcutta, the Association of Merchants, and the University of Calcutta.

For the purposes of the election, the municipalities and district boards are grouped in eight divisions, corresponding with the geographical charges of the official Commissioners of Divisions into which the province is divided, and two groups of each class, or four groups in all, will elect one member each. A seat in the Council being held for two years, each group will thus get its turn once in eight years. The votes of each municipality are valued in an ascending scale according to its income, a municipality with an income of 5,000 rupees having a single vote, one with an income of 250,000 rupees and upwards, eight votes. The various district boards have all equally a single vote. Each municipality or district board, as the case may be, which takes part in the election of the year, sends a delegate to the appointed place of meeting within the division, where the election is carried out by ballot, repeated if necessary until some one of the nominated candidates obtain a majority of the whole number of votes. The candidates nominated must be residents in that part of the province for which the election is being held.

The procedure adopted in Madras is somewhat more simple. Here also the Governor makes thirteen nominations, of which not more than nine may be of official persons; the nominations (or rather recommendations for the nomination) of the remaining seven councillors have been made over: to the Corporation of Madras, Chamber of Commerce, and University of Madras, one each; while the Municipal and District boards throughout the province are divided for the purpose of the election into two groups respectively, each nominating one candidate. Each Municipality and District Board has only a single vote, without regard to size or income.

For the Council of the Governor General the nominations to four seats have been made on the recommendation of the non-official members of the four provincial councils; a fifth nomination has been given to the Calcutta Chamber of Commerce.

A similar distribution of nominations has been ordered for the other provinces, provision being everywhere made to ensure that the Government shall command at least a small majority. This is obviously a necessary rule; the conditions of party government being altogether absent, the non-official members are not in the nature of an opposition who can become responsible for the consequences of an adverse vote by being called on in turn to take up the government. Their functions are to advise in legislative matters only, and they are under no sort of responsibility or liability for the consequences of their opinions and votes. The nomination of non-officials being still

CHAP. VII. to a certain extent left to the head of the Government in the different provinces, admits of a selection being made of representatives of classes and interests (so far as representation in the proper sense can be secured), which may have been left out in the selections made by the delegations, a very necessary protection. The first composition of the legislative councils as now established is principally notable in that the delegated nominations have been almost all of lawyers, and, but for the reserved nominations, the interests of the agricultural community, who form a vast majority of the population, would be almost unrepresented.

In thus remodelling the legislative councils, a further step has been taken towards the introduction of a system of debating, permission being given to discuss the annual budget, heretofore permissible only when legislation affecting taxation was before the Council, and also, under strict rules, to use the right of interpellation as it is called, or of asking questions about things in general.

This expansion in size and functions of the legislative councils, the proposal for which emanated from the Government of India, and the details for carrying out which are all in accordance with their recommendations, is thus the first beginning of what may possibly hereafter develop into something of the nature of parliamentary institutions as obtaining in other parts of the world. The step taken may not be a wide one; the mode of regulating nominations rests with the Executive Government; the bodies to whom this partial nomination has been entrusted are themselves elected on a very narrow and exclusive franchise, and have shown so far very little appreciation of, or interest in, the duties of municipal corporations, while they are not in the least representative of the majority of the class whose affairs they have to deal with. But the beginning of such a movement must needs be cautious and the scheme framed on modest lines. In a country where amongst the vast mass of the people the very notion of representation or elective government is still absolutely unknown, whose comprehension of such matters as the nature of government other than an absolute one, is as much below the knowledge of the least educated of the English people, as that of the latter falls behind the intelligence of a professor of constitutional law, the time is still far distant when representative institutions can be applicable. But so far as it goes the change appears to be all in the right direction, while the right of interpellation conferred by the rules should be of the greatest service to the Government, exposed as it is to constant attacks of a press, extraordinarily scurrilous and often openly seditious. Replies to questions put in the legislative councils will offer the Government the means which it has not hitherto possessed of exposing, not only current misapprehensions, but the wilfully false statements which form the staple matter of most of the vernacular newspapers. And it may be possible in this way to obviate the necessity which must otherwise sooner or later be imposed on the Government of placing some restriction on the press if the peace of the country is not to be subjected to the gravest risks. I venture to express the belief that the experiment—for it can hardly be called more than this—which will be watched with interest by all who desire the safe progress of India, may on the whole be regarded without misgivings, and with reasonable hope that it will lead the way to further advances in the same direction.

Municipal and rural District Boards.

In connection with this subject a short account may be useful of the local institutions, the municipalities and district boards to which the election of a part of the legislative Councillors has been delegated, and

CHAP. VII.

Municipalities.

which have been created and modified by various Acts, for the most part of recent date, of the supreme and local legislatures. There are altogether about 750 municipalities in India, a number which includes every considerable town and a good many small ones. The constitution of these municipalities varies greatly, from the large and public-spirited and practically self-governing corporations of Bombay and Calcutta, to small urban bodies the business of which is practically conducted by the magistrate and his officials, aided in little more than name by a few of the more respectable inhabitants nominated for the purpose. The total number of members of such corporations throughout India is about 10,000, giving an average of fourteen to a municipality. Of these the elected members (the electors also are very limited in numbers although on a low franchise), are rather more than one-half, and the officials about one-fourth of the whole. The incomes of these bodies amount in some of the smaller towns to a few hundred rupees only; the aggregate municipal incomes in all India amount to about $3\frac{1}{3}$ millions (Rx.), of which nearly one-third is realised in Bombay and Calcutta, and is derived in large measure (at the inland towns) from octroi duties levied on goods brought into the town, the most popular form of local taxation. Municipal government is of recent creation; the notable features of it are the growth of the elective system and the gradual reduction of the official and British elements. The whole urban population under municipal government is less than 16 millions, or about one-thirtieth of the whole population of the country, an indication of the fact that India is essentially an agricultural country. The incidence of taxation varies from about one-half of a rupee (sixpence) per head in Lower Burma to one-and-a-half rupees in Punjab and the Central Provinces; in the city of Bombay it is $6\frac{1}{4}$ rupees. On the whole local self-government in the towns shows signs of healthy progress, but during the past ten years it has been found necessary to close some municipalities from the inability to obtain the services of persons willing to take an interest in the business; the legal facilities created for municipal self-government are certainly not in arrear at present of the aspirations and wishes of the people.

District Boards.

The Local Board of each Indian district deals with the aggregations of villages comprised within it. The income of each district is collected and spent within it, and is derived from tolls, ferries, fees of various kinds, but mainly from a small cess on land. The total income of these boards in all India is a little more than two-millions (Rx.), of which about three-fourths comes from the land cess. These revenues, which are supplemented to a considerable extent by grants in aid from provincial funds, are applied for the most part to the repairs and maintenance of roads, usually of a simple and inexpensive kind, and valuable especially as feeders to the railways. Of late years sub-divisional boards have been formed in the larger districts—many of which are much larger than the average English county. These boards like the urban municipalities are in course of gradual development from an agency purely or mainly official, to bodies in a certain degree representative of the village communities. Altogether there are between thirteen and fourteen thousand persons serving on these boards, of whom about one-half are now elected. Small as are these numbers compared with the population they represent, they probably include every person of capacity or who wishes to take an interest in the business.

CHAPTER VIII

THE CENTRALISED DEPARTMENTS

CHAP. VIII.

BEFORE describing the system of district administration carried on throughout the country, in the efficiency of which the interests of the people are mainly concerned, and on which the security and efficacy of the British Government in India is mainly dependent, some account of the centralised departments may first be given.

Departments under the Supreme Government.

It has already been explained that the Government of India retains the direct control of various branches of the Civil Administration, the business of which is distributed among the following departments:—

Finance Department.

I.—*Finance and Commerce*:—Under the administration of the Financial Member of Council, whose functions correspond with that of the English Chancellor of the Exchequer, the Secretary of the department holding a position analogous to that of the Secretary of the Treasury. The head of the executive department of finance and account is the Comptroller and Auditor General, in whose office all the accounts of the country are brought together and compiled, who is responsible for the proper working of all the account departments throughout India, and is also the final authority for the disposal of all departmental or inter-provincial differences of account. The Comptroller General is also the

Currency Commissioner, and in this capacity exercises the functions which are performed for the British Government by the Bank of England.

The civil accounts of each province are dealt with by an Accountant General, with one or more deputies and assistants, who also conducts the detailed audit of all the civil expenditure. The proceedings of the Accountant Generals are supervised by travelling Inspectors who report to the Comptroller General. The Accountant General exercises twofold functions. As the representative of the imperial finance department he is responsible for the accounts of receipts and expenditure of the imperial revenues within the province—which form by much the larger part of the whole; as financial adviser to the local government he has charge of the purely provincial accounts of the province, as to which it may be observed that one of the difficulties peculiar to Indian accounts arises from the necessity for keeping these two kinds of receipts and expenditure separate and distinct, and of deciding upon the proper incidence of claim and charges between the two. The Comptroller-General is the referee in disputed cases, an appeal lying from him to the Government of India. The whole body of Accountant Generals, and their deputies and assistants, form a graded Accounts Department, whose promotion therein and transference from one province to another are regulated by the Finance Minister on the recommendation of the Comptroller General. But the provincial office establishments, although imperial, are localised, and the members of it are not generally liable to be moved about from one province to another. The department is partly officered, especially in the higher posts, from the Civil Service, partly from officers appointed direct to it in England by the Secretary of State, and partly from selected officers of the provincial establishments promoted to the higher branch.

CHAP. VIII.

Mints.

The two mints of Calcutta and Bombay are under the Finance Department. The coinage being of silver, with the very large subsidiary copper coinage required to meet the conditions of the country, a much larger coinage of pieces is needed than in a country like England which employs a gold currency, and where the economy of metal coins has been carried to a great point of refinement. In consequence the establishments and machinery of the Indian mints are on a much larger scale than those of the English mint. The customs, excise, salt, opium, and stamp departments, although dealing with the imperial revenue, are administered by the Local Governments concerned, under the supervision of the Finance Department of the Government of India.

PostOffice.

The Post Office, an imperial service under the Finance department, is administered by a Director General; under him come the Postmaster Generals of provinces, either civil servants or departmental officers advanced for good service, who form one body for the purposes of promotion, and are available for transfer from one province to another. The Indian postal rates are the cheapest in the world; a letter can be sent from one end of the country to the other, from Peshawur to Mandalay (three thousand miles) for half an anna, value a halfpenny. The postal service, which has had the good fortune to be administered by a succession of very able men, is remarkably efficient, and in respect of the facilities afforded is in some respects in advance of the English post-office. It is now self-supporting, bringing in a small revenue.

Revenue and Agriculture Department.

II. *The Department of Revenue and Agriculture*, which deals with the business denoted by its title, administers also the following departments:—

Survey Department.

Survey of India Department. This carries on three great branches of survey. (1) The Great Trigonometrical Survey, or general measurement of the country. This has been practically completed within India, but is now being carried on to the extensive regions on the north west frontier and in Burma which have recently come under British rule. (2) Various Topographical Surveys, among which may be mentioned more detailed surveys of the territories in Burma and Baluchistan, above referred to,* of tracts already surveyed on larger outlines. At the present time extensive surveys are also being carried out for demarcating the tracts set apart for forest operations, while the changes which the great rivers of India make in their annual floods, washing away great tracts of country in one direction and throwing up new islands and banks in another, give constant occupation to the Survey Department. (3) The Revenue Survey, for recording superficial areas and tracts as the basis of land revenue settlements. The business of surveying, in connection with the development of this great country, is one that necessarily has no definite limits. At the present time, an extensive and protracted series of operations is being carried on of tidal movements along the coasts of India, and for determining the differences of sea level at various points.

The Survey Department is organised at present for these various purposes in twenty-five parties. The whole service, which is presided over by a Surveyor General with three Deputy and three Assistant Surveyor Generals, comprises a staff of forty-five superior officers, of whom the majority belong to the Royal Engineer Corps.

Geological Survey.

A small staff of geologists attached to the government of India have been engaged for many years in a geological survey of India, whose services, apart from the scientific results achieved, have been especially valuable in the discovery of the Indian coalfields now in course of being turned to account, with economic advantage to the country which can hardly be overrated.

A systematic Archæological Survey of the historic

CHAP. VIII. and architectural memorials of India has also been for some years in operation; the researches of this department are so well known to all who take an interest in the subject as to need no detailed reference here. The Marine Survey of the Indian Seas is carried on by the Indian Marine, a branch of the service under Military (Marine) Department of the Government.

Forest Department. Forest Department.—Until the middle of the century the Indian forests were subject to no care or supervision, with the result that in those parts of the country whence timber could be brought to market, a wasteful spoliation of them was carried on by private speculators. In other parts the firing of grass in jungle tracts to prepare the ground for crops caused a wholesale destruction of timber, while in some of the Sub-Himalayan tracts the denudation of the mountain slopes, by the impetus given to floods, wrought great injury to the plain country at their base. About forty years ago a remedy began to be applied to this waste, and through the exertions of the very able and energetic officer charged with the duty, Sir Dietrich Brandis, and his successor Dr. Schlick, the process of destruction has been arrested, and a very efficient system of forest conservancy and improvement established throughout the country, under which the Indian forests already give a surplus of about three-quarters of a million (tens of rupees), and afford promise of becoming a prominent item of public revenue. The management of the forests in each province rests with the Local Governments, but the superior officers form one graded service for the purpose of promotion and employment; the establishment is recruited from the Royal Indian College at Coopers Hill. A general supervision of the whole operations of the department is conducted by the Director General attached to the Government of India.

Civil Veterinary Department. A Civil Veterinary Department has recently been established, officered from the Army Veterinary service, which furnishes the professional instructors for a veterinary college at Lahore, at which the native veterinary staff of the Bengal cavalry receive their training; the other officers of the department are distributed among the different provinces as advisers to the local governments in dealing with cattle disease and the improvement of cattle breeding, a small superintending staff being attached to the Government of India.

Home Department.

Home Department.—This department, which with that of Revenue and Agriculture is administered by the available civilian member[1] of the Governor General's Council, deals with all the business coming up to the Government of India other than the special affairs already detailed and public works, and is the general medium of communication with the provincial governments and Secretary of State, as well as the department in which all business relating to the Government collectively is dealt with, as for example rules for the conduct of business between the departments. The only branch of the civil administration directly administered by the Home Department is the Medical Service, the head of which is the 'Surgeon-General with the Government of India.' The Indian Medical Service, which is a military body in its constitution, supplies the medical staff to the regiments of the native army and shares with the British Medical Staff a proportion of the superior administrative medical staff of the Indian army, British and Native. The portion of the Indian Medical service so employed is under the orders of the Commander-in-Chief. But a large part of it is distributed among the different provinces for the exten-

Medical Department.

[1] The Council comprises five ordinary members, of whom one must be a lawyer, and not more than two may be other than Indian officials. The present military member not being in this category, the other three must belong to the civil service, of whom one has charge of the finance and another of the public works department (the appointment of a member for public works purposes being in abeyance), leaving one member available to administer both the home and revenue departments. The double charge, however, is not more arduous than any of the other single charges.

CHAP. VIII.

sive medical duties connected with the civil administration. While so employed, and detached from military service, medical officers are entirely under the orders of the provincial government under which they are serving, but the arrangements connected with first postings to civil duty, and transfers from one province to another or to military duty, are carried out by the Government of India through the agency of its Surgeon General. This official, in respect of the business connected with the medical officers in military employ and the collective body, including promotions, is attached to the Military Department; in his office are kept the records of service of the whole Medical Department directly or indirectly under his orders.

The Medical Service is the only part of the army in which the presidential system is still maintained. Although separate presidential designations have been abolished, and all the medical officers of the Indian army now belong to one 'Indian' Medical Service, the administration of the Surgeon General with the Government of India does not extend to Madras and Bombay, which have their own Surgeon General, and where the medical officers are limited in the sphere of employment to those two provinces respectively. The arrangement is of course no longer defensible; the medical staff employed on civil duties in either Bengal or the North West Provinces is much larger than that in Madras or Bombay. The separation cannot be much longer maintained. Now that the unification of army administration is at last to be carried out in all other respects this artificial distinction in regard to the medical service is obviously unmeaning and absurd, while placing the officers serving in those provinces at a disadvantage; and would cause, if persisted in, a great deal of needless trouble and complication.

Telegraph Department.

Public works, the administration of which forms another department of the Supreme Government, will be dealt with in a later chapter of this work. This department also administers the Telegraph Department (with a Director General at the head). This is a more appropriate arrangement than to place it like the Post-Office under the Home Department. The telegraph lines being carried in many parts through uninhabited forests and over wild mountain ranges, their construction and maintenance present greater difficulties than the transmission of messages.

Departments of the Provincial Governments.

Provincial Administrative Organisation.

The foregoing account deals with the branches of the civil administration which are administered directly by the Government of India. Each provincial government has also a corresponding organisation, controlled by a local secretariat. In the smaller provinces a single secretary's office deals with the business in all departments; in the larger provinces business is distributed between two secretaries, while Bengal has three.[1] The departments of customs, excise, assessed taxes, salt and opium, are all organised provincially, and administered by the local governments concerned, although the revenues collected by them are credited to the imperial exchequer. The opium department is organised in two agencies for the operations in Bengal and the North West Provinces respectively, but both are administered by the Bengal Government. The excise duty on the opium manufactured in the native states of Central India is collected by the Government of Bombay.

Police.

The police of India are organised by districts, a general control being exercised by the Inspector General of the whole force at the headquarters of the provincial government. The higher police appoint ments of district and assistant district superintendents,

[1] In all the provinces the chief engineer is also *ex officio* secretary to the government for the business of the public works department.

CHAP. VIII. and deputy inspector-generals (in the provinces where these are maintained) form a graded service for distribution and promotion, all British officers. This is the only branch of the service appointment to which until lately was still a matter of local patronage, now superseded by competition conducted in England. The provincial head of the police department is often a member of the covenanted civil service.

Jails. The jail department is also mainly on a district organisation, each district having its jail under the general supervision of the magistrate. But prisoners undergoing long terms of servitude are collected in central jails, of which there is usually one for each of the divisional or commissioner's charges in which the districts of a province are grouped. The administration of the jails in each province is controlled by an inspector general attached to the local government.

Education. Education, a branch of public business dealt with in the Home Department of the Government of India, is administered entirely by local organisation. Each province has its director of public instruction, and in most cases its government colleges and schools, with a staff of professors, masters, and inspectors of schools. The schools are divided into primary and secondary, represented in Bengal, where the business is on a larger scale than elsewhere, by nearly 70,000 of the one class and about 2,300 of the other. The greater part of these are government institutions or assisted by grants in aid; some of the largest and most flourishing of the latter are carried on by different missionary societies. In each of the larger cities and towns a high school or college is established, at which the education is carried up to the university standard, and there are various separate colleges or departments of colleges for special studies; of these the Sanskrit and Arabic Colleges at Calcutta, the Elphinstone College at Bombay, the Science College at Poona, the Muir College at

Allahabad, and the Sanskrit College at Benares may be specially referred to. At Calcutta, Madras, and Bombay there are state medical colleges, at which the subordinate staff of the medical services are trained, and a veterinary college has lately been established at Lahore. Universities have been established at Calcutta, Madras, and Bombay, and more lately at Allahabad and Lahore, examining bodies organised after the pattern furnished by the University of London, which confer degrees in arts, law, medicine, and engineering. During the year 1891–2 about 6,300 candidates matriculated in the five universities; but a great majority of these did not proceed further, and only about 1,300 students graduated in arts, law, and medicine.

The whole number of pupils under instruction throughout India in that year was nearly four millions, of whom one and a half millions were in Bengal—large numbers to deal with, but forming only a small proportion of the population. Of these again, by far the larger part were in the secondary schools, some of which are of an elementary kind, the instruction being given in the vernacular of the district, and in some cases not going even so far as reading and writing. The girls under instruction form only a minute part of the whole. The rate of school fees is throughout low, and the receipts are far from covering the cost of education. The whole expenditure on this head in India is about 30 millions of rupees, the fees amounting to less than 9 millions. The difference is met partly by local rates, partly by endowments, in making which many wealthy Indians have displayed conspicuous generosity; the balance of about 12 millions is a charge on the taxpayer.

The avidity with which the higher education put within their reach has been taken advantage of by the classes which throng the schools and colleges is a natural condition among a people always distinguished for acuteness of intelligence, and who had evolved an elaborate system of philosophy at a time when the Northern conquerors of Europe had not emerged from barbarism, and from that point of view must be regarded as a great success. But the system is open to two serious objections. The higher, as well as the primary education, is mainly gratuitous, and given at the cost of the general taxpayer. In India the bulk of the taxes are paid by the lower classes, especially the cultivator of the soil, the poorest of the poor. That these should be contributing to the cost of educating a wealthier class above them is indefensible. In the next place, the system of education is for the most part wholly literary, stimulating the unpractical side of the Indian character instead of remedying its defects. The educated classes of Indians, the Brahmans, have always been literary, and nothing else; the literature handed down from generation to generation for hundreds of years—modern Indian literature there is none—consists of a dreamy and unprofitable philosophy, or a mere travesty of history in the guise of extravagant fables, compared with which the myths of legendary Greece are sober narrative. The Indian displays great aptitude for pure mathematics, but none for its applications to science; the Indian university examination system plays up to this weakness. The encouragement given in English universities to the study of abstract science, suitable enough for the too practical Englishman, whose life is to be devoted to practical work, is peculiarly inappropriate for the Indian, who has no intention of handling any instrument but the pen. This unsatisfactory state of things arises from the traditionary claim of the Brahmanic class, handed down from time immemorial, to a monopoly of education and clerical employment. And it is perhaps natural that a department which deals only with education, and not with its results, should be inclined to foster this tendency, and to encourage the taste of this class for purely literary studies. But the teaching most needed for India is in physical science and technical art. In this last respect the Indian artisan displays remarkable aptitude whenever he gets the chance. In many railway workshops the whole of the machines are run by Indian workmen, who are found to possess all the skill and nerve required for the business; but this is the class which never finds its way into the colleges, while the students from the latter hardly ever turn to any practical or scientific occupation. The universities now send forth their hundreds—soon to become thousands—of graduates a year, the vast majority of whom look only to employment under Government or to the law for their livelihood. This unhealthy condition increases from year to year, and threatens to become a serious evil; we are artificially creating an ever-increasing class of hungry and discontented, because unsuccessful office-seekers. It is this class, educated at the expense of their poorer and uneducated countrymen, which fills the ranks of the vernacular press, the tone of which, with a few honourable exceptions, is scurrilous and mendacious to a degree unexampled in any other country, habitually and with uniform persistency misrepresenting the actions and intentions of the Government, and striving to foment disloyalty towards it, and hatred of the English in India. The higher education, of which this is one result, should at least be given at the expense of those who get it. Secondary education, on the other hand, especially in the vernacular languages, needs to be widely extended; so far the number of those who come under its influence are the merest fraction of the people. Still greater, perhaps, is the need for a widely diffused technical education. A beginning has been made in this direction, but a strong and sustained impulse will be needed from above to overcome the inertia of the present system, the tastes and preference for the showy and unpractical of both teachers and pupils.

CHAPTER IX

DISTRICT ORGANISATION

CHAP. IX.

Efficient government based on decentralisation.

THE different departments detailed in the foregoing chapter are organised for special purposes, necessary and important as part of the business of the State, but the members of which represent the Government only so far as their specific duties bring them into contact with the people. The business of these departments is conducted, so far as the higher officials are concerned, in English, and a man may serve a lifetime in them without learning to speak a consecutive sentence in any vernacular language. The Indians, other than his private servants, with whom he comes most in contact, are the English-speaking clerks of his office. So far as the people of the country generally are concerned, the government is represented by the district officers, the great body of officials who make up the bulk of the superior public service of the country.

The district the administrative unit.

The district is the administrative unit, corresponding with the 'department' of France and other continental countries which have a centralised form of government. The headquarters of the district station is fixed at the principal town, where reside the group of English officials with their establishments who represent the government of the province, and form the medium of communication between it and the people.

Extent of an Indian district.

The number of districts in the different provinces varies in some accordance with their size and population. Bengal, which is the most populous, and next after Burma the largest province of India, contains forty-seven districts, the North West Provinces with Oudh forty-nine, Burma forty-one, Punjab thirty-two, Bombay twenty-three, Madras twenty, the Central Provinces eighteen, Assam thirteen. The average size of a district varies considerably in the different provinces. Some of the Madras districts contain more than 12,000 square miles, a larger area than that of Belgium, and the average Madras district is a good deal larger than Yorkshire. In the North West Provinces and Oudh, which are densely populated, the district is somewhat smaller. In Bengal the districts vary in size from 1,200 to 6,000 square miles, and the average area is somewhat larger than that of Devonshire. The average population of a district is about one and three quarter millions in Madras, one and a half millions in Bengal, nearly two millions in the North West Provinces, three-fourths of a million in Bombay and Punjab.

Head district official the collector and magistrate. Duties of collector—in regard to land revenue;

The representative of the Government in each district is the officer who discharges the united but distinct functions of Collector and Magistrate. As Collector he is the agent of the Government for the collection of the district revenue, the principal item being derived from the land, of which, speaking generally, the Government is deemed to be the landlord or proprietor. His duties in this respect vary according to the nature of the tenures under which the land is held. In the greater portion of Bengal and a portion of the North West Provinces, the land has been leased for perpetuity in large estates at a fixed rent, under the arrangement known as the 'perpetual settlement,' effected by the government of Lord Cornwallis; and the ordinary business of the Collector in this connection is confined to receiving, at fixed dates, the sums payable by the landlords (zemindars), some of whose holdings are principalities in size, and furnish to them princely

CHAP. IX.

revenues. A part of the North West Provinces also is under the zemindari settlement, made in perpetuity; but generally the land revenue is determined by leases fixed for a term of thirty years, granted direct to the tenants, the community of each village usually taking a lease for its own lands. In Madras, while in a part of the province towards the north the zemindari system was established in the earlier days of our rule, the raiyatwari (or what may roughly speaking be termed the cottier) system obtains; the settlement is made with each individual holder of a field or fields, and in some districts the separate leases granted by the Collector number many thousands. The raiyatwari system obtains largely in Bombay also, and in the Central Provinces, as well as in Burma. In Punjab the system is generally similar to that of the North West Provinces. But the Indian land tenures present almost every kind of variety even in the same province, a result of the political convulsions to which the country has been subjected, combined with the antiquity of its institutions and the extreme conservatism of its people. The Collector's court is the office of registry, where are recorded all leases, and the particulars of all landed rights and transfers of land with which the Government is concerned. Besides performing these duties as Government land-agent, the Collector is also vested with certain judicial powers in executing the claims of Government against defaulters, and in determining claims which arise of tenants holding from Government against their under-tenants for arrears of rent—on the principle that, since the Government exacts punctual payment of its own rents, it is bound to afford its tenants the means of obtaining their rents in turn. He superintends the partition of estates, and regulates the distribution of the Government assessment among the different subdivisions. He has also in certain cases to assume direct management of the landed property of minors holding land

CHAP. IX.

from Government, acting in this respect in a capacity resembling that of the English Court of Chancery, in regard to the wards in his district.

other kinds of revenue;

The rent from land constitutes the principal source of Indian revenue, and its realisation is the subject which principally engages the Collector's attention. He is also the fiscal representative of Government for receiving all other descriptions of revenue levied from his district, acting as superintendent of excise, and assessor of the income, licence, or other personal taxes. Further he is the government treasurer, as well as the banker for the different public departments, which keep their public moneys in his treasury, and make all payments by means of cheques on the Collector. In addition to these specific duties, he has charge of the local funds for public works and other purposes appertaining to the district.

as district treasurer.

Duties of magistrate: general—

In his capacity of Magistrate the same official is the general representative of government within his district. With him rests the responsibility for peace and order being maintained, the superintendence of the police, and the management of the jail. It is to him that all classes of the people look for aid in times of disturbance, and by him would be initiated any proposals needful for cases of emergency, as well as, at all times, for the improvement or well-being of the district. In addition to these general responsibilities, the Indian Magistrate has extensive judicial as well as ordinary magisterial functions. As his name imports, his court is the tribunal for first investigation of all criminal cases; but only those involving a heavy punishment are committed to the court of session. The rest he finally disposes of himself, his powers extending to a sentence of two years' imprisonment, and fine of 1,000 rupees. This arrangement is derived from the system originally established by Lord Cornwallis in Bengal, which was gradually extended to the

magisterial—judicial.

Reason for junction of the two offices.

CHAP. IX.

other regulation provinces, as they came under British rule, and under which the offices of district magistrate and judge were united in the same person; although, it should be observed, the district judge had at this time no criminal jurisdiction, the jail deliveries being made by a separate court of circuit. The Collector was a separate officer, whose establishment dates from the time of Warren Hastings, when the management of the revenues of Bengal was first directly undertaken by the English. Subsequently, the duties of the magistrate were separated from those of the judge (as part of a reconstitution of the system of judicature which need not be detailed here)—the former, however, being vested with the judicial powers above mentioned, in view to relieving the pressure of business which had arisen in the higher court. Thus it fell about, that the office of collector having a higher salary attached to it than that of magistrate, the course of a civilian's promotion came to be from magistrate to collector; and the former grade was usually held by officers of comparatively small standing and experience. To remedy this practical defect, the offices of magistrate and collector were eventually united in the same officer. In the North West Provinces, Madras, and Bombay, this amalgamation was carried out many years ago; in Bengal the change is of comparatively recent date.

Joint Magistrate.

The Joint Magistrate and Collector comes next in rank of the district officials. This officer has passed all the tests imposed by the regulations of the service; and, as his name imports, he has co-equal powers with the Magistrate and Collector in the hearing of all suits brought before his court. He acts, in fact, as the deputy of the latter, for the disposal of such portion of the various business of the district in all departments as the Magistrate may make over to him. In Madras and Bombay this officer is styled Sub Collector and Joint Magistrate.

Assistant-Magistrate.

An Assistant Magistrate and Collector, with the official status of Subordinate Magistrate of the First or Second Class, is usually attached to each district, also a member of what until lately was styled the covenanted civil service; in the first instance *in statu pupillari*, with limited powers, which are gradually extended, until, after passing certain examinations, he is vested with the full powers of a magistrate, and is eligible for promotion to the post of joint magistrate on the occurrence of a vacancy in the province. These examinations are held annually, at some central point in the province, by committees consisting of civilians of standing, and embrace the subjects connected with the business of the administration—especially the vernacular languages, the land tenures of the province, the procedure of the courts, and the laws and regulations of the country.

Native district officials

These members of the Indian (Covenanted) Civil Service, the Magistrate and Collector, the Joint Magistrate and Collector, and the Assistant, represent (with the superintendent of police and his assistant) the English element of district administration, five men at most to perhaps a million of people. Next to them comes the executive branch of the provincial civil service, the seniors of which are the Deputy Collectors, in number proportioned to the size and population of the district (almost always with magisterial powers also), all natives of India, and almost all Indians by race. Next below them is the Subordinate Civil Service, all Indians, the principal members of this being the officers, usually styled Tehsildars, in charge of the subdivisions (tehsils), into which the district is divided.[1] The Tehsildars, also, as a rule, have magisterial powers.

The office establishments in all departments consist almost entirely of natives of India.

[1] The designation of these officers varies in different parts of the country. In Bengal the officer corresponding with the tehsildar is a sub-deputy magistrate.

CHAP. IX.

District court-house.

The central courthouse is of course at the headquarters of the district, and is generally placed a little outside the town, near the residences of the English officials. It contains a separate court for each of the officers above named, an office for the clerks, a muniment-room for the district records, and a strong-room for the treasury. The proceedings are conducted and recorded in the vernacular language of the district. The correspondence of the Magistrate and Collector with his superiors, and with the officials of other departments, is carried on in English. A Deputy Collector in each district has usually executive charge of the district treasury and accounts, under the general responsibility of the Collector.

District Police.

Until within a few years ago, the Magistrate was also at the head of the police of his district, and it was his duty to apprehend criminals as well as to try or commit them. A radical change was made in this respect about thirty years ago, by the establishment of the new constabulary; the police force of each district is now under the control of a Superintendent, who, as well as his Assistant is an Englishman. With respect to the distribution and movements of the police, the preservation of order, and the repression of crime, the District Superintendent occupies a position of subordination to the Magistrate, who in this as in other matters is the head authority and representative of government within his district. In matters connected with the general organisation of the force—the pay, clothing, training, and so forth—the District Superintendent is under the orders of the Inspector General of Police at the headquarters of the provincial government.

District jail.

The district jail is usually in charge of the District Medical Officer (who is styled the Civil Surgeon) under the general responsibility of the Magistrate. In this jail are confined all prisoners undergoing short sentences. Those sentenced to long terms—that is, extending beyond two years—are removed to central jails, of which there is usually one to every five or six districts. Persons condemned to penal servitude for life are transported to Port Blair, a convict settlement at the Andaman Islands in the Bay of Bengal.

Superintendence of excise,

It has already been stated that the Collector is the assessor of the income, licence, or any other personal tax that may be levied. He has also usually the superintendence of the excise within his district. In some parts of India the sale of spirits is a government monopoly, and the manufactories of spirits are government establishments, leased out to contractors, who pay duty on the amount of spirit they distil. In other parts the business is farmed out, the right to manufacture and sell spirits within the district, or a portion of it, being sold by auction to the highest bidder.

and of stamps.

A considerable part of the Indian revenue is derived from the stamp duties. Stamps are sold to the public by licensed vendors, who obtain their supplies from a depot kept in the collector's treasury.

The Commissioners of Divisions.

Intermediate between the Government and the District Officer comes the Commissioner, a superior member of the civil service, who has the superintendence of (usually) from four to six districts, both as regards affairs generally, and the collection of revenue more particularly, as to which the Commissioner's office is a court of appeal from the decisions of the Collector, who is subordinate to the Commissioner in all business except that connected with the trial or commitment of prisoners to sessions in the magistrate's court. The Commissioner, whose office is the highest in the regular executive line, is thus the head of the administration in the extensive territory which constitutes his division, and the representative and embodiment of the government therein, in fact the highest representative of government with whom the inhabitants will ordinarily

CHAP. IX.

ever come in contact. In revenue affairs there is a further intermediary between the Commissioner and the Government in the form of a Board of Revenue, or a single officer exercising the powers of one—except in Bombay, where the Commissioner submits revenue business direct to the Government. In Madras, on the other hand, the office of Commissioner has never been introduced, and the Magistrate-Collector is in direct communication with the Board of Revenue in respect of revenue business, and with the government of the province about everything else. It should be added that the Commissioners, when first appointed, in 1829, under Lord William Bentinck's administration, were judicial as well as revenue officers. They replaced the provincial courts of session which had been established by the government of Lord Cornwallis, and held periodical jail deliveries in the various districts under their supervision. These judicial duties were eventually transferred to the judges of districts, who until then had exercised a jurisdiction in civil suits only.

District judge.

This completes the list of the executive establishments. To turn now to the judicial department. The head judicial officer of the district is the Civil and Session Judge, a covenanted civilian, whose courthouse is usually established separate from, but in close proximity to, the collectorate. In this latter capacity he holds a monthly jail-delivery, for the trial of all prisoners committed by the magistrate or other officers having magisterial powers; he also hears appeals from the judgments of those officers. His powers extend to a sentence of fourteen years' imprisonment or transportation for life. Sentences of capital punishment must be referred to the High Court before they are carried out. On the civil side the Judge has a general superintendence over the course of proceedings in the numerous district civil courts of first instance. The lower class of

Native judicial officers.

court is that of the Munsiff, for the original hearing of all suits involving amounts not exceeding one thousand rupees. Selected Munsiffs have jurisdiction in suits up to two thousand rupees. The higher class of court is that of the Subordinate Judge, a somewhat inappropriate title, his jurisdiction being greater than that of the District Judge, since it extends to all civil suits irrespective of the amount involved, whereas the judge's jurisdiction is limited to original suits not exceeding ten thousand rupees. Appeals from the Munsiff and Subordinate Judge, in small suits, are preferred in the court of the District Judge; appeals from the decision of the latter, and of the Subordinate Judge in cases exceeding ten thousand rupees in amount, are made to the Appellate Court of the province.

Proceedings of district judicial courts.

The proceedings of all the courts are conducted and recorded in the vernacular of the district, the suitors being ordinarily acquainted with that language only; but the District Judge in all cases tried before him is required to take down a very full abstract of the depositions of the witnesses in his own hand, and to record his judgment in English. This abstract is in addition to the vernacular papers of the case, which contain all the evidence and other particulars in full detail. The record of every case is filed in the court where it was tried, available to be sent forward to the higher court if the case is appealed.

The High Courts.

The chief seat of judicature in the four older provinces is the statutory High Court, situated at the capital town of each, the judges of which consist partly of civilians, partly of barristers selected either from the Indian or English bar, and partly of pleaders in the Indian courts, the minimum number to be chosen from each class being specified in the Act of Parliament constituting the court in each case. These judges are appointed by the Crown, and hold their seats during good behaviour. The High Courts have original juris-

CHAP. IX.

Their jurisdiction and functions.

diction in the trial of European British subjects within the province (over whom the district courts have only a limited authority in criminal offences), and for offences committed by all classes within the limits of the capital towns as well as in civil suits arising out of transactions therein. One or two of the judges are usually wholly employed on this class of business, but the principal functions of the Court are performed on the appellate side. All capital sentences passed by district judges are referred to the High Court for confirmation before being carried out, and appeals are heard in it from the decisions of a district judge on the civil or criminal side, and in civil suits from the courts of the subordinate judges. The High Court has also a general superintendence over the procedure and conduct of the various courts of the province.

Bar of district and high courts.

The bar of the district courts consists of certificated pleaders whose qualifications are tested by examinations conducted under the orders of the High Court. The bar of the High Court consists of pleaders, native and English, and barristers-at-law. The bar may plead either in the vernacular or in English. Interpreters are employed in the High Court to translate the evidence of witnesses and the vernacular papers attached to the cases appealed, for the information of such of the judges as may not be acquainted with the native languages. The appellate court, as a rule, deals solely with the written record of the case, and admits not fresh evidence.

Free use of appeal permitted.

The system of Indian law provides for a very free use of the right of appeal in both criminal and civil cases. Every case tried in the lowest civil court, that of a Munsiff, can be appealed to the Judge's Court of the district, while all suits involving more than a certain sum can be carried in appeal from the District to the High Court, and others can be appealed finally to the Judicial Committee of the Privy Council in London.

Appeals in criminal cases can be carried from the court of the magistrate to that of the Sessions Judge and again to the High Court. This freedom of appeal has been deemed to be a necessary condition of the constitution of the Indian law-courts. The inferior social condition of the native judicial officers of the lower courts and the imperfect training of all the judges in earlier days; the total absence, so far as the district courts are concerned, of the restraint exercised in European countries by an honest and highly trained bar, and by the criticism of an intelligent press—rendered a supervision over the proceedings of the Indian law-courts from some higher authority especially desirable. A district court is never visited by any one except the suitors; the only record of the proceedings is contained in the judge's own report; and therefore the only check afforded on them is the review of the record on appeal by the higher court. Under these conditions, a free right of appeal is necessary to ensure the suitor a reasonable chance of obtaining a remedy; but the exercise of this right, and the complicated procedure enjoined by the regulations, render Indian lawsuits extraordinarily protracted and expensive; and it would be difficult to say whether the litigious character now manifested by the people in those parts of India where British law-courts are established, is a cause or an effect of those institutions. Certainly, the apparently capricious way in which the judgments of each court often appear to be upset by the next above, which renders the final issue of a lawsuit a matter of uncertainty until the highest court of appeal is reached, in a degree unknown in any other country in the world, is calculated to promote a spirit of reckless gambling in law, among a people to whom most forms of excitement are not available. At any rate, if the Indian system of appeal was favourable to the rich suitor who failed to obtain justice in the first trial, it as often as not barred the road for justice

Its good and bad effects.

CHAP. IX.

Small cause courts.

against the poor man, who practically was without a remedy at law until the introduction of small cause courts. These have long been established in the three presidency towns, with a jurisdiction over suits not exceeding 1,000 rupees, and limited to the class of cases which can be dealt with by the English county courts, and similar courts have been gradually established in every considerable town throughout the country. The judges are chosen, in the presidency towns from the European and native bar of the High Court, and elsewhere usually from the native judiciary. In the majority of cases, however, the office of judge of a small-cause court is held in conjunction with some other judicial office, but with separate records and procedure. The fees of these courts are moderate, the procedure simple, and no appeals are permitted from their decisions, except in special cases and under certain narrow conditions. Altogether, the introduction of these courts is one of the greatest improvements in legislative procedure which has been conferred upon the country.

Higher grades of civil service distributed in two branches, executive and judicial.

It will have been understood from this account of the district administrative system, that the official training of the civil servant up to a certain point is the same for all. It begins with his first appointment as an assistant magistrate and collector, and he continues to be employed on both magisterial and revenue duties until he reaches the position of joint magistrate and collector. In no other way could a better or so complete a knowledge of the people and their institutions be obtained. The great mass of the people being engaged in agriculture, most of them as owners in whole or part of land, a thorough knowledge of the complicated systems of Indian land tenure is the first qualification needed for efficient administration. This, which is needed equally by the judge as by the executive officer, can best be gained in the district revenue courts, while the conduct of the magisterial courts gives the needful experience in the criminal law, and an officer can become fit either for the charge of a district—and the efficient administration of the district is the first condition for the proper government of India—or for the exercise of higher judicial functions, only by training in the two kinds of business, the land revenue and the criminal law. On reaching the grade of joint magistrate and collector the civilian has, for further advancement, to make his final choice between the executive and judicial lines, electing either to remain in the administrative line and succeeding to the charge of a district, when the appointments of commissioner of a division (or group of districts) and to the board of revenue are available; or passing on to the office of district judge, with the prospect of eventual preferment to a seat on the high court of the province. Still higher appointments are the Lieutenant Governorship of a province or a seat in Council, but these, the prizes of the service, are practically monopolised by the secretaries to the different governments, whose services, if involving less real responsibility, bring them more prominently under the notice of the dispensers of patronage than are the administrative officers scattered about the country.

The civil service employed mainly on district administration;

It will also be understood from this account that by much the greater part of the civil service is engaged on district work. The men attached to the special departments and offices outside the regular line are the exceptions, but exceptions which the tendency of the times is to increase, as with the greater complexity of modern government the necessity is assumed to arise for creating new departments to deal with technical business. To the extent to which this goes on, and men are withdrawn from district-work to duties in offices at the headquarters of the different governments the business of which is carried on in English, the efficiency of the administration as an instrument for keeping the government in touch with the people necessarily suffers. The

CHAP. IX.

increasing acquaintance of the educated Indians with the English language operates in the same direction to diminish the necessity for a thorough familiarity with the vernaculars, and there is always a tendency among those in high places to forget that if a few thousand Indians can speak English, there still remain the millions whose thoughts and feelings can be arrived at only through the medium of their own tongue. A man may gain credit and preferment as a secretary who has forgotten what he once knew of the language and sentiments of the people, and can scarcely converse with even a native gentleman, much less with a peasant. And in the distribution of honours and preferments it seems to be too little borne in mind that the men who are actually administering the country, the magistrate-collectors each ruling over his million or million and a half of people, for whose well-being he is mainly responsible, and to whom he is the embodiment of the government, are really doing more important work than the office men at headquarters whose services come more immediately into view, still more than the irresponsible officials in England who to the advantages of well-paid and easy duty in a good climate may add whatever a large share of the titular honours bestowed for public service may be deemed to be worth. Yet if arduous duties carried on in a bad climate, with little relaxation or leave, receive but scant recognition, nevertheless the district officers and the superior officers who rise from their ranks are the mainstay of Indian administration. Of late years the tendency has been to overweight this class with an excess of multifarious duties arising out of the ever-increasing central departments at the headquarters of the provincial government, and with calls for reports and returns upon every conceivable description of public business. And the further this is carried, and the more the district officer is tied to his desk, the less efficient

important of all duties.

must he become for the discharge of the primary and most important of his duties—the administration of his district, which can be properly conducted only by leaving him sufficient freedom and leisure to make himself thoroughly acquainted with all parts of it and its people.

CHAPTER X

THE NON-REGULATION PROVINCES

CHAP. X.

Nature of the Indian Regulations.

In the foregoing account of the civil administration and of the duties of district officers, the system described is that obtaining in what are termed the 'Regulation' provinces—Bengal, the North West Provinces, Madras, and Bombay. The Regulations referred to, are, as has been explained in earlier chapters, the enactments of the Government which for many years constituted the body of public law. Statutory powers were first given by an Act of Parliament passed in 1773,[1] amended by an Act of 1781,[2] to the Governor General and Council at Fort William in Bengal, to 'make and issue . . . rules, ordinances, and regulations for the good government of the settlement.' It appears to have been tacitly assumed that the Act of 1773 gave also validity to all Regulations made previously to that year, but the matter was placed on a clearer footing in 1793, when the Bengal Government annulled all the Regulations promulgated by it up to that time, and began a new series of enactments, the first forty-eight of which, for the most part re-enacting in new form what had gone before, were passed on the same day (May 1) of that year. These and all subsequent Regulations, were extended to the North West Provinces on their annexation in 1801. Acts of Parliament passed in 1797, 1800, and 1807 gave to the Governments of Madras

[1] 13 Geo. III., C. 63. [2] 21 Geo. III., C. 70.

and Bombay the same statutory powers as had been given by the Act of 1773 to the Government of Fort William [Bengal], for their respective territories, and a similar system of Regulations was introduced by those Governments accordingly. In 1833, when the Government of Bengal became the Government of India, the power of the Governments of Madras and Bombay to frame Laws and Regulations was withdrawn, and the Governor General in Council was empowered to frame Regulations, henceforth termed Acts, for all parts of India, the Council being strengthened (as has been already mentioned [p. 118]) by the addition of a fourth councillor, for the business of making Laws and Regulations only. This arrangement lasted until 1853, when a Legislative Council of India was created by the addition to the Executive Council of a certain number of councillors for legislative purposes only. [The particulars of this measure, and of the subsequent changes in the composition of the Legislative Council and of the establishment of similar provincial bodies have been given in Chapter VII.]

The Regulations and Acts of the Government of India, which have thus the same statutory force in that country as have Acts of Parliament in the United Kingdom, provide, among other matters, for the establishment of courts of justice, and while determining the composition and jurisdiction of the various courts, and the functions of many departments of the administration, prescribe also the course of procedure to be adopted in the prosecution of suits. No code of laws was promulgated in the first instance. The course of justice was to be made conformable to the customs of the country, and to the precepts of the Mahomedan and Hindu law, so far as they could be ascertained and (on the criminal side) were not altogether repugnant to European ideas; and various enactments were passed from time to time, modifying those laws, altering the degrees of

CHAP. X.

penalties, declaring certain offences to be penal, and so forth. The bulk of the Regulations, however, had reference to the procedure of the civil and fiscal courts; they supplied by law a definitive procedure, which in England and elsewhere has been slowly developed in the practice of the courts through many centuries; and their result was to create artificially, and *per saltum*, almost as complicated a procedure as in countries of older civilisation has been brought about gradually by the accumulated pedantries of ages, and, under which the issue of an Indian lawsuit came to depend as much on the observance of nice and tedious formalities as on the merits of the case.

Certain districts exempted from their operation.

But whatever might be the opinion held by the framers of these Regulations, of the benefits conferred by them on the body of the people, it was seen that for some at least of the races of India, so technical and complicated a procedure was unsuitable and pernicious. And accordingly many territories acquired from time to time were never brought under the Regulations, while others have been removed from their operation and placed under a more simple system. But the Acts of Parliament dealing with India all assumed the British portion of the country to be distributed among the Presidencies, within one or other of which all British territory was comprised, and were silent as regards any other territory not allocated to a Presidency, the administration of which therefore fell to be undertaken by the Government in virtue of the act of conquest or cession. The most important cases in point were those of the extensive tract in Central India, long known as the Saugor and Nerbudda Territories, annexed after the Maratha War of 1817; Assam and the tracts bordering on the Bay of Bengal, acquired from the Burmese in 1826; Sind, annexed in 1843; Punjab in 1849; Pegu in 1852; Nagpur in 1854; and Oudh in 1856. For all these additional provinces, simple codes were drawn up

CHAP. X.

adapted to the circumstances of each, and the Regulations were applied to them only in respect of such particular localities and such special regulations as appeared suitable in each case.[1]

Regulation and non-regulation provinces.

Thus the provinces of British India come to be divided into two classes—Regulation and Non-Regulation, the procedure of the law courts of the one being of a highly elaborate and technical kind, and in the other of a simple and summary form, but not necessarily less precise and definite, and very much more so than the native system which it replaced. Further, the administrative staff of the two was differently constituted. Successive Acts of Parliament prescribed that all civil appointments, from that of Assistant Magistrate and Collector upwards, should be filled from the covenanted civil service, a very necessary provision to prevent jobbery and the appointment of improper persons which would certainly have otherwise occurred in the earlier days of our rule: they further prescribed indeed that all promotion throughout the service should be regulated by seniority except only as regards the members of council, a restriction formally removed only in 1861 by an Act of Parliament,[2] which also legalised the appointment of other than covenanted civil servants to offices, such as that of military secretary to government, and others, as in the engineering and educational line, requiring special technical qualifications. But the law notwithstanding, for the non-regulation provinces, as each in turn came to be dealt with, there was organised an administrative staff, consisting partly of civil servants drawn from the regulation provinces by the prospect of more rapid promotion, partly of military officers withdrawn from their regiments, the only other agency extensively available, and to some small extent

[1] For example, an Act of 1835 establishes the subordination of the law courts in Assam and on the Burma littoral to the Supreme Appellate Court of Bengal.

[2] 24-25 Vict., C. 54.

CHAP. X.

of officials, British and native, promoted from subordinate positions. Further, in all these non-regulation provinces a new designation was adopted for the district officers. The Magistrate-Collector was styled Deputy Commissioner. In the smaller provinces the Commissioner who came next above the District Officer was also the head of the administration, under the direct orders of the Supreme Government; to the larger provinces a Chief Commissioner was appointed, with one or more high officials to superintend the administration of the revenue and judicial courts, fulfilling in effect the functions discharged in the regulation provinces by the board of revenue and the supreme court of appeal.

Ambiguity of the law regarding the non-regulation provinces.

Thus the non-regulation provinces differed from the regulation 'presidencies,' both as to the system of law under which they were governed, and the form and composition of the administrative agency. But the former had for a long time no statutory recognition. The Act of 1833 does indeed apply to 'the British territories in India, and to all other territories . . . now in the possession and under the government of the said Company,' but the implication conveyed by the wording of the Act throughout is that all these territories are comprised within one or other of the presidencies, and it would almost appear as if the drafter of the Act had been unaware of the existence of any territories not so comprised. The first explicit recognition of the existence of territories without the limits of a presidency, if even this reference can be so called, is contained in an Act of 1854,[1] which empowers the Governor General in Council to take under his direct administration any part or parts of the territories in

Effect of Act of 1854.

[1] 17-18 Vict., C. 77. The professed primary object of the Act is to empower the President of the Board of Control to countersign the letters patent of Indian appointments in place of the Lord Privy Seal; it would appear as if the clause here cited was inserted as an afterthought.

the possession of the Company, and was introduced no doubt in view of the recent acquisitions of Punjab, which was being administered by a Chief Commissioner under the orders of the Government of India, and of Pegu, under a Commissioner. The Act thus gave legality to the administration established for the province of Nagpur, annexed in that year, and provided for the cases of other outlying provinces, as Tenasserim on the Bay of Bengal, Coorg in Southern India, and Singapur, which had been already for long in occupation. But it made no provision for the districts in various parts, which although not administered directly by the Governor General in Council, were yet removed from the operation of the regulations. A well-known case in point was the removal in 1855 from the operation of those regulations of the Santal District—a wild region on the north west frontier of Bengal, inhabited by a simple primitive people, who had been driven into rebellion by the exactions of the money lenders pressed through the agency of the law courts. This country was placed under a special commissioner (in subordination to the Bengal Government) who administered it under a code of simple character, adapted to the circumstances and understanding of the people affected, who ever since the change have remained peaceable and contented. The measure was carried out by an Act of the Legislative Council of India created in the previous year; nevertheless the validity of it appears open to question, in view of the fact that the administration of the tract in question was not undertaken directly by the Governor General in Council, but remained under the Lieutenant Governor of Bengal. At any rate, the law had never been repealed which prescribed that all civil appointments throughout India should be held by covenanted civilians only, and under which therefore the administrative constitution of all the non-regulation provinces,

CHAP. X.

and a great many appointments of various kinds within presidential limits continued to be illegal.

First statutory recognition of non-regulation provinces.

The first specific statutory recognition of the non-regulation provinces is to be found in the Act of 1861,[1] which also gives retrospective validity to all legislation previously carried out by the Government of India in regard to them, and authorises the appointment to offices therein (and elsewhere under certain conditions) of other than covenanted civil servants. The non-regulation provinces thus came to occupy a definite and recognised position as parts of British India in addition to the presidencies. But the distinction between the two in regard to the laws under which they were governed—the latter under laws passed in the Legislative Council, the former under laws passed by the Government of India in their executive capacity, has since then been almost obliterated. By the Act of 1833 a commission was appointed to frame a body of substantive law for India, whose labours after nearly thirty years bore fruit in the presentation of a series of Codes dealing with various branches of the law. The Indian Penal Code, introduced in 1860, and the Code of Criminal Procedure which followed it in 1861, were made applicable, with slight local modifications, to the whole of British India. Other great Codes have followed, dealing with civil procedure, and codifying parts of the unwritten law, as in regard to succession and contract. A great many other Acts, as those creating or altering the mode of taxation, relating to emigration, to cantonments and to railways, are also for the most part of general application. Further, every province has been made the subject of special legislation by the Governor General's Council.[2]

[1] 24-25 Vict., C. 67, sec. 25.

[2] For example, various Acts passed since the annexation of Upper Burma are concerned with the establishment of laws and administration for that province. In 1890 four Acts were passed which placed the administration of the newly acquired province of Baluchistan on a regular footing.

CHAP. X.

Distinction between two classes no longer in force,

Thus, the old distinction of regulation and non-regulation provinces has disappeared; every province is subject to regulation, but some have been under regulations longer than others and are subject to more. The only distinction that remains is of a personal kind, the designation of officials and the composition of the administrative staff. In the four older provinces all appointments in the regular civil line are filled by members of the Civil Service only, while in the other territories subsequently added to the empire, as well as those withdrawn from the operation of the Regulations—as for example the South West Frontier of Bengal—this condition is not acted upon. This distinction will also soon be a thing of the past. It is to be still maintained so far that military officers will continue to be eligible for employment in the civil administration only in what were termed the non-regulation provinces, but in other respects the conditions of appointment to civil offices have recently undergone a radical and very important change, which forms the subject of the succeeding chapter. It may be just mentioned here that the judicial and administrative systems pursued in these provinces present considerable variations according to the degree of advancement to which each has arrived. In Punjab the difference from the system obtaining in the older provinces is slight. The district officer is still called Deputy Commissioner, but judicial duties have been transferred from him and the Commissioner to a judicial branch of the service comprising District and Divisional Judges, while in place of the Judicial Commissioner of the province, a Chief Court has been established, differing from the High Courts of the older provinces in that it has been created by the Indian legislature and not by act of parliament, and that the judges are appointed by the Government of India instead of by the Crown. In Oudh the same separation has been made of administrative and judicial duties; but at the head of the

except as regards the administrative agency employed.

Variations of administrative system in different provinces.

CHAP. X.

judicial service are two Judicial Commissioners, with power of reference when their decisions do not agree to the High Court of the North-West Provinces. In the Central Provinces two superior judges hold office, appeals going to a Judicial Commissioner. In Assam also there are two judges, but there is no Judicial Commissioner, appeals going to the High Court of Bengal. In Burma, where a more simple procedure obtains, the Commissioners of Divisions continue to be also Sessions Judges; the highest court is that of the Judicial Commissioner, one for Lower and one for Upper Burma, but the Recorder of Rangoon has local jurisdiction approaching to that of a High Court, and he has jurisdiction also over European British subjects throughout the province, appeals lying from his court to the High Court of Bengal. In the different native states the Agents to the Governor-General have the powers of a high court for dealing with suits between British subjects, or criminal cases in which these are concerned within their respective charges.

Amount of judicial business.

During the year 1891 about one and three quarter millions of civil suits were instituted in the various courts throughout the country, and about one and a half million persons were brought to trial, of whom about 200,000 were tried for serious offences—theft, housebreaking, cattle theft, gang robbery, offences against the person, and murder. Of those tried about one half were convicted. About ten per cent. of these cases were appealed; 427 persons were sentenced to death for murders committed throughout British India, including the wild uncivilised tracts recently brought within it.

Moderation of scale of civil salaries.

A noteworthy point in connection with the staff of British officials which conducts the civil administration of India, is the moderate scale of pay which obtains throughout the service. We must not of course compare the Indian with the English civil servant; the one is a clerk, the other an administrator. The Indian civilian does not undertake clerical duties except in posts corresponding, so far as the analogy holds good, with the very highest posts, as of under secretary of state or secretary to a department, to which the English civil servant can rise. There is no public employment in England of the kind which occupies the greater part of the Indian Civil Service; the only corresponding cases are furnished by the civil services of the Crown Colonies, and compared with these the Indian rate of pay is low, especially since the fall in the gold value of silver. The Lieutenant Governor of an Indian province receives about the same rate of emolument as the Governor of Singapore or Jamaica; the colonial judges, with comparatively trifling duties, are nearly as well paid as those of the high courts in India, who hear the appeals from fifty to seventy millions of people. The same contrast between relative responsibility and remuneration runs through the whole scale of offices. The present rates of Indian civil salaries were substantially fixed by the government of Lord Cornwallis a hundred years ago, since which time the duties in all departments have become greatly more onerous, while the value of silver has fallen one half, and with this fall there is an end of one great attraction offered by Indian service, the comfort and freedom from anxiety about money matters which largely made up for the drawback of exile in a bad climate. The substitution of what was then a very liberal scale of salaries for the scanty recognised emoluments Lord Cornwallis found in force, was an act of statesmanship which transformed the whole character of the Indian public service, and brought it to the high standard of purity and efficiency which it has ever since maintained. It will be an evil day for India when public servants occupying important posts, and exposed—if they were once open to the suspicion of entertaining the notion—to peculiar

And recent depreciation of them.

temptations, come to feel as a daily pressing care the difficulty of making two ends meet. From the nature of the case the Indian official is without professional or commercial interest, and practically the only opening for his sons is in the public service, all the branches of which can now be entered only through competitive examinations. Education, therefore, is a heavy charge on his purse, especially as this is combined with the condition of finding a home for his children in England; while since the family income ends with his life, and he leaves no saleable goodwill or business behind him, it is peculiarly incumbent on him to save as well as spend. There are not wanting indications that the pressure of poverty, the difficulty of supporting a family, and the impossibility of laying by anything for their support, is already beginning to press heavily on the public service in all departments. The least evil effect of this will be the growth of a general feeling of discontent. And the restoration to the service of a scale of remuneration which shall be in substantial accord with the importance of the duties imposed on it and with what it has enjoyed in the past, is not the least difficult of the administrative problems with which the Indian Government must shortly be called on to deal.

CHAPTER XI

EXTENSION OF NATIVE AGENCY IN CIVIL ADMINISTRATION

CHAP. XI.

Civil administration carried on mainly by native agency.

THE foregoing account will have brought clearly to view that the civil administration of India is in fact carried on by native agency, supervised by a small body of Englishmen. During the last twenty-five years, notwithstanding the additions of territory made, the covenanted civil service has been reduced by 22 per cent., and, excluding Burma, the condition of which is for the time exceptional, there are now altogether only about 750 English officials,[1] including military men in civil employ and a few others, engaged in the civil administration, or about one to every quarter of a million of people. Besides these the higher judicial and executive service comprises about 2,600 officials, of whom, according to the latest returns, only thirty-five were Englishmen not domiciled in India. Four-fifths of these are Hindus, one half of them being Brahmans; the remainder, save a few Sikhs, Parsis, and unspecified classes, are Mahomedans. Under this class comes the subordinate civil service, including about 110,000 persons on salaries of 100 rupees and upwards, of whom 97 per cent. are natives of India.

Recent development of this.

The development of the native civil service to its present position has taken place in comparatively recent times. The great increase in the cost of the civil administration which has occurred during this

[1] This does not include the English officers in the police.

CHAP. XI.

period is due mainly to this cause—to the creation of new offices required by the needs of improved administration, to be held by Indians only; and to an advance in the rates of salary paid to the Indian members of the service, which are now sensibly higher than the rates obtaining in the indigenous civil services of France, Germany, and other European countries. But when the earlier editions of this work were published, our administrative policy was open to the charge that it took no account of the increasing aptitude and claims of the people of the country for advancement to a larger share in its administration, and that the system established by the Company and Lord Cornwallis, of a monopoly of all the higher posts for well-paid Englishmen, was adhered to long after the conditions which led to its establishment had passed away. This charge can no longer be sustained, and a brief account will be offered of what has been done to remove the stigma, and what there still remains to do in the same direction.

Introduction of competitive system

The monopoly, not of the civil service, but of Englishmen to appointments in that service, was put an end to by the introduction in 1854 of the competitive test for admission. That test, however, was imposed wholly in view of its substitution for nomination as the means of maintaining the supply of Englishmen. That Indians would come to England in large numbers to take part in the competition appears not to have been contemplated by the authors of the scheme. At any rate the opening has in fact been taken advantage of to only a very limited extent, and so far as it has occurred the result has been to substitute for those whom it was designed to secure, young Englishmen of superior ability and education, a class of Indians having these qualifications also, but drawn mainly from one country of India, and from one class of that country, and in no proper sense representative of the people of India generally. A Bengali civilian appointed to office in Punjab would be no more appropriately placed, than a Neapolitan or a Greek if set down in charge of a district of France or Prussia. The rule of this class, so far as can be told, has been distasteful in every country except Bengal, the only one practically which has furnished candidates to the competition. The ruling classes of the Hindus, and still more markedly all classes of the Mahomedans, to whose power we had succeeded, have held altogether aloof from these competitions.

As a means therefore of obtaining a representation of the higher classes of Indians in the upper ranks of the public service, the competitive system failed. It could not be said that the pledge had been redeemed which was made in the Queen's proclamation, that Her Majesty's subjects, of whatever race or creed, should be freely and impartially admitted to offices, the duties of which they may be qualified, by their education, ability, and integrity, duly to discharge. And it might reasonably be objected that the test of fitness as above defined was not fairly applied, when the condition was attached that it should be undergone in Europe. The class of Indians, whom on the score of fitness for ruling their fellow subjects it was most desirable to associate with ourselves in the administration of the country, were just those whom this particular test would certainly keep out. And apart from the condition attached of residence in Europe, the test was of a kind particularly unsuitable for the selection of Indians. In the case of Englishmen, the presumption is fully justified by experience that there is no incompatibility between the possession of intellectual power and of the moral and physical qualities needed in the rulers of men; that these will be found just as largely present in company with mental endowments as in those who are less fully equipped in the latter respect. But this condition does not hold of the people of India, of whom it may certainly be predicated, that the classes

Its unsuitability to the case.

CHAP. XI.

who crowd into our schools and colleges, and show an aptitude for acquiring the knowledge to be gained there as remarkable as gratifying to those who have fostered the development of education in India, belong for the most part to a section of the community who have never shown any capacity for rule, but have been from time immemorial a subject race, employed indeed in the public service, but never in positions of authority, and of whom it may be declared the people of the country at large would not wish to be ruled by them. A system of educational tests only, whether applied in England or in India, must have the certain effect of giving a monopoly of office to this class, to the exclusion of those whom it should be our aim to associate with ourselves in the administration, the natural leaders of the people whom they look up to and respect. The competitive system, therefore, even if by this means the introduction of Indians into the Civil Service had been distinctly contemplated, was in this respect a distinct failure. Even as a means of admitting any class of Indians, suitable or otherwise, to the higher public offices, the number who gained a place at the competition was so small as practically to leave the people of India still excluded. Meanwhile, the spread of higher education; the ability displayed by many Indians at the bar followed by the elevation of more than one successful lawyer to the bench of the High Courts, the highest tribunals of the country; the distinction others had obtained in commerce; and the integrity and good conduct generally exhibited in the native subordinate services, gave sufficient evidence of the claims established on every ground of justice and propriety for removing this bar against their further advancement, and redeeming the pledge given in the Queen's proclamation.

The means attempted to carry out this policy again took the form of a modification of the constitution of

CHAP. XI.

the Civil Service while retaining its character as a close body with a monopoly of all the higher appointments. An Act of Parliament[1] passed in 1870 provided that duly selected natives of India under regulations to be laid down, should be eligible for any of the offices heretofore reserved for the Civil Service. The regulations drawn up in accordance with the Act for the creation of a Statutory Civil Service, as it was called, were the subject of prolonged correspondence, conducted without any marked alacrity between the Home and Indian Governments, and were not carried into effect until 1879. They provided in effect for the nomination of the candidate being made by the Government of the province of which he was an inhabitant, and for the nomination being subject to the approval of the Government of India and Secretary of State. They contemplated that the statutory civilian thus selected should ordinarily be employed only in his native province—Bengalis in Bengal, Madrassis in Madras, Punjabis in Punjab; also that this branch of the Civil Service should eventually—at any rate as the first point of departure—amount to one-sixth of the whole body, and recruitment of the service at the examination in England was correspondingly reduced in this view.

Creation of Statutory Civil Service.

This new system was allowed only a short trial. In all about sixty persons were appointed to this Statutory Civil Service in the seven years following its introduction; but although the different provincial governments undoubtedly exercised their power of selection with great care, and sought so far as they could to make the service, in respect of the standing and character of the candidates chosen, representative of the classes in their respective provinces best fitted for high office—fitted to administer with talent and integrity, and to command respect, nevertheless the system was found to

Partial trial of it.

[1] 33 Vict., C. 3.

CHAP. XI.

Defects of the system.

come short of realising the desired aim. The higher classes did not come forward, and many of the candidates chosen were young men, who, but for this opportunity, would have been satisfied to enter the subordinate service.

New departure made.

In 1886 the whole subject of the constitution of the Civil Service, outside the covenanted service, was referred to a strong commission presided over by a distinguished public servant, Sir Charles Aitchison, then Lieutenant Governor of Punjab, and composed of fifteen members, English and Indian, representing many phases of opinion and much diversity of interests. The Commission, after visiting various parts of India and taking a great quantity of evidence, submitted their report in the spring of 1888, which was referred to the Secretary of State with the opinions and recommendations on it of Lord Dufferin's Government in the autumn of that year. The final conclusions and orders of the Secretary of State in Council on the whole case were embodied in a despatch to the Government of Lord Lansdowne, of September 1889, to the following effect.

Indian civil service to be partially recruited from provincial services.

Heretofore, as has been explained, the administrative and judicial staff of the public service (omitting the special and technical branches, public works, telegraph, education, &c.), had been divided into two parts: one the small covenanted civil service, the other the whole body of public servants who, down to the humblest clerk, were dealt with under the general title of the uncovenanted service. The salaries of these, who outnumber the covenanted service in the proportion of some hundreds to one, were determined by the office held in each case, but they were all placed under the same conditions as to leave, length of service for pension, and other general regulations. This organisation, if such it could be called, was altogether anomalous and out of date, and is to be replaced by a new system. In every province the civil employees are to be divided into two bodies:

a Subordinate Civil Service, comprising the holders of clerical and minor offices; and a Provincial Civil Service to embrace the class engaged on executive and administrative duties. To these last, to be styled the Bengal Civil Service, Madras Civil Service, and so on, admission will be obtained under tests to be laid down by the Government of the Province (subject to confirmation by the higher authorities) and also by promotions of deserving members of the Subordinate Civil Service. Further, which is the important point in this connection, the members of these Provincial Services are to be eligible for any of the offices heretofore reserved for the covenanted service. The advancement will be gradual; the Secretary of State anticipates, and the opinion will be shared by everyone acquainted with India, that while men fit for promotion to the higher judicial posts will soon be forthcoming to the extent required, the development in any considerable number of Indian officials qualified to take the executive charge of districts can be looked for only by degrees. Meanwhile the recruitment of the civil service in England is to be so regulated that it may suffice eventually to fill only five-sixths of the posts now held by it. Some years must elapse before the change can be carried even so far, and speculation as to any further development the system may be found capable of taking when that point is reached would, in the light of the limited experience now available, be premature and unprofitable. When time shall have shown that Indian magistrates can carry on the charge of districts with firmness and judgment in circumstances of stress and difficulty—and such occasions will surely arise as the years go by—it will be soon enough to frame rules for their advancement to still more responsible posts. We may be sure that the desire to maintain the pledge in the Queen's proclamation will increase rather than diminish as time goes on, and that no limit will be placed on the em-

CHAP. XI.

ployment of Indians in all civil offices save that determined by their own fitness and the necessity for securing the efficient government of the country, which must always be the first condition to keep in view.

Abolition of title 'covenanted' for civil service.

With these changes in the organisation of the other branches of the civil service, the title of 'covenanted' for the portion appointed from England is very properly to be abolished. It arose out of a great reform introduced by Lord Cornwallis, who found the civil servants of the Company miserably paid, but allowed to make their livelihood by trading. He succeeded in abolishing this vicious practice and procuring for the service a scale of emoluments liberal at the time, and which, although gradually reduced, would still be adequate but for the great fall in value of the rupee. From this date the civil servant on appointment was required to enter into a covenant with the company, whereby he undertook among other conditions, not to engage in trade; and thus a term, which in reality implied a precaution against a pernicious privilege, became in its survival a title of dignity. The designation of the body which bore it has now been changed to the 'Indian Civil Service.' The term Uncovenanted Service, which had even less appropriate meaning, has also been discontinued.

No special legislation has been entered on in order to carry out these changes, the Home Government being advised that the Act of 1870 contains the needful authority for giving effect to them. The same Act will continue to empower the Government of India as before to select any fit person outside the provincial services for the superior offices. So that the idea of engaging the natural leaders of the people in the government of them which for the present has been dropped, may at some future time be revived.

With this change it may be said that the road is now fully open to the Indian which leads to the highest offices of the state, and that the pledge conveyed in the

Queen's proclamation has been at last redeemed; while those who are acquainted with the present state of India will probably unite in feeling hopeful that the native civil service will soon prove itself equal to the opportunity. And all friends of India will watch the development of the new system with sympathy and interest. One further change appears to be distinctly called for. The competitive examination held in London should now be limited to British-born candidates. It is perhaps the smallest objection to leaving it to be still open to Indians, that to the extent to which the opening is availed of, must the channel of admission in India to higher offices through the new system be contracted. No one who has a claim to be heard would contend that a competitive examination is the best, or even a proper mode for the selection of Indians for posts needing other qualities than the power of assimilating knowledge. The new system which aims at selecting men for advancement from an already carefully selected service, on the ground of proved ability in the discharge of public duties, gives a full guarantee for their efficiency, while the promotion being provincial instead of through all India, the system ensures that the ruler set over the people shall be a fellow-countryman and not a stranger from some other part of India. But the essential consideration is that a certain number of Englishmen are required for the business. The present strength of the Civil Service gives quite as small a proportion as is sufficient if India is to be governed in a safe and rational way—at any rate for the present. Some people profess to look forward to the time when the English element in the Government will be represented by the Viceroy and a few Governors, presumably with a British army still maintained to keep the peace. When we get to that point the change assuredly will not stop there. We are, however, a long way off from such a state of things, and if the Home Government

Competitive system should be limited to English candidates.

will have the courage to declare that the selection of civil servants made in England is to be for the English portion only of that service—a portion steadily decreasing, but the strength of which cannot be left to chance, and must be maintained at the numbers considered to be necessary; such an announcement will be approved by all whose judgment is based on reason and experience.

CHAPTER XII

RISE AND DEVELOPMENT OF THE INDIAN ARMY

CHAP. XII.

Company's forces raised in Madras.

THE first establishment of the Company's Indian army may be considered to date from the year 1748, when a small body of Sepoys was raised at Madras, after the example set by the French, for the defence of that settlement in the war which had broken out four years previously between France and England. At the same time a small European force was raised, formed of such sailors as could be spared from the ships on the coast, and of men smuggled on board the Company's vessels in England by the crimps. An officer, Major Lawrence, was appointed by a commission from the Company to command their forces in India.

Hostilities between the English and French were terminated in the following year (1749), on the receipt of news of the Treaty of Aix-la-Chapelle; but about the same time the settlements of both nations began to take an active part in the politics of the peninsula, and the engagements into which the English entered with the parties whose cause they supported led to a rapid increase of the Madras native army, stimulated further by the outbreak of the Seven Years' War in 1756.

Rise of Bengal Army.

During this time Calcutta remained a purely commercial settlement, and the military force with which Clive retook that place in 1757 from the Nawab of Bengal, and won the Battle of Plassey, was principally composed of troops, native and European, belonging to

CHAP. XII.

the Madras establishment, with part of a royal regiment of foot. On the English becoming virtual masters of Bengal, Clive proceeded to raise a Sepoy force after the Madras pattern, commanded by English officers, and supplemented by a local force of European infantry and artillery. The complications which soon followed in Bengal politics, arising out of the deposition of successive Nawabs by their new masters, and the efforts of the party of the emperor to recover that country, led to a rapid augmentation of the Bengal army, which, in 1772, consisted of 21 native battalions, 3 battalions of Europeans, and 4 companies of artillery. The native battalions were about 800 strong, and were commanded each by a captain, with a few subalterns attached; the European battalions and the artillery companies were more fully officered, but were usually very weak in men. In all, there was a nominal strength of about 3,500 Europeans and 24,000 natives, with more than 600 officers. The army was divided into seven brigades, the battalions of which were attached to them permanently. Each brigade was commanded by a field-officer, the whole army by a general officer commissioned by the Company, a charter of 1753 vesting them with authority to raise troops and appoint officers. It was with an army so constituted that the campaigns were fought which terminated in the final subjugation of Behar, and placed the Emperor and Nawab-Wazir of Oudh at the mercy of Clive, on his second return to India in 1765. The Bengal army had previously supplied a considerable detachment to the Madras coast, which afforded material aid in the struggle between the French and English in the South of India, ending in the final overthrow of the former, and the capture of Pondicherry, in 1761.

With the grant to the English of the diwani or treasurership of Bengal, and the fall of the French power in India, all contests for the possession of that province ceased; but the English almost immediately afterwards entered into more extensive engagements. In 1773 their troops occupied Allahabad, in view to hold that place on behalf of the emperor against the Marathas; in 1774 they undertook the defence of the Nawab of Oudh's dominions, and their garrisons were moved up to Cawnpur and Fateghar; in 1778 the Bengal Government joined in the operations then being undertaken from Bombay against the Marathas, and a Bengal column was despatched across India to aid the western presidency. These measures involved a considerable augmentation to the Bengal army, which in 1786, at the time when Lord Cornwallis assumed charge of the government, consisted of 36 battalions of Sepoys, which had been formed into 18 regiments of 2 battalions each, and 6 weak battalions of Europeans; the whole organised in 6 brigades. The European battalions were fully officered; the native battalions were commanded by a captain, with a subaltern to each company. Under the organisation followed up to this time the promotion of the officers had been regulated in one list for the whole army, from which they were posted to the various battalions. In all matters connected with pay, equipment, and the audit of accounts, the army administration partook of the general laxity and disorder which had pervaded every branch of the Company's Government in India, the greater part of the officers' emoluments being derived from irregular perquisites; while, as to the quality and discipline of the early Company's army, the history of those days records a succession of mutinies, in which the black and white troops were alternately employed to coerce each other. The latter were composed of the scouring of almost every European nation, kidnapped or wheedled on board ship by crimps, for the Company's recruiting depot was not established until 1781. The class from which the Sepoys were obtained was familiar with the scenes of

CHAP. XII.

turbulent violence which at that time were being enacted at every court in India. These conditions were quite incompatible with the formation of a well-disciplined or well-organised army, such as has been sometimes represented to have existed at this time. Discipline and sound organisation were the products of a later date. The redeeming feature of the troops of all classes was the gallantry and endurance exhibited in the numerous campaigns and protracted expeditions on which they were engaged.

Increase of Madras Army.

While the Bengal army was thus in course of gradual development, the Madras army also underwent a rapid augmentation. The overthrow of the French power, in 1761, left it indeed for a time without a rival; but the Madras Government had now undertaken the defence of the Carnatic on behalf of its ruler, whom it was rapidly supplanting from all but the nominal sovereignty, and the engagement involved the maintenance of a considerable force. In the year 1772 the Madras army contained about 3,000 European infantry and 16,000 Sepoys, with an establishment of more than 600 officers, the greater part of the cost being defrayed by the Nawab of the Carnatic. This force was shortly afterwards further augmented in consequence of the war with the Marathas and with Haidar Ali. The first contest with the latter, as is well known, involved a struggle for the very existence of the English settlement, Haidar extorting a peace (1769) from the Madras Government under the walls of Fort St. George; in the second war with him and his son Tipu, which terminated in 1784, neither side manifested any decided superiority.

Bombay Army.

The Bombay Presidency during this period, and for many years afterwards, comprised no territory on the mainland of India. But a military force was maintained for its protection, which was increased during the Maratha wars. In 1772 it consisted of about 2,500

Europeans and 3,500 Sepoys, with nearly 200 officers. The expense of this army, as of the Bombay civil establishments, then and afterwards was defrayed from the revenues of Bengal, or by the produce of loans.

In 1773, when the first Governor General was appointed under the Act passed in that year, and the Crown interposed to nominate the members of the Government, the Company's army consisted nominally of about 9,000 Europeans and 45,000 natives.

Royal troops in India.

The first regiment of the British army sent to India was the 39th Foot, which arrived at Madras in the year 1754. This regiment formed part of the force which went with Clive to the relief of Calcutta in 1756, and it was present at the Battle of Plassey in the following year. In 1758 it was nominally sent home, but in effect was broken up, the men being invited to volunteer into the local force, and the officers offered commissions in the Company's army. The English garrison in Bengal then consisted for a time wholly of the Company's forces. Madras remained without royal troops until 1758, when in pursuance of the elder Pitt's vigorous plans for pressing the war against the French in every quarter of the globe, a newly raised regiment of the line, the 79th, was sent out, followed by the 84th, commanded by Lieutenant-Colonel Eyre Coote, and the 96th. In 1759 Coote's regiment was transferred to Bengal, and he was appointed by the Company Commander-in-Chief of their forces in that presidency. On the peace of 1763 the British line was again reduced to 70 regiments, and India remained without any royal troops until 1779, when the 71st [then numbered 73rd] Foot was raised and despatched to Madras. Four other new regiments followed, to aid in the war against Haidar Ali.

Lord Cornwallis, who was appointed the first Governor General in India after the passing of the Act of 1784, which gave that personage authority over the

CHAP. XII.

three presidencies, was appointed also Commander-in-Chief, and was thus vested with supreme authority over both civil and military affairs throughout India. Up to this time it had been usual to confer a step of local brevet rank on all lieutenant colonels of the royal service, an arrangement which naturally caused dissatisfaction among the Company's officers, whose own commissions were moreover often not recognised by the former as giving valid rank. The high authority conferred by the rank and military reputation of Lord Cornwallis, enabled him to procure the repeal of a regulation which was repugnant to his sense of justice. Through his representations the local brevet promotions were withdrawn in 1788, and brevet commissions in the royal service were granted by him as Commander-in-Chief to all the Company's officers, with corresponding dates to those of their substantive ones. This arrangement was continued until the abolition of the Company's government in 1858.

Gradual augmentation of native armies.

From 1772 until 1796 the strength of the Indian army underwent a gradual increase, occasioned by the Maratha war of 1778, and that in the Carnatic with Haidar Ali and Tipu. These wars were, however, undertaken rather for defensive than aggressive purposes; and until the accession of Lord Mornington to the government, the policy of the English, although at times marked by great oscillation of purpose, was on the whole based on the principle of recognising the political equality with themselves of the principal native states, and maintaining the balance of power throughout India. Lord Cornwallis, indeed, when forced into hostilities with the ruler of Mysore, displayed a degree of decision and vigour at that time quite unusual in the conduct of the English military operations. The burden of that war, which ended in the complete humiliation of Tipu and the confiscation of a large part of his territory, was borne principally by the Madras and Bombay armies, which received the largest share of the augmentation rendered necessary of the aggregate military establishment.

At the commencement of Lord Cornwallis's government, the establishment of royal troops consisted of one regiment of dragoons and five battalions of foot. In 1788 four regiments of the line were raised for service in India, and thus brought up the complement to nine battalions, which remained unaltered until 1797. Of these nine battalions only one was stationed in Bengal; two belonged to the Bombay Presidency, the remaining six, with the regiment of dragoons, to Madras. In the year 1794 the total strength of the Indian armies, including royal troops, was 70,000, of which 13,500 were British. The Madras and Bengal establishments of native troops were each about 24,000 strong, the Bombay establishment about 9,000.

Reorganisation of 1796.

In 1796 the organisation of the Indian Army was entirely recast. Heretofore the officers belonging to the establishment of each presidency had been borne on one seniority list, from which they had been distributed among the different regiments; and the proportion of junior to senior grades was exceedingly unfavourable for promotion, there being about eight subalterns to every captain. They were now divided into separate cadres, one for each native regiment of two battalions, to which henceforward the respective officers were permanently attached, their promotion up to the rank of major running in the order of regimental seniority. The lieutenant colonels and colonels remained on separate lists for each branch of the service, to which the regimental majors were promoted in order of army seniority, on succession to vacancies. The establishment of each regiment was fixed at 1 colonel (non-effective), 2 lieutenant colonels, 2 majors, 8 captains, 22 lieutenants, and 10 ensigns, with the result of a great advancement in rank throughout the army.

CHAP. XII.

This system of promotion was maintained until the reorganisation of 1861. The regiments of artillery and engineers were at the same time organised on a similar footing to that of the infantry. An establishment of generals was also formed for the Company's army, the officers of which, owing to the power previously conferred on the Company to grant generals' commissions having been withdrawn, were not at this time eligible for promotion byond the rank of colonel. It was also provided that a specified number of the divisional commands should be held by major generals of the royal army. These were fixed at two for Bengal, and one each for Madras and Bombay; until after the Mutiny these, with a limited number of brigade commands, were the only appointments on the staff of the Indian army which could be held by officers of the British service.

The year 1796 was further marked by the introduction of furlough regulations, which entitled officers to visit England without resigning the army, and also to quit India on sick leave, retaining their Indian allowances and appointments during absence. The privileges conferred by these regulations were, however, partly withdrawn in 1854, and they were still further curtailed, virtually, by the operation of the amalgamation measure of 1861. They were restored with more favourable conditions by the furlough rules of 1868, which have in turn been superseded by later regulations, more in keeping with the conditions of the times and the increased facilities for communication between India and Europe.

Subsequent increase of forces.

Lord Mornington (Marquis Wellesley) arrived in India in 1798, and immediately entered on a new line of policy, the object of which was to sweep away the appearance of equality of power between the English and the principal native states, and to establish the undisputed supremacy of the former throughout the country.

The era of war and conquest which marked his tenure of office, and resulted in the advance of the British cantonments to beyond Delhi in the north, and over the whole of the Dekhan and the Maratha territories, involved of necessity a large increase to the army. The Bengal infantry was raised from twenty-eight[1] to fifty-four battalions, that of Madras from thirty to fifty battalions, and that of Bombay from twelve to eighteen battalions. A considerable augmentation was also made to the native cavalry and the Company's artillery of all kinds. The British troops in India were also largely increased; but the Company's European infantry, which had always been far below its nominal strength in rank and file, was reduced to one regiment per presidency.

CHAP. XII.

In 1808, after the great Maratha war had been finally brought to an end, and the military forces reduced to a permanent peace-footing, the Indian establishment was constituted as follows:—

Indian Army in 1808.

	Royal Army		Company's Army			
	Regiments Cavalry	Battalions, Infantry	Battalions, European Infantry	Battalions, Artillery	Regiments, Native Cavalry	Battalions, Native Infantry
Bengal . .	2	5	1	3	8	54
Madras . .	2	8	1	2	8	46
Bombay .	—	7	1	1	—	18
Total . .	4	20	3	6	16	118

The strength of the three armies being, in round numbers—

	British	Natives	Total
Bengal . . .	7,000	57,000	64,000
Madras . . .	11,000	53,000	64,000
Bombay . . .	6,500	20,000	26,500
Total . .	24,500	130,000	154,500

At this period, it will be noticed, the Bengal and Madras native armies were nearly of equal strength,

[1] The number of battalions had been reduced in 1796 from 36 to 24, and again raised in 1797 to 28 battalions.

CHAP. XII.

but the latter had a larger proportion of British troops serving with it. The cavalry and artillery were on a small scale in proportion to the rest of the army; but this was in accordance with the organisation in force at that time for the British army at home.

In 1823 the two-battalion regiments of native infantry were separated into regiments of one battalion each. The officers of a regiment under the new organisation consisted of—

	1 Colonel (non-effective)
	1 Lieutenant Colonel
	1 Major
	5 Captains
	10 Lieutenants
	5 Ensigns
Total	23

Further development.

The period from 1805 to 1827 was marked by several important wars, and considerable annexations of territory. The war of 1817–18, conducted by the Marquis of Hastings—which led to the dethronement of the Peshwa and further contraction of the other Maratha states, and the expansion of the Bombay Presidency into one of the great provinces of India—as well as the first Burmese war of 1825, involved some considerable additions being made to the army, principally to the Bengal and Bombay establishments. In 1843 a second European regiment was added to the Company's army at each presidency; a third was added in 1854. The artillery also underwent considerable augmentation. The number of British regiments remained almost unchanged, but, in consequence of the large additions made to the territories occupied by the Bengal army, a gradual transfer took place of line battalions from the Madras and Bombay establishments to that of Bengal.

Establishment in 1856.

In 1856, the year preceding the Mutiny, the establishment of regular forces in India was as follows:—

CHAP. XII.

	Bengal	Madras	Bombay	Total
Regiments, British Cavalry . .	2	1	1	4
Battalions, British Infantry . .	15	8	4	22
" Company's European Infantry	8	8	8	9
Battalions, Artillery (European and Native)	12	7	5	24
Battalions, Native Infantry . .	74	52	29	155
Regiments, Native Cavalry . .	10	8	8	21

with three battalions of sappers and miners.

The native battalions were 1,100 strong in Bengal, and 900 in Madras and Bombay. The British line battalions had a nominal strength of 1,000 rank and file. The cavalry regiment had in the British service 730, in the native 500 sabres.

Additional native infantry regiments.

There were also in Bengal, besides the 74 battalions of native infantry, a few additional battalions which had been raised at different times, and which, although not numbered, took their place as a part of the regular army. These had three officers each, detached from the regular regiments.

Irregular cavalry.

The cavalry of the line bore a very small proportion to the infantry, and the disproportion was the more remarkable, when it is remembered that the plains of India are particularly adapted for the use of that arm. But a force of eighteen regiments of what was termed 'irregular' cavalry, was attached to the Bengal army, in addition to the ten regular regiments. The force thus styled was drilled and trained on the same method as the cavalry of the line, and was subject to the same discipline and to the Articles of War. The points of contrast were, that their officers (three per regiment) were taken from the regular regiments, and that the men, recruited from a superior class, yeomen for the most part, possessed of independent means, were engaged under different conditions (as to clothing, arms, and the supply of horses) from those which governed the rest of the army. The Bombay establishment also comprised some regiments of the same kind.

In addition to the regular army, various local regi-

CHAP. XII.

Local troops.

ments had been raised from time to time in Assam, Arracan, and other places which were exceptionally unhealthy for unacclimatised troops; while on the annexation of Punjab, a strong local force of fifteen regiments—five cavalry, ten infantry, was organised for the defence of the frontier, recruited principally from the mountain races of the border, and placed under the orders of the provincial government. The formation of these local forces, as the empire was increased, was deemed preferable to an expansion of the regular army, which in course of time had lost something of the mobility which distinguished the native troops first raised by the English; it was recommended also on grounds of state policy. It was felt that the regular army of, at any rate, the Bengal Presidency, was already too large a body, raised as it was almost entirely from one recruiting field, Oudh and the North West Provinces, and composed mainly of one class, high caste Hindus, united by the strongest bonds of common prejudices and interests. Accordingly, in 1854, on the annexation of Nagpur, a local force was raised on the Punjab plan; and again, on the annexation of Oudh, in 1856, another considerable body was formed, to aid the regular army in garrisoning those provinces. The Oudh local force, which was composed of almost precisely the same material as that which supplied the regular army, was the last addition made to the Indian armies before the outbreak of 1857. At that time the total military force in the pay of the Company was about 280,000 men, of whom about 45,000 were British soldiers. Of the latter, rather more than one half belonged to the royal army.

Contingents.

Further, besides the Company's troops of all kinds, regular, irregular, and local, a considerable supplementary native force had gradually arisen which was practically at the disposal of the British Government, in the various 'contingents' of native states. The first, as well as the largest and most important of the kind, was the Hyderabad or Nizam's Contingent, consisting of two strong brigades of infantry and cavalry, with a proportion of artillery. This force was originally established in order to strengthen the position of our ally the Nizam in his own dominions, and with respect to his neighbours, and also in order to give the British Government the aid which would be available from the alliance, were a portion of his army rendered efficient by discipline. The contingent was commanded by European officers taken from the regular regiments of the Indian army, and was paid for by the Nizam, the payment eventually taking the form of an assignment of territory in perpetuity. This example was in course of time followed in other places, and in 1857 almost every native state had its contingent based on the same plan, and paid for in the same or a similar way. These troops were not under the orders of the Commander-in-Chief, but were under the direction of the Foreign (or diplomatic) Department of the Government of India, the officer in command receiving his instructions through the Resident at the native court in question. The aggregate strength of these contingents was about 35,000 men, largely recruited from the countries (North West Provinces and Oudh) which furnished the greater part of the regular army, certainly the best fighting material we had found in India until we came across the people of Punjab, and which had carried the British flag over every part of the country.

Officering of irregular troops.

All the battalions and regiments additional to the regular army—extra regiments of the line, irregular cavalry, local troops, and contingents—had each a complement of three European officers, selected and specially appointed to them from the regular regiments. To supply these officers, the effective strength of the latter, which was nominally two officers per troop and company, was thus correspondingly reduced; and as appointment to the irregular service in every branch carried with it an

CHAP. XII.

increase of pay and higher relative position, it was eagerly sought after. Thus, from an early date, the system of officering the irregular service tended to lower the efficiency and credit of the regular army. But this was a small part of the evil. The whole of the extensive army staff and the military departments—commissariat, pay, stud, &c.—were all supplied in the same way by officers borne on the effective strength of their regiments; and the drain on the latter was still further increased by the formation of the mixed commissions of civil and military officers, for the administration of the different non-regulation provinces as they came under British rule. The employment of military officers in diplomatic duties, and as judges and magistrates (under the titles of commissioner, deputy-commissioner, &c.), dates from the earliest period of British rule; but the great drain of this kind was caused by the annexations made by Lord Dalhousie of Punjab, Nagpur, and Oudh, when, simultaneously with the formation of large new local forces, a great number of officers were appointed to the civil administration of those provinces. The Court of Directors authorised a slight addition to the army to meet this demand, a sixth captain being added to each regiment of cavalry and infantry in 1843, and a seventh captain and eleventh lieutenant in 1854; but these augmentations were but a slight alleviation of the evil, and at the outbreak of the Mutiny, out of the nominal strength of twenty-five officers there was scarcely a regiment in the country with a dozen officers attached to it. The greater number of the Bengal regiments had much less, and the majority of these officers were ensigns and junior lieutenants, who had not yet qualified for staff employ.

With-drawal of officers for civil duties.

Its ill effects.

But the paucity of officers was the smallest part of the evil, for a dozen officers under a good system should have been an ample complement for a native battalion. The mischief lay in the unhealthy feeling of dissatisfaction with which regimental duty came to be regarded, as the last course, only to be undergone by the minority who could get nothing better. If it had been a question in each case of making a definitive choice between the irregular and regular service, or between a civil and a military career, no doubt many aspiring and able soldiers would have elected to remain with their proper regiments, foregoing present advantages for the chances of future distinction. But, as matters were arranged, a man sacrificed nothing of his regimental position by accepting staff or civil employ. He rejoined his battalion in his proper standing if it were ordered on active service, and in most cases he reverted to it on promotion to field officer, when as a matter of course he took the command, no amount of absence on civil duty being deemed to make him ineligible for that position. Under these circumstances, when every consideration tended to attract an officer from his regiment, it must have been almost impossible that any man should voluntarily elect to remain permanently on regimental duty with the regular army; and in fact almost all the abler officers escaped from that employment, which had come to be regarded as what must needs be accepted either in default of good-luck, or as a mere rest-house on the way to preferment in some other direction. The effect of this prevailing sentiment on the tone of the native army was only too apparent during its latter days. It was impossible but that this degeneracy of feeling should be reflected by the men; and the paucity of officers, from the manner in which it came about, was unquestionably one of the many causes which led up to the great Mutiny.

Other defects of system.

Other causes combined especially to impair the tone and discipline of the army. Two field-officers were nominally attached to each regiment, a major and a lieutenant colonel, but there was not, on the average, more than one available for duty. Now the majors, as

CHAP. XII. has already been explained, belonged to their respective regiments, from which they could not be removed, while the lieutenant colonels were borne on one general list for each branch of the service, infantry and cavalry. In order therefore that the field officers should be distributed equally, it followed that the lieutenant colonels had to be posted to those regiments of which the majors were absent on leave or staff employ; and they were always liable to transfer, on the return of the major, or the promotion of an effective captain to that rank, to some other regiment in want of a field officer. A system which thus made a convenience of the commanding officers, was subversive of all sense of individuality and responsibility on their part, in fact the lieutenant colonel's position was thoroughly humiliating. To which evil must be added the excessive centralisation of the army administration, which deprived commanding officers of all authority; this, combined with the system of promotion maintained, under which all the non-commissioned and native commissioned grades were filled up solely by seniority—the senior private in the regiment succeeding as of right to the first vacancy among the corporals, and so on through all the senior ranks, and the permission accorded to the soldiery to petition the Commander-in-Chief privately touching any supposed regimental supersession or other grievance, rendered the commanding officer a perfect cypher in his regiment.

Seniority system.

The same vicious practice of seniority extended to the higher commands, every officer being held to be entitled to succeed to the charge of a brigade and afterwards of a division when it came to his turn, although this might involve his waiting unemployed for many years, possibly in England. The duties of command when he succeeded to it were little more than formal, mostly of superficial regimental inspections, and passing on references to army head-quarters.

The army staff and departments were officered in the same way. Once on the staff always on the staff; the man who succeeded in getting appointed to the adjutant general's or quartermaster general's department, perhaps as a subaltern, remained in it till he rose to the top after twenty or thirty years' service therein, during which he saw little of the army save through the medium of reports and returns.

The system was little better as regards the staff and generals appointed from the British service. These were mostly selected from the old army which had fought in Spain and Waterloo, men young and vigorous in the earlier part of the century, old and usually inefficient as the years passed by, when officers succeeded to the command of divisions, and of the Indian armies, after long periods passed on half-pay, and came to India for the first time worn out in health, and utterly ignorant of the country and the troops at the head of which they were placed.

Ill discipline.

Drill and military training were of a simple stereotyped kind. The long periods of rest were alternated by campaigns, latterly bloody and desperate, but of short duration; in peace time the troops had little to do. Discipline in the proper sense of the term had long ceased to govern them. They would obey a customary order, and when nothing occurred to interfere with their prejudices or recognised claims, the sepoys were singularly docile and well conducted; military crime, as commonly understood in armies, was almost unknown; but the history of the army was a record of repeated mutinies treated usually with culpable weakness, and so far as could be hushed up; while the want of conduct often shown before the enemy was glossed over, from a natural but mistaken feeling of regimental pride on the part of those who witnessed it.

The Bengal army with its attached contingents and local forces was over one hundred and fifty thousand

CHAP. XII.

Bengal Army over-grown.

strong, men, both the Hindus and Mahomedans, raised mainly from one particular part of the country; the former imbued with overweening pride of caste; all united by the strongest bonds of class feelings and common interests. Flattered, petted, feared, and conscious of its strength, this army was a magazine of explosive matter which a spark would kindle. The great augmentations made from time to time as one new acquisition after another was added to the Empire, had been accompanied by no corresponding increase of British troops, which had been withdrawn from many of their old stations to occupy the new frontier. The guard of almost all the forts and magazines had been entrusted to sepoy garrisons. Many among the officers saw dimly the dangers of the situation, but public opinion took its tone from army headquarters, whence the word was passed to make things pleasant and show the confidence felt there in the aspect of affairs. In this state of things a catastrophe of some sort was inevitable, for the army of 1857 was rotten to the core. The motive action was supplied by the greased cartridges.

Mutiny of 1857.

In the Mutiny only a remnant of the Bengal army remained faithful. All the contingents connected with it joined, sooner or later, in the rebellion. The Punjab Frontier Force—which formed a separate army, recruited from a different country, and which had never been brought into contact with the regular army—came eagerly to the aid of the small British force in the Punjab, and took a highly prominent and distinguished share in the suppression of the rebellion. The Bombay army, although recruited to some extent from Upper India, generally escaped the contamination. Of the Madras army, which was recruited entirely in Southern India, one regiment only of cavalry showed a mutinous spirit, and was disbanded.

During the Mutiny large reinforcements of British troops were sent to India. On the pacification of the

CHAP. XII.

Subsequent increase of British troops.

country these were again reduced, but the establishment retained was much more considerable than that kept up previously. This establishment underwent gradual reduction from time to time, till in 1882 it had been brought down to 60,000 men—or about 15,000 more than the nominal establishment of the pre-Mutiny days. The events on the frontier in 1885 with the new military responsibilities then brought to light indicated that the reduction had been carried too far, and the British portion of the army in India was increased by 10,000 men, partly by the addition of some batteries of artillery and three battalions of infantry, partly by strengthening the rank and file of both cavalry and infantry. The establishment now stands at nine regiments of cavalry and fifty-two battalions of infantry, against four of cavalry and thirty-one[1] of infantry in 1857. But as three additional battalions of infantry are now detached for the occupation of Upper Burma, annexed in 1886, the number of additional battalions in India itself is only eighteen.

Reorganisation after the Mutiny. Reductions made.

The end of the Mutiny found the Bengal native army again almost as large as that which had disbanded itself. A very few of the old regiments had remained faithful, but a great number of new regiments had been raised, the greater number in Punjab of excellent troops, the others in the North West Provinces, levies hastily raised of inferior material. A natural reaction had set in against the high caste Hindustani Sepoy, but the low caste soldiers who were in favour for a time wanted the needful fighting quality. On the pacification of the country being accomplished, all the three Indian armies were largely reduced; a number of regiments were disbanded and the strength of the remainder in rank and file was cut down. At the same time the nine battalions of local European infantry, with three regiments of European light cavalry which

[1] Nine of these belonged to the Company's service.

CHAP. XII.

had been raised during the Mutiny and officered from the unemployed officers of the mutinous Bengal cavalry —a force in which the Court of Directors had a special interest—were transferred to the British army. The three presidential regiments of artillery also were absorbed into the Royal Regiment. The reduced Indian armies now consisted of native cavalry and infantry only, distributed as follows:—

	Battalions Infantry	Regiments Cavalry
Bengal	49	19
Madras	40	4
Bombay	30	7
Punjab	12	6
Total	131	36

with three sapper battalions.

Of this force, the Punjab army, which had five batteries of native artillery attached to it, continued to be under the orders of the Punjab Government. The Hyderabad Contingent of four cavalry and six infantry regiments was retained. This force is commanded by a general officer under the orders of the Resident at Hyderabad. The various contingents and local regiments which had mutinied were not restored, but two regiments of local horse and five of local foot were maintained in Central India, under the Foreign (Political) Department of the Supreme Government. The strength of cavalry regiments was fixed at 500 sabres or lances, that of the infantry at about 700 of all ranks. The total strength of the reorganised native army was therefore 120,000, or about one half the strength of 1857, and less than it has been at any date since the time of Lord Cornwallis.

This great reduction became possible only by the general disarmament of the people of the country carried out after the Mutiny, and by the transfer to a newly organised police of a large part of the duties formerly undertaken by the army, especially the escort of treasure from place to place, and the guard of the district treasuries; and there is no country in the eastern hemisphere where the military force bears so small a proportion to the population, and where, apart from the liability always present that the army may be called on to take the field, even the large cities are so slightly guarded in peace time. City for city, the military garrisons of India are now smaller than even those of England.[1] The Indian army, in fact, has been placed on the footing of a very limited peace establishment, and without any capacity for rapid augmentation.

The mode of officering adopted for the reorganised army will be described in the following chapter. It will be sufficient to say here that as regards the native officers and non-commissioned officers, the vicious system of promotion by seniority throughout all ranks, in itself sufficient to destroy the discipline of any army, was abolished, and by the new Articles of War commanding officers were vested with considerable powers, both for reward and punishment.

Subsequent changes.

For the next twenty years the native army underwent little change in strength and composition, although the British troops were gradually reduced. The Afghan war brought out prominently the insufficiency of the then existing organisation for service. A battalion 700 strong, when recruits, depot and sick were left behind, took the field at starting a very weak body, and under the stress of campaigning soon dwindled away to a handful of men little stronger than the company of a continental army, and this although the enemy was formidable rather from the advantage of

[1] Delhi, for example, the imperial city with a population of 200,000 abounding in dangerous elements, is occupied by four weak companies of British infantry, a garrison battery, a detachment of native cavalry and a battalion of native infantry. The province of Bengal, with 70 millions, has three British and five native battalions to guard it. All the obligatory points are held by such small garrisons that it is no exaggeration to say that, in order to furnish a division for foreign service, a strain has to be put on the army which is felt from one end of the country to the other.

CHAP. XII.

occupying strong positions and a difficult country, than from fighting quality. It was not, however, in view of reforming the tactical unit but under financial pressure that the change was carried out in 1882, of a large reduction in the number of regiments maintained throughout the Indian armies, accompanied by an increase to the rank and file of those retained. The strength of the native infantry battalion was raised from 712 to 832 of all ranks, and a fourth squadron was added to the Bengal and Bombay cavalry regiments, the general result being—with a considerable saving in cost—to leave the strength of the army practically the same as before, but with its organisation certainly improved even for a peace establishment. In 1885, however, the advance of Russia up to the frontier of Afghanistan, and the liability involved—then imminent and henceforward to be kept in view—of being called on to aid in the defence of that country, involved the necessity for an immediate increase to the army, which was carried out to the extent of 30,000 men, the 10,000 British troops already referred to, and 20,000 native troops. The augmentation in the latter case took the form, partly of an increase to the strength of regiments, the infantry cadre being raised from 832 to 912 of all ranks in the Bengal army and Punjab Frontier force,[1] and the cavalry cadre of these and the Bombay army to 625; partly by raising new regiments from the more warlike classes. In particular several new battalions were raised of Gurkhas, the dominant race in Nepal, soldiers of the highest quality. This increase was, however, to a great extent absorbed by the annexation of Upper Burma in the following year, the occupation of which was effected without any addition to the army. But as no cavalry is stationed in Burma, and the infantry garrison of that country is furnished mainly from the Madras army

Augmentation of 1885.

[1] Two (Baluch) regiments of Bombay infantry also were put on the higher establishment.

which it would not be proposed to employ on the North West Frontier, the increase made in 1885 so far as effective strength goes is all to the good. With respect to the augmentation of British troops, the three infantry battalions added to the Indian establishment have indeed been absorbed by Burma, but those remaining in India have been raised from about 900 to about 1000 rank and file, and the considerable increase of artillery is all available in India.

Present strength of army.

The augmentation of 1885 brought up the Indian army to 70,000 British and 130,000 native troops in round numbers, or 200,000 men in all, at which strength it has practically remained. But during the last eight years some important changes have been made by the substitution of new for the old material in several regiments, the men serving in them at the time of conversion being discharged altogether, and an entirely fresh class enlisted, obtained mainly from Punjab or the warlike races on the frontier. Some of these regiments have been localised in the territories in which they have been raised.

CHAPTER XIII

BRITISH OFFICERS OF THE INDIAN ARMY

CHAP. XIII.

Pre-mutiny system of officering regiments. Degradation of the regimental system.

It has been explained that, up to 1857, all the British officers of the Native Army were borne on the rolls of the different regiments composing it. Each infantry regiment had an establishment of twenty-five, and each cavalry regiment of twenty-two officers, of whom rather more than one half were permanently absent from it, serving with so-called irregular regiments, or on the staff, or in some civil employment. To rescue regimental employment from the state of degradation to which it had thus been reduced, was among the reforms most urgently needed, and it was wisely declared almost as the first act of positive reconstruction of the native army, that henceforward employment with a native regiment should be in the nature of staff employment, for which officers would be specially selected. Whereas heretofore the number of officers with an irregular regiment had been three (a commandant, second-in-command, and adjutant), and with a regular regiment usually from ten to twelve, according to the demands of other departments, a fixed regimental establishment was now laid down, at first of six officers, subsequently increased to eight for the infantry and nine for the cavalry;[1] to each situation in the regiment a specific

Reorganisation of 1861.

Reform of regimental system.

[1] In the infantry a commandant, two wing commanders (the senior being also second in command), adjutant, quarter-master, and three available to take the place of the others when absent and learning their work. The companies are commanded by native officers. In the cavalry—the commandant, four squadron commanders, adjutant, and three others spare.

staff salary was attached, in addition to the officer's pay of his substantive rank, and appointment to the regiment and to each particular post in it was to be made by selection at the pleasure of the Commander-in-Chief. Officers detached for appointments on the staff, the tenure of which is for five years, are borne as supernumerary in their regiment during absence, and substantive appointments are made to it in their room.

Creation of the Staff Corps. For the purpose of regulating substantive promotion, all the officers of the Indian army were to be borne on a Staff Corps, of which one was established for each of the three presidencies, and in which promotion was to be regulated by length of service, eleven years to captain,[1] twenty to major, twenty-six to lieutenant colonel; so that the service continued to be one of pure seniority (largely tempered however by the effect of brevets, officers of the staff corps taking rank among each other according to dates of army commissions), but in which office and employment were independent of rank and wholly by selection.

Merits of the system. As a means of supplying the wants of India for officers, a system such as that of this Staff Corps is very suitable. Its merit lies in that it has no fixed establishment, but consists simply of the number of officers required to fill the various posts, regimental and others, maintained at any time, and so expands and contracts automatically with the varying wants of the day; the regulation of promotion by length of service prevents the block in or too rapid promotion which might arise with a fixed establishment. The improvement wrought by the new regimental system simultaneously introduced cannot be too highly appraised. But the manner of carrying out this great reform was not so happy as its conception. The old Bengal army having disappeared, it was a simple matter to post the unemployed officers to the new regiments which replaced it. But the Ma-

Blunders made in introducing it.

[1] Twelve years in the first instance.

CHAP. XIII. dras army, and the greater part of the Bombay army, had remained unaffected; the result, therefore, of applying the new system at once to these bodies was that a part of the officers were placed in a new and much more satisfactory position with increased salaries in every case, while the remainder found themselves put out of employment. It would not have been difficult to arrange for the gradual introduction of the new system, or to defer it altogether as regards these two armies until a reduction in the number of officers should have enabled the change to be made without doing the injury which, thus carried out, it inflicted on the existing interests of the less fortunate officers.

The introduction of the staff corps system was also a measure which would with propriety have been made applicable prospectively, to the young officers entering the service after its introduction; its application to the army as it then stood involved obvious difficulties and complications, only to be successfully overcome by careful forethought and consideration to adjust the new system to the varying circumstances to be dealt with. These precautions were wholly absent from the handling of it. The scheme as sent out cut and dried from the India Office to the Government of India, prescribed that all officers then serving in any staff or extra regimental employment, including in that term service with regiments under the new conditions, that is practically all the officers employed in any capacity, should have the option of joining the staff corps; but that the names of the officers so transferred should still be borne on the lists of their old regiments, to regulate the promotion of their juniors. Since even the moderate rate of promotion guaranteed under staff corps rules was much quicker than that obtaining in the old army, this option was largely availed of, so that the unemployed officers found themselves largely superseded by their more fortunate brother officers. They naturally protested, and claimed the right of succession to the vacancies caused by transfer of the latter to the staff corps. It fell to a succeeding Secretary of State to compose the differences which arose on this and various other points—notably in regard to the claims advanced to compensation for the abolition of the old retirement purchase funds, which had been maintained in almost every regiment, as to which it might and should have been foreseen that a difficulty would certainly arise. It was finally decided on the first point, with which alone we are now concerned, that the staff corps should be thrown open to the whole army, and that while the names of officers electing for transfer to that corps should continue to be borne on their old cadres up to the grade of lieutenant colonel, on reaching that grade the officer's name was to be removed from the regimental list and substantive promotion to that rank made in his room. It might seem at first sight that such a rule would have provided at most only a very moderate rate of promotion for the men who elected to remain in their old lists; but inasmuch as the offer of transfer to the staff corps was very generally availed of, the result was that in several regiments one officer after another rose in rapid succession to the lieutenant colonelcy, and was struck off the regimental list to make way in turn for his junior. If the officer so removed had joined the staff corps, the promotion being nominal only did not benefit him; his pay and rank were determined by his standing in the staff corps; but if the officer had declined the offer of transfer to that service his promotion was substantive; several officers in this way were advanced to the rank and pay of lieutenant colonel in even so short a time as eleven or twelve years, the average rate for promotion to that rank having previously been over thirty years, and having been fixed for the staff corps at twenty-six years. Army promotion was thus made subject to unforeseen and unexpected

CHAP. XIII.

chance, and the lucky lieutenant colonels thus prematurely advanced to that rank being for the most part unemployed, a large and unnecessary charge was imposed on the finances. Another mistake was made with far-reaching consequences. The introduction of the new system of a smaller but fixed establishment of officers for each native regiment, simultaneously with the sweeping reductions made in the number of regiments to be maintained, necessarily threw a large number of officers out of employment. The fixed establishment of officers with the native army had been about 4,300; the actual requirements under the reorganisation came short of this by about one thousand, after making provision for all the extra regimental appointments, military and civil, filled by military men. And every consideration of sound administration indicated the expediency of at once reducing the establishment to this extent, and that a supply should be maintained of young officers brought in at the bottom of the list in succession to vacancies, so as to secure a due proportion of strength in the various grades throughout the list. This was fully recognised when the great reduction was carried out in the strength of the Royal Navy in 1871. In that year a large number of officers in all ranks, down to the sub-lieutenants, were induced to retire by the offer of special pensions; but the establishment having been thus brought down at once to the reduced scale, the supply of young officers proportionate to the requirements of the new establishment was maintained without any intermission. In the case of the Indian army, on the other hand, the unfortunate decision was made to work off the superfluous officers, who were to be brought back to active employment in succession to vacancies, after a longer or shorter period of inaction, during which they had necessarily become less fit for duty with every succeeding year of enforced idleness. This process of reduction took about thirty years to carry out, and many officers were never brought back to duty at all. Special retirements were indeed offered to a small portion of the redundant officers, but on terms not sufficiently attractive to achieve even the limited scope of the measure. And simultaneously, but most unwisely, special inducements were created to retain officers in the service. Heretofore the prizes held out to the old officers had been the 'colonel's allowance' attached to the nominal colonelcy of a regiment, which was usually reached after about twelve years' service as lieutenant colonel. As the latter rank was seldom reached till an officer had served considerably over thirty years, the colonel's allowance was virtually a retirement in old age. But a large number of regiments had disappeared, and to meet the case it was provided that the colonel's allowance, instead of being attached to succession to the colonelcy of a particular regiment, should be acquired after twelve years in the rank of lieutenant colonel. Thus the fortunate men just referred to, after twelve years spent in doing nothing, retired in middle age on a pension much larger than any pay they had ever drawn when in so-called active employ. Certainly the reconstruction of the Indian army was carried out with scrupulous regard to the interests of officers, but so carried out it involved a heavy public charge of which the burden is by no means yet extinguished.

Costly remedies applied.

The cost of the measure was, however, not the greatest evil caused by the ill-considered way in which it was carried out. The Madras army, which had sustained few casualties in the Mutiny, has been especially a sufferer from the unfortunate decision to work off the superfluous officers by degrees. For nearly a quarter of a century virtually no fresh appointments of young officers were made to that army, and the men who were at the bottom of the list in 1861 occupied the same position in 1876. Their rank had advanced, but

Bad effects of mistakes made, especially on Madras army.

CHAP. XIII.

they were still performing a subaltern's duties.[1] It is unnecessary to comment on the disastrous effect of such a state of things upon the spirit of the whole body; in fact, it gave the final blow to the efficiency of the Madras army. Officers so situated could not have any heart in their work; regiments thus officered with men grown grey in the performance of subordinate duties, and without prospects of advancement, formed a most unsatisfactory school for the young officers eventually posted to them.

The officers of the Madras army thus growing old all together reached the age for retirement together, seniors and juniors, making sudden gaps in the list, which, the establishment having now been brought down by effluxion of time to the required strength, were filled up by the appointment of young officers in numbers far exceeding the proper average yearly supply. The first comers of this accession have had exceedingly rapid promotion, and the Madras regiments are now for the most part commanded by captains. But those who come below these lucky seniors will in their turn be very unlucky. The Madras officers are all very much of the same age again, all young men, just as the men they succeeded were all old men, and another block in promotion is impending. And some special measures will be needed to prevent a recurrence of the disastrous circumstances of the past. The needful degree of prevision to deal with this is perhaps hardly to be expected from the Government of India, the members of which hold office for only brief terms, and are very fully employed on the business to be dealt with from day to day. And a

And further evils to come.

[1] In a certain Madras regiment, not long ago, the eight British officers comprised seven colonels and lieutenant colonels and one lieutenant. From 1861 the two junior officers of a regiment were officially styled 'wing subalterns;' it occurred to the authorities, after some years, that this title was hardly appropriate for field officers, and it was altered to that of 'wing officer.'

Secretary of State, who comes to his office absolutely ignorant of India and its affairs, seldom holds it long enough to master administrative problems much more important than even the organisation of the army. But the Council of India, whose members have no executive business, whose functions are limited to offering advice, and who have abundant leisure, should be just the body from whom an exhibition might be looked for of the needful foresight to draw attention to evils to come. Past experience however does not encourage the expectation that this form of statesmanship will be exhibited by that body.

Amalgamation of the three Staff Corps.

It remains to mention about the Staff Corps that it was originally constituted in three separate bodies: the Bengal, Madras, and Bombay Staff Corps respectively. Inasmuch as the officers comprising them are serving under identical conditions as to pay and promotion regulated by length of service, and that they are all equally eligible for employment extra-regimentally in any part of India, this separation into three corps was obviously unnecessary. Their amalgamation into one 'Indian Staff Corps,' repeatedly proposed by the Government of India, has at last been carried out. The title is obviously inappropriate for a body only a small fraction of which is employed on the staff. But a difficulty in the way of making the desired change in this respect has existed so far, that the title 'Indian Army' has been given to the minority of the officers of the old army who elected not to join the staff corps. These, however, are a rapidly decreasing body, consisting now of seniors only, and on their disappearance, when the Indian army and the Staff Corps will mean the same thing, it may be hoped that the latter unmeaning title will be discontinued.[1]

Title should be changed.

[1] There is also a body of officers, appointed in the years 1859-1861, termed the 'General List.' Their case is too technical to be dealt with here; it is sufficient to say that no difficulty would arise in dealing with them in the same way as with the staff corps.

CHAPTER XIV

ARMY ORGANISATION

CHAP. XIV.

Causes which brought about the presidential system of organisation.

THE circumstances under which the Indian army was originally created and has gradually attained its present form, have already been described briefly in earlier parts of this work. In the first instance the three armies which arose out of the requirements of the times were separate and independent organisations. The Government of Bengal had indeed from an early period a general authority over the Governments of the other Presidencies, but this was not exerted in matters of detail, and the three armies had only the degree of uniformity due to the respective Governments they served being under the orders of their common master, the Court of Directors of the East India Company. Each army recruited its native soldiers locally, and received its European reinforcements direct from England; it served only in its own Presidency, and was separated from the other armies by wide tracts of country under independent native rule. From an early date indeed the Commander-in-Chief in Bengal was recognised as being also Commander-in-Chief in India, but the authority thus conveyed applied only to control over the military operations in the field and to a certain limited extent over the discipline of the King's troops serving in that country. The native troops and the Company's European troops in Madras and Bombay continued to be wholly under the local Commander-in-Chief and Government. Gradually the three armies came in contact as they spread over the whole country, and gradually also the Supreme Government came to exercise a more direct control over the administration of the Madras and Bombay armies. From the first, indeed, the financial responsibility for finding ways and means for defraying all military expenditure had rested with the Government of Bengal, as the supreme authority was then called. For long after it maintained an army, the Bombay Presidency had no revenues to speak of, and the Madras Government was never able to meet its military charges; but this responsibility was not clearly recognised until a system of annual estimates and appropriations was introduced, when by degrees a definite financial control was established and the authority of the two minor Governments to sanction military expenditure gradually came to an end. The military system continued however to be organised on the presidential basis; three separate departments of account were maintained; three departments of commissariat, ordnance, and so forth, all engaged in disbursing money supplied directly by the Supreme Government, and all acting under regulations laid down by that authority. The two local governments came into the business only in personal matters. Appointments to and promotions in the departments at Madras and Bombay were still made by those Governments, a striking case of patronage divested of responsibility; but this patronage, and the assumed loss of dignity which would be suffered by change have been largely instrumental in creating the opposition long maintained to the introduction of a more rational system.

This gradually became unworkable.

In the progress of events the Madras and Bombay armies, as has already been explained, were gradually pushed forward beyond the limits of those Presidencies to occupy the different territories added from time to time to British India. From the beginning of the

CHAP. XIV.

century the Madras army has occupied Mysore and Hyderabad, states with the affairs and administration of which the Madras Government has no concern; more recently it has been called on to furnish garrisons for the Central Provinces, the maritime districts of Burma, and even portions of Bengal and Bombay. Similarly, on the occupation of Central India and Rajputana after the last Maratha War, in 1817, a portion of the garrisons of these countries was allotted to the Bombay army, which latterly has also detached some of its regiments to remote Baluchistan. The complications involved in carrying on the military business of the Indian Government in this disjointed fashion have long been extraordinarily troublesome and inconvenient; the state of things arising in war was in the last degree embarrassing. The Government of India which was alone responsible for the conduct of military operations, had not even the advantage of choosing the generals and staff to be employed, the nomination of which for the contingents supplied from the Madras and Bombay armies rested, according to the etiquette obtaining, with their respective Governments. If we suppose that in a case of an expeditionary force sent abroad from the United Kingdom, the selection of the troops to go from Ireland and the Channel Islands with their generals and staff, were to be vested in the Lord-Lieutenant of Ireland and the Governor of Guernsey respectively, we should have a reproduction of the practice which has hitherto obtained in India. The Indian Government in effect took the field with an army of allied troops, under all the disadvantages attending such a condition and with none of the countervailing benefits; the whole responsiblity for results and the burden of meeting the charges remained with that Government.

The serious evils and the flagrant absurdities involved in this state of things were first brought under public notice in the earlier editions of this work, more than a quarter of a century ago, in which also was proposed a definitive plan for carrying out a comprehensive reform, to bring the organisation of the Indian armies into accord with the requirements of the day, based on the principle that the entire control over them should pass to the authority on which already rested the whole responsibility, financial and administrative. Recognising the extreme importance of maintaining the segregation of the different armies and their difference of composition, and pressing indeed that this should be carried out more rigidly than had been customary of late, the author pointed out that the nominal interposition of the Madras and Bombay Governments in the administration of their now scattered armies, which were serving under regulations in the framing of which they had practically no part, and stationed for the most part in countries with which they had no concern, so far as it was not directly mischievous was simply productive of needless expense and delay in the disposal of business. The remedy proposed was obvious and simple. Those armies should be maintained intact, but they should be removed from the control of the local governments, the various disbursing departments and the offices of account and audit being brought directly under the Government of India and the local Commanders-in-Chief placed directly under the Commander-in-Chief in India.

Evils of maintaining system brought to notice in previous editions.

And reforms proposed.

On the other hand the Bengal army called for disintegration. The old army had become dangerous because an overgrown homogeneous force, all recruited from one part of India and from one class. This error, which mainly was the cause of the transient success of the great Mutiny, had indeed been avoided in the reconstruction of that army, and it now consisted of two distinct and nearly equal elements, Hindustani and Punjabi. But the principle of segregation had been lost sight of; the two classes of regiments had been mixed up together, all over northern India, Hindustanis serving

CHAP. XIV.

on the Peshawur frontier, and Punjabis at Calcutta. Moreover, the Bengal army was spread over a country far too extensive for a single command, and every consideration pointed to the need for dividing it into two separate armies, to be kept entirely apart from each other in peace time, for the eastern and western parts of the north of India, which from their position and composition would accurately be called the armies of Hindustan and Punjab, the name Bengal being dropped altogether. Always a misnomer, since there has never been a Bengali serving in it, it had become more than ever inappropriate, and indeed absurd, now that only a very small fraction of that army was serving in Bengal. The commanders of these two armies would be placed on the same footing as the Commanders-in-Chief at Madras and Bombay; the Commander-in-Chief in India, dissociated from his present immediate connection with the Bengal army, would occupy the same position towards each of the four armies, and would be responsible in the same degree for the discipline and general efficiency of all.

This proposal to substitute for a condition which had been suffered to grow up unchecked without any attempt at progressive reform, to adapt it to the altered circumstances of the times—for a system, if such it can be called, full of anomalies, violating all sound financial principles, which worked only with infinite friction in peace time, creaking at every joint, and must infallibly break down in war: the proposal to substitute for this ill-ordered state of things an organisation symmetrical, simple in form, and based on the principle universally recognised everywhere else, that administrative power must go with the authority that is responsible, met with general approval except at the India Office and Horse Guards. At the one it encountered opposition natural from men wedded to a system in which they had been brought up; at the other the nature of the proposal was not understood. The years passed by, but the authorities at home showed no disposition to take any action in this direction, when the Afghan war of 1878–80 and the revelations of presidential mismanagement which followed made plain the impossibility of maintaining any longer the existing state of things. And the Government of Lord Lytton appointed a Commission to enquire into the organisation of the Indian army. The ostensible cause for action was the desire to reduce military expenditure at a time of financial embarrassment. But cost and organisation were bound up together; the war had been illustrated by instances of grievous mal-administration and improper appointments to responsible posts, and the instructions to the Commission—a very strong one with the Lieutenant Governor of Bengal, the most important civil official in India after the Governor General, at the head, were wide and general. Their copious and exhaustive report, in addition to proposals for reduction of expenditure, recommended a complete re-organisation of army administration corresponding in all essential respects with that proposed in this work—the unification of army administration under the Supreme Government, the detachment of the Bengal army from the direct command of the Commander-in-Chief, and its division into two armies for Hindustan and Punjab respectively. Lord Lytton left India shortly after the presentation of the report, which fell to be taken up by the Government of Lord Ripon, and the adoption of the leading proposals contained in it was strongly pressed by them on the authorities in England. The latter, however, received it but coldly. To some members of the Indian Council any change upon the state of things obtaining in their day was repugnant, others were indifferent, those who approved of the reform were lukewarm in supporting it. At the Horse Guards the scope of the proposals seems to have been misapprehended; that office is not

which after protracted opposition and controversy

CHAP. XIV.

familiar with the organisation of the Indian army, and its criticisms on the case, so far as they are known, were hardly relevant to it.[1] They were mainly directed to the danger of overcentralisation in military affairs which was assumed to be contemplated. The fact that the Madras and Bombay armies had remained faithful when the Bengal army mutinied was ascribed to the fact that they were serving under separate governments, and it was argued that their loyalty would be strained by the transfer of their services to a distant authority. Further, that in the event of a recurrence of rebellion, a great advantage would be lost if the local governments were not in a position to command the services of the local armies at a time when perhaps communication with the Supreme Government might be cut off.

To this the Government of India replied that while overcentralisation, in the sense of concentrating all power in a central authority, dealing with matters which might with propriety and advantage be disposed of by the local officials, was undoubtedly to be deprecated, their proposals did not involve anything of the kind. Segregation of the armies would be maintained as before, while the division of the Bengal army into two carried the principle of segregation much further. So far from the existing arrangements securing the desired result, as a matter of fact great practical difficulty had been found in restraining the authorities in Bombay from persistently recruiting in Northern India from among the classes which supplied the Bengal army, in violation of the regulations prohibiting the practice. As to the supposed attachment

[1] The Commission, in their report, rather unfortunately used the term 'army corps' to denote what would, in fact, have been four separate armies, kept as distinct from each other as they were before the change; possibly it may have been apprehended that there would be a loss of patronage because the local commanders-in-chief were to be abolished. They were, however, to be retained under another name, and the number of them was to be raised from two to four.

of the local armies to their government, inasmuch as they were serving for the most part in territories beyond the jurisdiction of that government, with which they seldom if ever came in contact, and as the military code under which the troops were serving was not that of the local government, which equally was not responsible for the pay or clothing or equipment of the troops, the connection between them must necessarily be of but a shadowy kind. As to the supposed safeguard, in the event of internal troubles hereafter, of maintaining the nominal connection of two out of the eight provincial governments of India with military affairs, the degree of energy and skill which might be displayed by the civil authorities of any province cut off from outer communication, and forced to act for itself, would depend on the character of the Government. The Governor who showed the highest example in this respect during the Mutiny was one who had nominally no control over the army serving in his province. On the other hand, if centralisation in the bad sense was to be condemned, unity of command and control was an essential condition of proper army administration. The existing system, with the nominal interposition of the authority of the two local governments in the concerns of armies dispersed for the most part in territories beyond the limits of their own administration, was productive of nothing but embarrassment and delay, and must sooner or later be recognised on all sides as a mischievous survival of a state of things which had long passed away. Meanwhile, the liability was always present that the outbreak of war might find the administration of the Indian Government still encumbered by this defective military organisation. The correspondence was pursued for some years on these lines, the Indian Government continuing to press its demands for the reform, the India Office repeating its objections in a half-hearted way as if growing ashamed of its obstruc-

CHAP. XIV.

tion; but while refusing to accord definite sanction to the proposal, the Secretary of State gave the case away bit and bit. One by one, he sanctioned the transfer of the different army departments in Madras and Bombay from the nominal control of the local governments. In 1876, the three departments of military account and audit were consolidated into one with an Accountant-General attached to the Government of India at the head of it, and on this change being made, what control over army administration had still nominally remained with those governments practically came to an end. The three presidential Stud Departments were amalgamated in 1881. The unification of the Ordnance Departments followed in 1884; and later on of the Army Transport and Commissariat and the Clothing Agencies. The Madras and Bombay Governments had never been concerned with the charge of the barracks and other military buildings occupied by their armies outside the limits of those presidencies, the provision and custody of these having been entrusted to the governments of the different provinces in which the troops were stationed, while the harbour defences and other fortifications throughout the country were carried out by the Government of India through the agency of the Military Works Department, which had also the charge of the military buildings occupied by the Bengal army. In 1888, this department, reorganised in four branches, each under an Inspector General, with a Director General at the head, took over the charge of all military buildings throughout the country. Lastly, the three separate presidential staff corps were amalgamated into one Indian Staff Corps.

Meanwhile the military operations which followed upon the annexation of Upper Burma in 1886 brought into prominent relief again the evils of what still remained of the presidential system. The troops employed were furnished from the three presidencies, and nearly one half of the Madras army was diverted to that country—although the Bengal and Bombay troops took the leading part in the operations, and the general commanding, acting of course in immediate communication with the newly appointed governor of the province, took his orders from the Commander-in-Chief in India, who was responsible to the Supreme Government for the conduct of the war, and indeed went himself to Burma for a time to superintend affairs from the spot. Nevertheless, Burma being a command nominally attached to the Madras army, the fiction was maintained that the Madras Government, in some sort of way which no one could pretend to define, was responsible for the business, and for a time the general commanding submitted formal reports to that government of operations about which they had otherwise no other information than was to be derived from the newspapers. This absurdity was eventually dropped, but the Commander-in-Chief at Madras continued to be the medium of communication between the general officer on the spot and army headquarters in India.

are at last in course of being carried out.

At last, in 1888, the authorities at home could no longer withstand the irresistible reasons for putting an end to a state of things repugnant to common sense and amounting to an administrative scandal, and the Indian Government were authorised to prepare the necessary orders for finally giving effect to this long withstood reform. These, which were to be framed in detail, were to provide for the assumption by the Supreme Government of the direct administration of all the Indian armies. So far the change would be little more than formal, the transfer of this administration having in fact been already gradually taken over, but the further important change was now to be carried out, an essential part of the reform originally proposed, of dividing the Bengal army into two armies, each under a general officer having the same status and authority

CHAP. XIV.

as the commander-in-chiefs of the Madras and Bombay armies. The immediate connection of the Commander-in-Chief in India and headquarters staff with the Bengal army would thus be severed, and the great patronage heretofore exercised by him of all the appointments and promotions connected with that army would be transferred, with the command, to the heads of those two armies to be created. On the other hand the Commander-in-Chief in India was now to undertake fully the functions indicated by his title, occupying the same degree of supervision and control over all four armies, while as a necessary condition of the responsibility attaching to that position he would naturally have a potential voice in selection for the higher posts throughout all those armies. The measure, while thus establishing unification of command and administration, was aimed at providing also in a large degree for decentralisation, by devolution of authority to the four army commanders and the local departmental heads. Everything was thus made ready for carrying out the change in 1890, but delay arose in obtaining the statutory authority considered necessary for severing the connection between the Commander-in-Chiefs of the Madras and Bombay armies and the governments of those provinces. This was obtained by a short Act of Parliament passed in 1893, and there only remains for the Secretary of State to signify approval to the proposals of the Government of India for giving effect to the measure in its various details in order that this most important and long delayed reform should at last be carried out.

Reforms proposed in 1870 no longer suitable to circumstances of case.

But meanwhile the march of events has already outstepped the slow and reluctant movement of the Home Government, and the arrangements first proposed so many years ago and now approaching accomplishment, have already ceased to be appropriate to the state of things with which we have to deal. The original scheme of four armies, the Bengal army being formally decomposed into its two distinct elements, the Hindustani and Punjabi, necessarily presented a considerable inequality; the Punjab army to be created would be much the strongest numerically of the four, besides being the superior in fighting quality; the Hindustan army also was considerably larger than the other two. This inequality was accepted as a necessary condition of taking things as they were, and altering as little as possible the existing organisation. But since 1881 the Madras army has been largely and the Bombay army considerably reduced, while additions have been made to the troops on the North West Frontier; and the inequality in strength of the four divisions has now become so great that the new system will be found impracticable to work as soon as it comes into operation. Recent changes made in the composition of the armies increase the inequality still more. Of the thirty-two infantry regiments of the Madras army remaining after the reductions of 1882, seven have been converted into local Burma regiments recruited from Northern India, a change made partly in order to relieve the Madras Sepoy from unpopular service in that country, and partly because of his insufficiency for the work there. These seven regiments, although they continue to bear their old numbers as well as their new ones, are practically severed from the Madras army. Moreover, sooner or later, it will be found necessary to constitute Burma a separate command, the general holding it to report direct to army headquarters. With this change, which should have been carried out from the first occupation of Upper Burma, the last shadow of reason will disappear for maintaining even a nominal connection between these Burma battalions and the Madras army. Besides these local battalions, seven battalions of the regular Madras infantry are stationed in Burma, so that the Madras command will be limited, as regards native

CHAP. XIV. troops, to eighteen regiments of infantry,[1] three of cavalry, and a battalion of sappers, and including British troops will comprise only about twenty-seven thousand men, or less than one-seventh of the Indian army. It will not be justifiable to keep up the apparatus of a commander-in-chief and staff sufficient for an army on account of this body. The native portion is smaller than the Punjab Frontier Force, the command for thirty years of a brigadier-general with a single staff officer.

A similar disintegration has taken place in the Bombay army, which must inevitably be carried further. The portion of that army serving in Sind has always been a local force of two so-called Baluchi infantry regiments and three regiments of Sind Horse, consisting of men raised on the frontier and in Punjab. A portion of the garrison occupying the more advanced position lately taken up at Quetta and other points beyond Sind and Punjab has however been furnished from the regular regiments of the Bombay army, coming and going in the periodical reliefs, a service unpopular with men raised in the tropical districts of India, and for which they are physically unfitted. Of these battalions, five in number, three have lately been broken up, and the men in them replaced by a new enlistment from the border tribes for local service; so that, although the old numbers have been retained for the present, these regiments have practically severed their connection with the Bombay army. The Quetta district has always been directly under the Commander-in-Chief in India. The Bombay army, even before the conversion above mentioned, furnished only a smaller portion of the whole force there, and now is represented by only two battalions of infantry. In any redistribution of commands, the small force in Sind, which can be approached from

[1] These regiments have a considerably less strength in rank and file than the regiments in Northern India.

Bombay only by sea, would naturally be attached to the frontier command of which it forms a base. If this be done, as on military grounds is much to be desired, and would certainly be done if war were imminent, then the Bombay command would be reduced to about thirty thousand men, also little more than one-seventh of the whole Indian army. CHAP. XIV.

On the other hand, the Western or Punjab army will have become very much more than an army of Punjabis only, and will be brought up to a strength of about seventy thousand men, a larger and incomparably stronger military force than the Madras and Bombay armies put together.[1] The fact is that during the last few years the military centre of gravity has moved further towards the west. The necessity has arisen of strengthening the frontier position, while in pursuance of the policy which has always been acted on of inviting into our ranks the best material available, there has been a large substitution for other classes of the hardy races on the frontier which have come under our rule and influence. The result is a state of things obviously incompatible with the fulfilment of the original scheme of four commands with equal staffs and establishments for dealing with armies of nearly equal strength. The inequality resulting, if that scheme is persisted in, would be nearly as great as it is under the system to be replaced; an early modification of that scheme is inevitable.

It is certainly necessary that unity of military purpose should be secured on the frontier. But the extent

[1] The composition of the four armies would be as follows:—

	British Troops	Native Troops	Total
Madras army .	9,000	18,000	27,000
Bombay army .	12,000	18,000	30,000
Punjab army .	23,000	33,000	56,000
Hindustan army	23,000	47,000	70,000
	67,000	116,000	183,000

In addition there would be about 4,000 British and 10,000 native troops in Burma.

CHAP. XIV.

of this is too great for the personal supervision of a single commander. To attach any part of this frontier, with its garrisons of local troops, different from the Bombay troops in race and language, to the Bombay command, would be highly impolitic. It would be equally so to attach these local troops—Baluchis and others—to the Punjab army. The principle of segregation should, above everything, be scrupulously maintained under the new organisation. These considerations all point to the necessity for dividing the frontier into two commands: that is, the present Quetta district, with Sind added for its base, should continue to be a separate command directly under the Commander-in-Chief in India. This would reduce the overgrown Punjab army by about fifteen thousand men.

Another equally appropriate reduction would be to maintain the separate autonomy of the Punjab Frontier Force. This distinguished force, with a splendid record dating from its first formation, nearly fifty years ago, which comprises twelve battalions of infantry and five of cavalry, with five native batteries, was transferred from under the orders of the Punjab Government to those of the Commander-in-Chief in 1888. It guarded the border from Kashmir to Sind, except the Peshawur district, which has always been garrisoned by the Bengal army, and interrupted its continuous line of border-posts held by the former. Towards the south this condition no longer holds, some of the posts lately established in the extensive territory of Baluchistan overlapping those of the Punjab Frontier Force behind them and below the mountain passes; but it should not be difficult to redistribute the different posts, and to concentrate the Punjab Frontier Force on one portion of the frontier. The original proposal of the Commission of 1880, adopted in this respect by the Government of India, contemplated the maintenance of this force as a separate body from the four regular armies, and every consideration seems to press for adhering to this purpose. Unity of administration should be insisted on, no doubt; no conflict or co-ordination of authority is permissible in any reasonable military system; but this has now been secured, and it is equally important to secure decentralisation, and above all, to avoid a repetition of the blunder of building up one overgrown native army overshadowing the others.

Modifications desirable.

Under this view the Indian army would be organised in seven commands, the native portion of each being a separate and distinct army, the strength of which would be susceptible of modification from time to time, to accord with the changes in the military situation inevitable in the future. It may be pleaded as an objection to such an arrangement that all the army departments —ordnance, commissariat, transport, account, &c., have recently been organised in four branches, so that the commander of each of the four armies originally contemplated might have the aid of a local departmental head in each department. But it should not require a great exercise of administrative skill to adapt the original scheme in this respect to the more flexible system here advocated. Sooner or later, it must be recognised that the plan of four equal armies, or four armies of any sort, has ceased to be appropriate to the actual military position, and it appears highly desirable when carrying out the impending reform, to do so in a way calculated to be lasting and stable.

Patronage how to be regulated.

One matter, of detail comparatively, but of great importance, needs to be carefully provided for. The four-army scheme provided that the selection for all appointments—regimental as well as staff—in the Madras and Bombay armies would remain as at present with the generals respectively commanding them, and that similar powers would be vested in the commanders of the two bodies into which the Bengal army is to be

CHAP. XIV.

divided. Thus the Commander-in-Chief and army headquarters in India were to part with the whole of the great patronage of the Bengal army now vested in them. If the larger subdivision of the Indian army here suggested is carried out, the temptation to retain this patronage may not unnaturally assert itself, on the plea that it cannot be transferred with propriety to officers, the generals commanding in Burma and Baluchistan and the Punjab Frontier Force, of less standing and authority than was contemplated when the original plan was proposed. The importance of decentralisation in these matters however can hardly be rated too highly, and it should not be difficult to deal with it in a satisfactory way, whatever be the units of organisation determined on, which should be flexible enough for adaptation to the variations in the composition and strength of the different armies which will certainly be found necessary as time goes on. Patronage in the Indian army is of two kinds. There is the first appointment of the young officer on his arrival to a particular army, and to the cavalry or infantry branch of it, and also his posting to a particular regiment in that branch. Heretofore candidates for the Indian army have been obtained from British regiments, mainly from the regiments serving in India, and the distribution of them was made by the Government of India, the young officer being usually appointed to the particular army with which his regiment happened to be serving.

Of first appointments.

This mode of supply has lately been abandoned, and candidates for the Indian army are now appointed direct from Sandhurst to the Indian Staff Corps into which the three separate staff corps have happily been amalgamated. The distribution of the candidates among the different Indian armies is made by the Indian government. And the question is, how this distribution should be regulated. Appointment to the army or armies on the frontier will naturally be most in request, but as the candidates are unknown to those with whom rests the distribution, the latter have nothing to guide them but the solicitation of friends. Patronage exercised under such conditions is indefensible, and the only satisfactory way of regulating the business is to give the candidates their choice, in order of their standing on passing out of Sandhurst, of succession to the available vacancies in the different armies. This, however, does not dispose of the difficulty, because there is keen competition for appointment to the cavalry and to particular regiments—as of the Gurkhas—in the infantry. This part of the business has been dealt with by the respective commanders-in-chief, and the patronage has no doubt been valued as a means of obliging friends; but it is an unsatisfactory form of patronage, because from the nature of the case its disposition cannot be determined by the merits of candidates whose qualifications have still to be tested. And under patronage pure and simple, however conscientiously exercised, bad riders have found their way into the cavalry, while undersized officers are clearly as much out of place in Sikh regiments as in the Guards; equally are officers six feet high out of place in regiments of Gurkhas who run to about five feet in height. Subject to this last condition the most satisfactory way of settling the matter would be to give the young officers their choice of regiments, as of army, according to their standing on leaving Sandhurst, while first appointments to the cavalry should be provisional, to be confirmed only after the candidate has undergone a searching test of fitness for that branch; a bad rider with Indian cavalry (and there are many such now in the service) may do incalculable mischief.

Of regimental posts.

Patronage, however, only begins with first appointments. Every one of the eight posts which make up the complement of a native regiment (nine posts in the cavalry) is a staff appointment to which any officer may be appointed, either of that regiment or from

CHAP. XIV.

another regiment.[1] It is this freedom of selection, and the right which the Commander-in-Chief possesses of transferring officers from one regiment to another which perhaps more than anything else has conduced to the efficient officering of the Indian army. The right is limited by the condition always acted upon, although not prescribed by any regulation, that the regimental standing of officers shall correspond with their length of service. Inter-regimental transfers seldom occur except to adjust special instances of inequality in the rate of regimental promotion, while if an officer is superseded in the command of his regiment, it is generally understood that he shall be removed also from active employment.

To the staff.

There is, further, the selection for the staff proper. An officer appointed to the staff—except to some of the higher posts—continues to be borne as a supernumerary, on the strength of his regiment, to which he reverts on the completion of five years' service on the staff. The practice in this respect is similar to that which obtains in the British service, at home and in India, although in both armies it occurs that the services of some officers are deemed to be so indispensable that their tours of staff service are almost constantly renewed either in the same or a fresh capacity. Now in regard to both classes of appointment, the regimental and staff, the selection is made with a full knowledge of the qualifications of the men to be dealt with and under a due sense of the responsibility involved in making the selection. Patronage of this sort, which is the only kind that should be exercised by any authority, should be interfered with as little as possible. It only remains to determine with whom lies the best means of forming a right judgment, and the most complete responsibility. As regards regimental appoint-

[1] An adjutant or quartermaster cannot however be of field rank.

ments and the junior posts on the staff, it may be said that, be the army large or small, the army commander is clearly indicated as the proper authority in whom to vest the patronage. The Commander-in-Chief being responsible for the efficiency of the Indian army as a whole should certainly have a potential voice in the selection of commandants of regiments as well as for all the higher staff appointments, and this should be made by him, for all the armies, on the nomination of the local commander.

CHAPTER XV

INDIAN ARMY PROMOTION

CHAP. XV.

Promotion to colonel.

Promotion in the Indian staff corps, which will soon embrace the whole Indian army, as has been explained, is regulated by length of service; eleven years to captain, twenty to major, twenty-six years to lieutenant-colonel, and onwards according to the peculiar system now obtaining in the British service. Until lately promotion to the rank of brevet colonel, when not gained by distinguished service in the field, could be obtained by a specified term of service as lieutenant colonel in command of a regiment or other qualifying appointment, originally fixed at three, but subsequently extended to five years. The list of qualifying appointments was enlarged from time to time till it embraced practically every situation, regimental and departmental, in the active list, so that promotion to colonel became in effect like that to the grades below it, a matter of simple seniority attained in thirty-one years, except when given earlier for war services. A few years ago this system was superseded by a new one according to which appointment to certain specified staff situations was to carry with it substantive promotion to colonel, the condition being added that only lieutenant colonels of three years' seniority and upwards should in future be eligible to hold these offices. The warrant embodying these changes for the British army having been promulgated, the Indian Government were instructed to apply its provisions to their army. Two very notable conditions were involved in the change. In place of the long-established principle that promotion to colonel should be earned by approved service in an office, appointment to the office was to carry promotion with it; the selected officer was to get the appointment (and promotion) first, and to prove his fitness for it afterwards. And regimental command ceased to be a qualification for promotion. Now, whatever may be thought as to the importance of regimental command in the British army, in regard to the Indian army, at any rate, it has always been recognised that its efficiency must depend before everything on the discipline and good leading of the regiments; the command of a regiment has therefore always been held to be a higher and more important charge than any of the ordinary staff appointments, a distinction accentuated by the higher emoluments attaching to the former. Except in the case of a few men employed at head-quarters, the duties of a staff officer are of a routine kind, needing business habits and physical activity, but carrying with them no personal responsibility, and are best fulfilled by comparatively junior officers. To require that none but lieutenant colonels of three years' standing should be appointed to these situations would involve that the assistant adjutant general at the end of his tour of office should be a man of nearly thirty-five service, much too old for efficiency on the staff in India. Moreover, while in the British service the tenure of regimental command is limited to four years, and the lieutenant-colonel is therefore eager to pass on at the end of it to a staff appointment which carries promotion, instead of being placed on half-pay, the command of a native regiment is held for seven years; the commandant will naturally be unwilling to descend from this to the less responsible office of a district staff officer; yet as the warrant stands this is the only way of securing the coveted promotion. As a matter of

CHAP. XV.

fact the provisions of the warrant in this respect have not yet been applied to India, and the district and other staff appointments continue to be held in part by junior officers.[1] The loss resulting to the Indian army of promotions to the rank of colonel is to be made up by the selection of a certain number of lieutenant-colonels for promotion without reference to the appointments held by them. The case of this warrant, thrust upon the Indian Government without previous consultation with them, is one of many indications how little knowledge appears to be possessed by the Horse Guards of the organisation and needs of the Indian army, about which nevertheless it has often a potential voice.

Promotion to general officer.

The mode of dealing with the promotion of general officers is in its way as curious as that of the colonels. According to the wording of the present regulations promotion to major-general and upwards is to be determined by selection. For this in peace time no better way of ascertaining an officer's fitness for promotion could be found than that afforded by the discharge of the actual duties of command. The opportunity for making selections after these trials is constantly afforded. Second-class Districts as they are called—brigade commands—are held by selected colonels with the temporary rank of brigadier-general, and not unfrequently colonels are appointed to the command of first-class districts with the acting rank of major-general. So also promotion to the head of the great administrative departments of the army—ordnance, commissariat and transport, and military works, or to the army staff as adjutant or quartermaster-general or as inspector-general of cavalry or artillery, carries with it acting promotion to major-general.[1] Here then the amplest

[1] Some of these appointments are held by officers of the British service, with which we are here not concerned, but the principle involved is obviously applicable to all branches of the army.

opportunity is given for testing the officer's qualifications; and if appointment to a specified post is to carry with it promotion at once, still more the efficient discharge for five years of the duties of an office might surely be accepted as the most satisfactory possible test. But this obviously fitting test of selection is disregarded, and the officer after completing his term of duty in one or other of these high and responsible offices, involving perhaps the command of from ten to twenty thousand men, reverts to the rank of colonel, to take his turn of promotion to major-general with others who have in the meantime been holding subordinate posts or altogether unemployed.

For this state of things the India Office is responsible, so far as the Indian army is concerned. When absolute seniority for promotion to general officer was given up in the British army, it should have been recognised that the public interests demanded its abolition in the Indian army also; that the appointments to be held by general officers being few, the list of generals, now reduced, should be maintained only for those who should establish a claim to it by actual service in that rank. Unfortunately a too scrupulous adherence to the supposed claims of officers to promotion by seniority prevailed, not only of those on the so-called active list, but the still larger class who have been virtually retired; and it was decided that these should be moved up through the different grades of general officer *pari passu* with their former contemporaries, the most copious of the many measures for degrading military rank taken of late years, the like of which has never been applied to the army of any other country.

A defect of present system.

It has been mentioned that admission to the Indian army is now obtained direct from Sandhurst. Heretofore, when the channel was through a short preliminary term of service with a British regiment, the possibility of obtaining a transfer practically depended on the

CHAP. XV.

young officer being posted to a regiment stationed in India, and if the applications for admission exceeded the vacancies there were no satisfactory means of deciding between the conflicting claims. It is perhaps to be regretted that the opening should be closed to candidates from Woolwich; but the choice of a career must be made sooner or later under any rules, and that the candidate should be allowed to make his choice between the two services if sufficiently high in the class list is as satisfactory a plan as could be devised. The material thus obtained is as good as could be wished for; the outcome of public school life and the pursuit of athletics tempered by competitive examinations gives to the army a body of young officers with which the country they represent may well be satisfied. The subsequent training has perhaps this defect that the numerous courses of instruction to be undergone,—in musketry, signalling, surveying, and what not, take the young officer away from his regiment just at the time when the mind is quickest to acquire a new language. In former times the old Court of Directors used to give their cadets when they came up to present themselves before sailing for India a piece of advice—the only thing they gave them, for his passage money was defrayed by the friends of the cadet—to study the language, advice usually followed in the absence of other occupation. In those days the course of military training was short and simple, life was monotonous and distractions few, and the officer at starting was thrown very much among his men, and soon became proficient in their language. Nowadays, the young officer spends a large part of his first years away from his regiment, and sees little of his men except in the drill season, and so loses the first and best opportunity of becoming an expert linguist. The same difficulty occurs in the civil service, in the great increase of English correspondence thrown on civil officers of all ranks, and of special and centralised departments at the headquarters of Government, attractive to the abler men of the service as are staff appointments at army headquarters to military officers. Both classes while so withdrawn from direct contact with the people of the country, except their domestic servants, make no progress in their knowledge of the vernacular languages even if they do not lose ground in them, and equally make no progress towards a real knowledge of the people of the country and the native soldiery. The evil is a very real one, although it is not easy to find a remedy.

Comparative emoluments in India and elsewhere.

To these remarks regarding the British officers of the Indian army, it may be not inappropriate to add that the notion popularly held as to the comparative superiority of Indian pay over English and colonial pay is no longer supported by the facts. A comparison between the two rates would be fallacious; the English rate is supplemented by various allowances, and the officer is provided with free quarters, and one or more soldier servants. In India no perquisites of any sort are recognised; the officer receives a fixed rate of pay, and has to find his own house and servants, and on the march to supply his own tent and the means of carrying it. This system is invariable for all ranks from the general downwards; only when travelling on duty by railway is his fare paid. With the fall in silver the rupee pay has undergone a depreciation which puts the officers of British regiments in India very nearly on an equality with those serving at home; in this respect the officers of the Medical Staff in India are distinctly at a disadvantage. The officers of the Indian army are not much better off, if their comparatively slow promotion be taken into account, and that they have usually to find their own passage when going on and returning from leave to England. On the other hand the Indian army has the advantage of a much more liberal rate of retiring pensions.

CHAP. XV.

The same thing holds good of the prizes of the service, the district commands held by general officers. The real equality between home and Indian rates is disguised by the allowances and free quarters attaching to the commands at home and abroad, whereas the Indian general receives a consolidated salary in lieu of all demands. And there are only as many hundred men in the ordinary colonial command as there are thousands in the Indian one. The pay of the Indian first class district is on a higher scale, but there are no posts of corresponding importance out of India, except Aldershot and Ireland.

CHAPTER XVI

NATIVE OFFICERS

CHAP. XVI.

The old regimental system.

THE regimental organisation of the native army of India has already been briefly described. The unit of organisation is the battalion in the infantry and the regiment in the cavalry.[1] The seniority system obtaining for the British officers was equally applied to the native soldiery, and in a still more rigid way, extending throughout the regiment. The sepoy, usually drawn from the agricultural class, enlisted as a private and rose to the non-commissioned grade by length of service in his regiment. A knowledge of reading and writing in the vernacular was required for promotion, but subject to this small qualification the senior private, if of good character, was entitled by custom to become a corporal (naik) and then sergeant (havildar) in order of seniority in succession to vacancies. Advancement to the commissioned ranks of native officer, and promotion from the lower to the higher grade in that rank was regulated in the same way, by pure seniority, the senior sergeant of the regiment having a recognised claim to succeed to a vacancy among the jemadars and the senior jemadar becoming in turn subahdar. The subahdar-major (the senior native officer) was consequently, as a rule, the oldest man in the regiment and always an old man. The native officer held a very subordinate position; the troops and companies were

[1] The Gurkha regiments are organised in two battalions, which however are practically separate regiments, the officers attached to them rising in their respective lists.

CHAP. XVI.

commanded by British officers, generally lieutenants and ensigns. The same system obtained in the regular cavalry; the various ranks differed from those of the infantry only in name. Pensions regulated by the rank of the soldier were claimable after twenty-one years' service, and higher rates for still longer service. It was thought that this system, with the certainty held out of pension for long service, was a guarantee for loyalty, especially among the seniors who had so much to lose by misconduct—an expectation entirely falsified by the event. In the Mutiny the regiment either revolted in a body, or stood firm together with a very few exceptions, and its old native officers continued to command it throughout the war. The Bengal army was recruited mainly from the high-caste Hindu peasantry in Oudh and the adjacent British districts; but a fourth of the men in each regiment might be Mahomedans. This mixed composition, which was no doubt adopted in the first instance as a protection against combination, proved quite ineffectual. Class feeling proved stronger than race and religious antipathy; the two classes might possibly have clashed afterwards, had the rising been successful, but while the struggle lasted they held together. Shortly before the Mutiny, admission to the army was accorded to Sikhs from the lately conquered Punjab to the extent of ten per cent. per regiment. But this further attempt at establishing diversity of interests proved equally inoperative. The people of the Punjab indeed, when the Mutiny broke out, showed themselves eager to pay off old scores against the Indians, their hereditary foes and recent conquerors when led by British officers. The regiments of the Punjab Frontier Force, raised in 1849, formed a very distinguished part of the army which put down the rebellion, and the new regiments hastily raised by Sir John Lawrence in that country were filled up at once, and many of them were organised in time to take an active and most useful part in the war. But the Punjabi elements in the old army were altogether too small and too scattered to withstand the professional influences to which they were subjected. These young soldiers, for the most part, threw in their lot with their regiments.

CHAP. XVI.

The so-called irregular cavalry, which formed the larger part of this branch of the Bengal army,[1] was organised on a different footing. It was recruited from a higher class, mostly yeoman or landholder, each man bringing his horse with him and depositing a substantial sum in the regimental chest. Against this he was debited with the cost of his uniform and equipment, and credited in turn with their value on leaving the regiment, when the balance of his deposit was repaid to him. The rate of pay included the cost of maintaining the soldier's horse which was provided by himself. Originally a native gentleman or a man of substance on enlisting might bring a certain number of relatives or retainers with him, and he drew pay for them, the portion distributed in turn to them being a matter of private arrangement. Later on this individual footing was gradually altered to a regimental system, under which the horse as well as the forage was found by the regiment, which was self-contained and self-managed, both as to the supply and up-keep of horses and equipment, the Government merely issuing gross pay per head and leaving all arrangements for maintenance. and equipment to be managed regimentally, exceptional charges on the regimental funds from loss and wear and tear of equipment on service being met by special grants in aid. Promotions in this branch of the service were made by selection on the nomination of the commanding officer; the commissioned ranks were filled partly by direct appointment of native gentlemen from the military class, and partly

[1] Ten regiments of Regular Cavalry; eighteen Irregular.

CHAP. XVI.

by promotions from the non-commissioned grade, in which were generally serving many men of good family. The irregular cavalry (a perfectly inappropriate title, because its regulations, although special to the service, were as regular as simple) was in fact in the nature of a yeomanry force permanently embodied; and, although less well mounted than the regular cavalry, which as well as the British cavalry and artillery was horsed from the government studs, was composed of a class very superior socially to the ordinary Sepoy. There being only three native officers per regiment, the commandant, second in command, and adjutant, the squadrons were commanded by native officers. The cavalry in Madras and Bombay was organised on the regular footing, the three local regiments of the Bombay army serving in Sind being however on the irregular footing. Thus the irregular cavalry was the only service for a respectable career open to Indian gentlemen. The rest of the army was composed of peasants, but peasants, like the Roman legionaries of the early republic, who were yet thoroughly aristocratic by caste, regarding all other people except Brahmins and Rajputs as their social inferiors, separated from them by an impassable gulf of caste distinction. The irregular cavalry occupied a still higher social position, and it might have been expected that this branch of the service so differently constituted from the bulk of the army would withstand the influences which acted fatally on the other. But the character of the whole army had been sapped by the laxity of discipline and incompetent administration so long prevailing, while the horror excited by the greased cartridges (the actual cause of the Mutiny) affected the Mahomedans who formed a large proportion of the cavalry equally with the Hindus; and the greater number of the irregular cavalry regiments joined in the general outbreak, some taking a specially conspicuous part in it.

In reconstructing the Bengal army the old irregular

CHAP. XVI.

The new system.

system was adopted for all the cavalry and extended to the whole of that branch of the Bombay army. As regards the infantry, a reaction had set in against the high caste sepoy, and several regiments of low caste troops were raised, but on trial some of these proved insufficient in fighting quality, and a better material was eventually substituted. The place of other disbanded regiments was taken by Punjabi troops of high quality, and the number of battalions of Gurkhas, the ruling race in the mountains of Nepal, men whose gallantry and soldier-like qualities are the admiration of all who have served with them, has been increased from two to thirteen.[1] The Gurkhas, to whom the summer heat of the Indian plains is little more bear·able than it is to the British soldier, are distributed at various points in the Himalaya Mountains, and, with the British infantry stationed in the same region, form practically the only reserve available. The old Hindustani sepoy of Oudh and the North West Provinces, of whom there were formerly 120,000 in the service, and with them we conquered India, is now represented by only fifteen regiments, for the most part organised in separate castes or classes. The latest change of organisation, the substitution of local regiments on the North West frontier, recruited from the warlike and formerly hostile inhabitants of those regions, for regiments sent up for relief from tropical India, has already been referred to. One Bengal and three Bombay regiments have already been so converted, and the process must undoubtedly be carried still further in the future. The vicious seniority system of promotion has been put an end to. Selection by fitness is now the only recognised mode of promotion; commanding officers have been vested with large authority; discipline is strict, although with a soldiery sober and well

[1] Five regiments of two battalions, and three single-battalion regiments stationed in Assam.

CHAP. XVI.

conducted in a remarkable degree, punishments are few; and as a fighting machine the Indian army now ranks very high. But in one important respect the organisation remains unchanged and defective. While the judicial service has long been mainly filled by natives, who are represented also on the bench of the highest courts, and while under the most recent changes every branch of the service, judicial and executive, has now been thrown open to them, the army, save with a few very exceptional cases, continues to be what it always has been—an army of peasants, or a class little removed above them; an army of native soldiers commanded by English officers. So far, indeed, it may be said to be organised like the British army, in which the men and the officers form two separate classes; but then that is a British army led by British officers, and this makes all the difference.

Its defect, in not offering a career for the Indian higher classes.

In the cavalry the position of the native officer has even gone back, for whereas formerly he could rise to the command of a squadron, the squadrons are now commanded by British officers, the most junior of whom takes precedence over the oldest native officer. So far then as the army is concerned, the Queen's proclamation on assuming the direct government of India is a dead letter. This proclamation declares that 'Our subjects, of whatever race or creed, shall be freely and impartially admitted to office in our service, the duties of which they may be qualified by their education, ability, and integrity duly to discharge.' To a very large number of a most important class of Indian gentlemen, descended in many cases from ancestors who held high military office under former rulers, the only palatable, and indeed the only form of public service practicable and possible for them is the military, and that is closed to them. While this is the case it cannot be said that the promise held out in the proclamation is fully acted upon. It may be replied, indeed, that the class in question is excluded from service by the condition of fitness laid down, by reason that is of their defective education. And certainly in regard to a service the routine business of which is conducted in the English language, this contention may be held to be good, if the proclamation is read in a literal sense, without regard to the spirit which animates it. Some very gallant and distinguished native officers, among them hereditary chiefs who have brought their clansmen by the hundred to join our standards—men who closely resemble in many respects the chiefs of the Highland clans a hundred and fifty years ago—have been unable to read or write in any language; yet men labouring under the same deficiency have carved out kingdoms for themselves. A man of this sort, a thorough gentleman in manner and feeling, if illiterate, with all the pride and bearing of birth and high family tradition, leading his own kinsmen like the Highland chief of old, will by his chivalrous example show his men the way to victory, and that, after all, is what has to be aimed at in choosing officers. Moreover this state of things is fast passing away, if it has not disappeared already. Education is making great strides among all classes in India, and if the desired goal can be reached by that course, the needful standard in this respect would soon be attained. To make education the only test, indeed, or to introduce competitive examinations for admission to the army would be an absurd misapplication of what is perfectly suitable for Englishmen. The military class in India, whether prince or peasant, is distinguished from all others in a degree which it is difficult for anyone unacquainted with that country to appreciate, there being nothing analogous to the difference in any section of European society. Men and women are hardly marked off more distinctly from each other than the military and non-military class in India; to throw open the army to competition would

CHAP. XVI.

produce a result absolutely grotesque, if it would not involve the destruction of the army as a fighting machine. The selection of officers must be determined by other qualifications than that of education, which is by no means a necessary one. The first thing needed for a good officer is that he shall be a man who can lead and whom his men will be ready to follow. The military instinct is something apart from and far more valuable in stress of battle than any product of education. It would however be quite practicable, in deference to common prejudice on this head, to require a certain educational standard in addition to other qualifications. Such institutions as the Mayo College at Ajmir, established a few years ago for the princes and gentlemen of Rajputana, may easily be adapted to the purpose, and similar facilities, if required, could and would be afforded elsewhere.

It may be, indeed has been, said that the change of policy here advocated would be dangerous; that men of rank and influence raised to high military position might take advantage of the position; that the Mutiny might have had a very different ending if there had been men of rank and ability in the army to take advantage of the opportunity. Plain speaking is here the best. Nothing will be concealed by silence, for this defect in our military system is so prominent as to be the subject of constant comment. The studious exclusion of Indians from all but the humblest places in our army is so conspicuous, that only one inference can be placed upon it—that we are afraid to trust them. And the danger from one point of view may be freely admitted. The Indian people are not held to us by any feelings of attachment. When in almost every country of Europe men are found plotting against their fellow-countrymen; with the experience of Ireland before us, it would be absurd to expect that loyalty in India should take a higher form than expediency—the recognition that our rule is the best available at present, and that it is too firmly established to be attacked without risk. But apart from any question of justice or good faith, it is surely safer as a matter of policy to have men of talent and ambition with you, their interests enlisted in our system as offering possibilities of high advancement, than that their only chance of escape from a life of obscurity and inaction should be felt to lie in subversion of our rule and the anarchy attendant on such a revolution. There can be little room for doubt on which side the choice should be taken. Too much time has already been lost before entering on the course indicated by policy as well as good faith. Meanwhile contrasts, not to our advantage, are publicly made between the Russian system, its ready assimilation of the races brought under its influence, the utilisation of ability which might otherwise be dangerous, and our hard and fast repressive system. And when the step forward is taken in the right direction, it will be satisfactory to consider that while the army necessarily contains the elements of danger inherent in every body formed under such conditions, it has been rendered of late years a much safer as well as a more efficient weapon. No one class has been disproportionately increased in strength, while for the indiscriminate fusion of class and caste, the separate class and caste regiment has been largely substituted. For precaution, the army must be held to its duty by liberal terms and strict discipline; a still more effectual precaution would be that indicated by considerations of justice and policy —that the military classes equally with all other classes should feel that to them a career suitable to their tastes and aspirations is open, bounded only by their capacity to take advantage of it; that service under the Queen may offer more than can be hoped for by any other way.

The practical difficulties of carrying out such a reform, especially at the outset, may no doubt be recog-

CHAP. XVI. nised. The Indian Mahomedan from long contact with the Hindus, has imbibed caste ideas as to food and other matters unknown to those of his religion elsewhere, such as to make it no easy matter to bring him into the practical working of the military system in the upper grades. Between the English officer and the native officer who will not sit at table with him, and to whom it would be an offence even to refer to the existence of his wife or female relations, there cannot readily be that intimate fellowship which is found among the officers of the British army in all grades. There may, however, be mutual respect. A more difficult point would arise when the native officer became senior to the British officer entering the service after him. This however might be avoided as regards the regiment at least, if the native officers, instead of being distributed among different regiments, were attached to certain regiments only, the first one appointed as junior of all, then as second junior on the occurrence of a vacancy, and so on until the regiment so selected for the purpose was officered wholly by native gentlemen. Later on would come the fresh difficulty of the two races coming together in mixed bodies, and of the native officers as senior taking the command of a force containing British troops. This difficulty however would not arise for some years to come; the change must be gradually and cautiously made if it is to have a fair chance—it has taken fifty years to build up an efficient judicial service; meanwhile, the British soldier would become familiar with the idea of the native as a commissioned officer, and if the latter showed himself to be thoroughly efficient this would cease to be unpalatable. If, on the other hand, the prediction of those who contend that the native will never become an efficient officer should be verified: if he does not come up to the proper standard, then the experiment will have failed and be abandoned; but at any rate justice will not be satisfied till the experiment has been fairly made.

CHAPTER XVII

PUBLIC WORKS: ORGANISATION AND DEVELOPMENT

CHAP. XVII.

Technical meaning of term Public Works in India.

In India the term 'public works' was in former years applied to every kind of building operations undertaken by the Government, and included therefore the construction and repairs of all State buildings, civil and military, as well as the prosecution of roads, irrigation works, and eventually railways. Until the middle of this century, indeed, the operations of the Indian Government were confined almost wholly to works of the former category, which were public works only in the sense of not being private ones; while the greater part of the State expenditure under this head was incurred in the maintenance of the barracks and subsidiary buildings required for the European garrison of the country. The native troops built their own dwelling huts from an allowance made for the purpose, and the only State buildings required for native regiments were the hospitals and magazines. The civil buildings of the country were mainly the various district court-houses, and the maintenance of these unpretending edifices formed but a trifling item in the whole expenditure. In the Madras and Bombay Presidencies, the tanks which from time immemorial have supplied irrigation to the cultivators of the soil, were repaired and superintended by the State; and the maintenance of the extensive system of dykes or embankments which protect the Gangetic delta from the sea and from the

CHAP. XVII.

floods of the great rivers discharging into the head of the Bay of Bengal, was also undertaken by the Government, the landholders interested defraying a portion of the expense. But the bulk of the charges incurred under the head 'public works' was, as above stated, for repairs to military buildings, and the department charged with the duty was not unnaturally deemed to be a department of the army, and was placed under the superintendence of the Military Board at each of the three presidencies, a body composed of the heads of the different civil departments of that branch of the service.

Want of roads in India formerly. Traffic how far affected by it.

India was at this time destitute of roads, and journeys could be made only on horseback or in a palanquin. The facilities for travelling were not however altogether so small as might be inferred from the analogy of European countries. In a climate where the rainfall is limited almost entirely to one season of the year, and in a country the greater part of which is a level plain, the absence of well-made roads, or of roads of any kind, does not produce the extreme inconvenience that it would occasion in temperate regions. For three months of the year all travelling was suspended, but during the remainder it could go on uninterruptedly. The large rivers were crossed by ferries or boat bridges; the small ones could be easily forded. Any track served for a road, and the worst inconvenience occasioned was the tediousness of the journey to the traveller and the costliness of transporting merchandise on an unmetalled (unmacadamised) track.

Its effect on Indian military system.

From a military point of view this state of things had even its advantages. The want of roads taught Indian armies how to do without them. The whole system of military transport and supply being necessarily adapted to a roadless country, the ordinary requirements under this head during peace differed in no material degree from the requirements of a time of war.

CHAP. XVII.

All the subsidiary military establishments were framed on a scale and plan to admit of the troops moving readily across country in any direction; and when regiments were transferred from one station to another in ordinary course of relief, they took the field just as completely as if they were about to enter on a campaign. Thus to pass from a state of peace to that of war involved no change of system; the ordinary business of peace time constituted in fact a regular training for campaigning; on the breaking out of war nothing had to be improvised, and the troops took the field without difficulty or confusion. Succeeding, as did English rule, to the state of constant warfare which had obtained throughout the country, this preparedness for action was a necessary condition. It explains the extraordinary promptitude with which the wars of the Indian army have been so frequently entered on. The remarkable efficiency of the Indian commissariat and transport service is, no doubt, to be ascribed in great measure to the same cause.[1]

First progress in road-making.

These conditions serve in some measure to explain the complacency with which the older school of Indian statesmen—of whom Lord Metcalfe was a notable example—regarded the absence of any progress towards the material improvement of the country. The first beginning in this way may be referred to the administration of Mr. Thomason, Lieutenant-Governor of the North-West Provinces from 1843 to 1853. That country is peculiarly adapted for the construction of roads, from the dryness of the climate, its flatness, and

[1] Not the least important part of the training which this rough-and-ready system afforded, was the practice in marching which the troops obtained in the course of the annual reliefs. A regiment often spent three or four months, moving at the rate of twelve or fifteen miles a day, in passing from one station to another, and at the end of the march the men were in the highest possible condition for entering on a campaign. With the introduction of railways, these long marches became of course unnecessary, but with their discontinuance a good deal of that familiarity with camp life must be lost, which Indian troops, native and European, have hitherto exhibited.

CHAP. XVII.

the excellence and cheapness of the material for a road surface available throughout its extent, a nodular limestone (kunkur) found in thin horizontal layers at a short depth below the surface alluvial soil; and, through the influence and exertions of Mr. Thomason, practically the first governor appointed for the purely civil administration of a province, considerable progress was made towards the construction of metalled roads to connect the different large cities throughout his jurisdiction. About the same time a trunk road was undertaken to connect Calcutta with the Upper Provinces, and carried on with energy. The bridging somewhat lagged behind, and the road was not available for horsed carriages until 1850, when mail-carts began to run between Calcutta and Delhi. But the first great impetus was given to road-making in India, and public works generally, on the annexation of Punjab. The development of this province occupied the particular attention of Lord Dalhousie, who, both on military grounds, and in view to its general improvement, at once prescribed a course of vigorous action. A special engineer department for undertaking road and irrigation works was established for this province, unconnected with the Bengal Military Board, and, a fortunate selection being made for the head of it,[1] the progress made soon placed Punjab in this respect on a level with all, and in advance of most other parts of the country.

Lord Dalhousie's reform in organisation of Public Works Department.

Up to this time the presidential system had full sway in the arrangements of the Public Works Department, which was divided into three branches, to correspond with the three Indian armies; and except in the Madras and Bombay Presidencies, where the limits of the civil and military administration were coextensive, the various civil governments had no share in the control of the

[1] The first Chief Engineer of the Punjab, from 1848 to 1856, was Lieutenant Colonel Robert Napier, afterwards Field Marshal Lord Napier of Magdala.

CHAP. XVII.

departmental operations carried out in their respective provinces, which were conducted directly by the Government of India, through the agency of the Bengal Military Board.

In 1854 an important reform was effected, under Lord Dalhousie's administration, by the removal of the management of public works from the Military Board, and the formation of a separate department (or secretariat) of the Supreme Government for conducting the business. Simultaneously with this change, the immediate executive control of the public works was transferred from the supreme to the provincial administrations, and a Public Works Department was formed for each province. This example was shortly followed in Madras[1] and Bombay, where also public works affairs were removed from the control of the local Military Boards, and constituted a part of the business of the civil administration. From this time great and steady progress was made in the prosecution of works throughout the country, and largely increased grants of public money were provided on this account. In 1849–50 the State expenditure in India on public works of all kinds, including military buildings, was about 600,000 Rx., of which 122,000 Rx. was for roads; the grant provided for 1870–71 amounted to nearly seven and a half millions (Rx).

Executive agency.

Under the departmental organisation introduced by Lord Dalhousie a Chief Engineer was placed at the head of the Public Works Department in each province, who is now also secretary to the provincial government. Under him are the Superintending Engineers of Circles, while the actual execution of work is conducted by the next grade of officers, styled Executive Engineers, aided by Assistant Engineers, with a staff of subordi-

[1] The management of irrigation works in Madras had been for some years vested in the Board of Revenue. A separate department was now organised for all public works.

CHAP. XVII.

nates. As a rule the same engineer carries out all the works, whether roads or civil buildings, within his district or division; the more important lines of road are made special charges, divided into sections of convenient length. But in course of time, with the development of irrigation in various provinces, that branch of public works was separated from the rest and organised as an Irrigation Department, with its special staff of a chief engineer [and Joint Secretary to the Provincial government], superintending, executive, and assistant engineers.[1] The Public Works Department continued for some time longer to carry out all other works, military (including the work of the barrack master's department and other services connected with the accommodation of the troops) as well as civil. But upon the transfer of the administration to the provincial governments, which had no concern with, or responsibility for, any other branch of army business, the arrangement was soon found to be very unsatisfactory. The care of military buildings received insufficient attention, with the result of some discreditable constructive failures, which led to the removal of this duty from the cognisance of the provincial governments, and the formation of a military works department under the administration of the Indian War Department, which provides for the expenditure in the military estimates. The operations of this Department, which is officered from the Royal Engineers, has more recently been extended to the whole of India. Railways have from the first been dealt with as a separate branch of the service.

Department divided into four branches.

The staff of the Public Works Department, while organised in one body as regards rules of service, pay, pension, and so forth, is thus divided into four branches: roads and buildings, and irrigation, both organised provincially; railways; and military works.

[1] In the North West Provinces the administration of the great canal works was from the first kept separate from that of other public works.

CHAP. XVII.

The members of it are interchangeable between the different branches (the members of the military work department being, however, all military officers and held to be on military duty), but practically such transfers are rare, and with few exceptions an officer serves in the branch, and (except in the military branch) in the province to which he is first appointed, the position of the engineer being in this respect similar to that of the civilian. In the two provincial branches promotion runs in separate lists for each province, and each branch within the province, and is made by selection of the provincial government; but in regard to the higher appointments, the Government of India intervenes to a certain extent to secure that the claims of the seniors in the different provinces shall be fairly considered.

Composition of staff.

The staff of the Public Works Department consisted in the first instance of the officers of the Indian Engineers Corps, only a small part of whom were employed in peace time with the sapper battalions, supplemented by officers drawn from other branches of the service. Cautley, the designer and constructor of the Ganges Canal, the greatest work of the kind, was an officer of the Bengal Artillery; to which regiment also belonged Captain (now General) C. H. Dickens, the engineer of the Sone Canal. With the development of public works the staff of engineers available from these sources soon became insufficient, and large additions were made of civil engineers, some of those appointed in the first instance being men of professional standing and experience, but generally young officers selected in England and sent out by the Secretary of State to join the service in the junior grades. In 1871 the Royal Indian College at Coopers Hill was established, from which, since 1874, all first appointments in the country have been made. The service is also recruited to a certain extent in India, where various institutions have been

CHAP. XVII.

established for the education of engineers. The Thomason College of Engineering was established at Roorkee in the North-West Provinces near the head of the Ganges Canal about fifty years ago, primarily to supply a native subordinate staff for the canal department. The instruction of the classes formed for this purpose is conveyed in the vernacular, but a class of European soldiers was soon added, for training as overseers in the Public Works Department, and also a small class for the education of civil engineers. This last has supplied some engineers who, under the practical experience gained in the service, have proved very valuable officers, but the educational staff and appliances have never advanced beyond the very rudimentary stage on which they were first instituted, and are utterly insufficient for the purpose in view. There are also engineering schools or departments of schools at Calcutta, Madras, and Bombay, which give an elementary education in engineering, and which furnish the subordinate departmental staff for these and the adjacent provinces. The education at these institutions is practically gratuitous, and although they are starved in teaching staff and appliances, the cost of each pupil turned out from them is out of all proportion to the result. Indigenous engineering schools are very necessary, but those now in existence need to be thoroughly reformed and placed on a more efficient and business-like footing.

Expenditure how provided.

Up to the year 1867–8, the public works expenditure, which, as has been explained, comprised all outlay for public buildings, civil and military, as well as that incurred for the material improvement of the country, was provided for out of revenue; the amount allotted to this purpose necessarily varied from year to year according to the state of the budget. In the years of deficit, the loans raised to cover it were dealt with as supplementing the finances generally, and no part was allocated specifically as debt incurred for public works, although the deficit would in many cases not have occurred if this public works expenditure had not been undertaken. But in the year 1868–69 it was determined to provide specifically by loans for the capital expenditure on remunerative works, leaving the charge for other works only to be met from the ordinary revenues of the year. Under this arrangement the construction and repair of roads, the maintenance of existing irrigation works and the construction of such new ones as although necessary were not likely to be directly remunerative, together with the State outlay on guaranteed railways, arising chiefly for the land taken up by them and for the government controlling establishments, were to be provided for out of revenue. The construction of such new irrigation works as were expected to prove directly remunerative to the extent of defraying the interest on the public debt incurred on their behalf, and the capital expenditure on railways undertaken directly by Government agency, were defrayed from loans. This arrangement was so far modified about ten years later, that one and a half millions was set apart annually as a provision against famine, on the understanding that so much of this sum as was not required for the actual relief of famine should be applied to the construction of railways and irrigation works, the increase of capital debt for these works being to that extent prevented. This is the so-called Famine Fund, to which further reference will be made in a later chapter.

The cost of maintenance necessarily goes on increasing with the extension of roads, and forms a heavy charge on the revenues. The amount devoted to new roads for some time past has been about one million (Rx) a year, sufficient for the construction of about 1,000 miles. With the extension of railways, the importance of road-making has fallen into the background in popular estimation, but it continues to be

CHAP. XVII.

as necessary as ever; in fact every new railway creates a fresh requirement for road feeders, and the day is far distant when India will be adequately equipped in this respect. The cost of bridging the great rivers as part of the road system is prohibitive; these works are practicable only in connection with railways; the main lines of road are for the most part supplied with excellent boat bridges which can be maintained for the greater part of the year, while during the rainy season there is little traffic.

India generally is well provided with material for road making, but ordinarily and in most parts of the country, and where trunk lines have already been made, an extension of first-class roads is not what is most wanted. The goods traffic of the country, which consists mainly of agricultural produce, takes place after the harvest, at a season when the smaller rivers are almost dried up, while for the great majority of the travellers, extended facilities for slow travelling in every direction are more needed in the present state of things than a few perfect lines; to meet these requirements most beneficially, the outlay will be directed in the first instance to making fair-weather roads. Bridges will be regarded as supplementary works to be provided subsequently and by degrees, the smaller streams being bridged first, and the larger rivers left to be crossed by fords or ferries, till the expansion of traffic and the progress of the country justify a large outlay on specific localities.

Comparative advantages of roads and railroads.

In some parts of the country the great cost of road-making indicates the propriety of constructing railways in the first instance on all lines of importance, instead of beginning with roads and following up with railways. This is especially the case in Bengal, from the magnitude of its rivers, the need for high embankments, and the want of proper materials for a road surface. Persons whose experience is confined to

Europe may find it difficult to realise the idea of a perfectly flat country, extending for several hundred miles in every direction, and where there is not so much as a pebble to be found throughout its whole extent. Such is Bengal. Stone if used must be brought from enormous distances, and the only possible substitute for it as a road surface is the expensive and imperfect one of broken bricks.[1] The difference in cost between a railroad and what at best will be a very imperfect road would therefore merely arise from the addition of sleepers and rails. There is no question of tunnels, cuttings, or gradients in this country, and the embankment which serves for the road would do equally for the railway. It is indeed often forgotten, when comparing the cost of the two things, how much of the expenditure for a railway is due to provision for carrying the travellers, whereas the travellers on a road find their own conveyances, and that while the maintenance of a road is a permanent charge, a railway will at least pay its working expenses. Bengal, however, if a difficult country to make roads in, has been bountifully furnished with natural means of communication in its numerous perennial rivers and tidal channels, through which the great trade of that country has been called into existence; and money would probably be much more effectively spent in improving these natural highways than in attempting to surmount the difficulties which they present to the construction of roads. On the line from Calcutta to Madras, no amount of expenditure in reason would suffice to make a first-class road accessible in all weathers, for the line crosses the whole drainage of the country and several great rivers, and the large sums involved in such a project would produce little or no useful effect. A line of communication in

[1] Until railways brought stone from the interior within reach, the roads at Calcutta were macadamised with stones brought as ballast by ships visiting the port.

CHAP. XVII.

this direction is only possible if undertaken on the scale suitable for a railway, and a railway is now in course of slow construction between these two points. But the rivers that are crossed, and which are too large to admit of being bridged for a road, serve as most useful feeders for a canal between the two places, while the features of the country are in all other respects most favourable for the construction of that class of works. And a canal also connecting the two places has long been in course of being gradually carried out.

Canal navigation in Northern India.

The extensive irrigation canals of Northern India, running as they do through a highly populated country, are very favourably situated for the development of an extensive navigation, but the use made of them for this purpose has proved to be quite insignificant. The rapid current of these artificial rivers renders haulage against the stream expensive and slow, while in the desire to keep down the first cost of the undertaking the works connected with the navigation were constructed on an insufficient scale. The locks are too small to admit steamers of any power, and the bridges are not high enough to admit the passage of large or heavily laden boats. These defects of construction are being gradually remedied, but it seems improbable that the traffic will ever be much more than a traffic one way, mainly of timber floated down the stream.

Road-making transferred to provincial governments.

The construction of roads to keep pace with the extension of railways, involving not only the first cost, but an annually increasing charge for maintenance, must always continue to form an important obligation on the State and a great and increasing liability on the finances of India. The business has long been too large and scattered for the central authorities to deal with properly, and the finance and administration of it has been entirely localised, and made over to the different provincial governments, with whom it now rests to find the necessary ways and means for the prosecution of the work.

CHAPTER XVIII

IRRIGATION WORKS.

CHAP. XVIII.

Importance of Indian irrigation works.

THE liability of India to drought and its attendant famine; the remarkable benefits resulting from irrigation in all seasons, good as well as bad; and the magnitude of the undertakings carried out by the Indian Government in this connection, make the subject of Indian Irrigation one of special interest and importance.

Different systems of irrigation.

Various modes of irrigating the soil artificially are practised in India. Leaving out the use of wells, in which case the earth itself acts as the reservoir, the most simple, as well as one of the most effective kinds of irrigation is derived from tanks. The ordinary Indian irrigating tank is formed by intercepting the drainage of the country by an embankment. If a gorge between two hills be selected for the place of construction, a single embankment across the lower part of the valley is sufficient for the purpose; but where, as is most commonly the case, the scene of operations is a gently sloping plain, the embankment must be constructed on three sides. In these tanks the depth of water is of course greatest against the lower embankment, and gradually becomes shallower towards the opposite end, till the bed rises above the level of the water. Sluices are constructed at the lower end of the tank, in the embankment, whence the water is led off and distributed among the fields below it.

Tanks.

CHAP. XVIII.

For the construction of these tanks, a moderate and equable slope of the country is required. If the fall of the land be great, an excessive height of embankment becomes necessary; if it be slight, the shallowness of the tank, and consequently the extent of surface in proportion to its contents, causes great waste from evaporation, while the area of land occupied by the tank is disproportionately large.

The configuration of the coast of the Carnatic, or eastern portion of the Madras Presidency, is peculiarly favourable for tank irrigation, and the whole of this part of the peninsula is studded with these reservoirs, some of them enormous works many miles in circumference. These were almost all constructed before the occupation of the country by the English, whose connection with them has been limited to their maintenance and in some cases restoration. Tank irrigation is also largely practised in Bombay and Central India, as well as in Behar. But this last country has too small a surface inclination to admit of the full development of the system, and the water from the tanks has there to be lifted into the irrigating channel, usually by manual labour.

Irrigation from rivers. Madras system.

The other system of irrigation practised is by the diversion of river-waters. This is differently carried out in Upper and Southern India. What is generally known as the Madras system of irrigation, consists in the construction of a dam across the bed of a river to raise the level of the water, which is then diverted into side-channels, and thence distributed over the surface of the country. The irrigation system of Northern India is also based on the damming-up of the rivers, but the conditions of the two cases are very different. In Madras the most fertile lands are those adjacent to the coast, which form the deltas of the different rivers, and the use of the water commences in the immediate vicinity of the dam. The fall of the country is here extremely small, the regime of the river channel has been thoroughly established, and the management of the water is easily under control. Moreover, the difference of level between the river and the country through which it flows is so slight that a very moderate height of dam suffices to lift the water into the irrigating channels. Similar physical conditions would be met with in the delta of the Ganges, and on a much larger scale; but this part of the country is comparatively independent of artificial irrigation, by reason of its abundant rainfall; it is in the upper course of the Ganges and its feeders that the use of their waters is wanted, where they flow through the comparatively dry country of the North West Provinces. And here too the agricultural conditions are very dissimilar from those in Southern India. On the Coromandel coast only one crop is raised in a year, and this is irrigated in the rainy season; so that the system of irrigation deals mainly with the rivers when they are in flood, and comparatively simple works effect the desired object. In Upper India, on the other hand, there are two harvests in the year, and the corn, cotton, and other crops which most require irrigation are grown during the cold season, when the rivers are at their lowest. The Ganges, after it issues from the Himalaya, runs in a valley which it has excavated for itself in the course of ages—five or six miles wide, and from eighty to one hundred feet below the level of the great plain which forms this part of India. The general slope of the country from the Himalaya to the sea is from a foot to eighteen inches in the mile; this, which would be an excessive slope in a great river, is counteracted by the tortuous course of the Ganges, which meanders from one side to the other of the valley within which it runs. To dam up the river at any part of this course, would therefore involve the construction of a weir across the whole width of this valley, as well as very extensive

Canal system of Northern India.

CHAP. XVIII.

cuttings to convey the water into the adjacent country; and the level at which the water would strike the surface of the country could only be reached at a considerable distance lower down the course of the river than the site of the weir, so that the country adjacent to the upper part of the river's course would be unprovided with irrigation. These considerations led to a different plan of operations being undertaken. The waters of the Ganges are intercepted at the point where the river issues from the Lower Himalaya in a firm well-defined channel, whence they are carried to the centre or watershed line of the Doab,[1] down which the canal is conducted nearly to the point of junction of the Ganges and Jumna. The watershed line once reached, the canals in that situation afford highly favourable conditions for effective irrigation. Distributive channels are constructed on each side at intervals of a few miles, whence the water is led to the surface of the country, and from these again smaller channels convey it for distribution over the fields. The excess in the slope of the country, beyond what is required for a moderately swift current—and for this a few inches per mile suffices—has to be overcome by numerous weirs, over which the waters of the canal are discharged. Although the work is spoken of as one canal, it consists in fact of a network of branches, which convey the water, right and left, over the surface of the Doab, the whole system, with its main lines, branch lines and distributory channels, resembling the reticulations at the back of a mulberry leaf. Unlike a river, the canal becomes smaller instead of larger in its course;[2] and

[1] *Do*, two; *áb*, water—a country lying between two rivers. The great plain between the Ganges and Jumna, which forms the greater part of the North West provinces, is known *par excellence* as *The* Doab.

[2] This is, however, not true of all Indian rivers. The Cuggur and Sarsatti, which rise in the Lower Himalaya between the Ganges and Jumna, and at certain seasons are considerable streams, both disappear before the Indian desert is reached; partly taken up in irrigation, and partly absorbed by the sandy soil through which they run.

only sufficient water for the purpose of navigation is retained in the main channel, which finally, an attenuated stream, rejoins its parent river at Cawnpur. Unlike a river, also, the canal flows along the highest instead of the lowest line of the country.

The foregoing account is generally applicable to the principles of construction adopted for all the canals of Northern India—those taken off from the Ganges and the left bank of the Jumna in the North West Provinces; from the right bank of the Jumna, the Sutlej, the Ravi, and the Chenab in Punjab. The problem in each case is to divert the course of the river from the valley of its natural line to the crest of high land running parallel with it, and to make the force of gravitation take the place of mechanical agents for distribution of the water. Such a mode of irrigation is clearly only adapted for a flat country, where the high crest spoken of is in fact a very gentle undulation, only perceptible to the test of the surveyor's level.

Irrigation works on the large scale (other than the large tanks scattered over the country), and which involve the application of hydraulic engineering in the proper sense, are confined and have attained the greatest development in the three provinces above mentioned (Madras, North West Provinces, and Punjab), as well as in Bengal, where some large canals have been constructed within the last twenty-five years, and in Bombay. Of these it may be said that the works in Madras are of the most critical importance, in the sense that they are absolutely necessary for securing a harvest in all years. This is explained by the physical character of the country. The rainfall of India, generally, takes place during the prevalence of the south-west monsoon, a local trade-wind, which blows with great force from May till September, and is occasioned by the sun's progress to the north in summer, combined with the rotatory motion of the earth. But the supply of

CHAP. XVIII.

moisture deposited upon the peninsula generally by this wind, is intercepted from the Coromandel coast by the mountain ranges to the west, and the time of the rainy season in every other part of India is a dry season there. For their supply of rain the districts on that coast are dependent on the north-east monsoon, also a periodical wind occasioned by the return of the sun to the south, which blows from October till the beginning of the succeeding year; but this wind, which rises in the Bay of Bengal, is much less powerful and distinctly marked than the other Indian trade wind, which comes from the Southern Ocean, and it brings only a precarious supply of rain. This coast is therefore almost wholly dependent on artificial irrigation for good harvests. In Northern India, on the other hand—although there is seldom a season in which artificial irrigation, when available, is not made use of, and the demand becomes more extended and sustained as habit teaches the cultivators to insure themselves against the chances of the seasons—artificial irrigation is yet merely an auxiliary to the ordinary course of farming, and a palliative of occasional drought. In favourable seasons good crops can be raised without its aid.

Canals in Madras.

The irrigation system in Madras, in addition to the maintenance and development of the great tanks scattered over the country wherever the surface has admitted of their formation, comprises the works of damming up the great rivers which fall into the sea on the east coast by masonry weirs, at the points where their deltas begin, and distributing the waters over the surface of the country by canals. The principal tracts thus dealt with are the deltas of the Godavari at Rajamundri, the Kistna at Bezvada, the Penner at Nellore and Sangam, and the Cauveri at Trichinopoli. There is also a canal system in the interior of the province from the Tungbhadra river with head works near Kurnul, where the river issues from the hilly country to the westward. These last-named canals were originally constructed by a joint stock company formed under a guarantee of five per cent. on a capital of one million sterling. This sum proved quite insufficient for the purpose, and after making large further advances the Government eventually took over the works which cost altogether over two millions (of ten rupees). They have not as yet paid their working expenses and are the only unprofitable undertaking in the province. A large project is also in course of being carried out for irrigation from the Vaigai river near Madura, on which about half a million has been spent. The total capital outlay on all these undertakings amounts to about five and a half millions (Rx.), and the present revenue from irrigation is about forty lakhs, giving a return from the completed works of $7\frac{1}{2}$ per cent.; this although the account is loaded with the commercially unprofitable expenditure on the Kurnul Canal system. Altogether about six millions of acres are under irrigation in Madras, of which rather more than half are watered from tanks, old and new, and the rest from the new canal systems.

In Bengal. Artificial irrigation in Bengal is of comparatively modern date. Bengal proper, which is under the full influence of the summer monsoon, receives ordinarily a plentiful supply of rain, but in the south-western province of Orissa which forms part of the administrative province of Bengal, a complete failure of the annual rains occurred about thirty years ago, which in the absence of any sufficient means of communication by land or sea caused a grievous famine. Consequent on this a Joint Stock Company was formed, without a guarantee, for undertaking irrigation works from the river Mahanadi. The capital raised of one million sterling sufficed only to complete a part of the project. No more could be obtained, and the affair was on the point of collapse when the Government came to the rescue of the shareholders and purchased the under-

CHAP. XVIII. taking from them. Joint stock enterprise is altogether inapplicable to irrigation works. The best sites economically have already been taken up, and each new project is likely to be less directly profitable than those undertaken before. The canal system in Madras, although very economically constructed, gives a much smaller return on first outlay than the primitive tanks previously constructed. Moreover, the construction of the works is only the beginning of the business. The distribution of the water from day to day—the ultimate duty of those concerned, is by far too delicate a matter to be entrusted to an agency interested only in getting the largest possible return on its capital; it can be properly conducted only by the department of government directly responsible for the welfare of the people, or by a body of public servants in immediate communication with, and subordinate for revenue business to that department. Anyone familiar with the extortion sometimes attempted to be practised by the subordinates attached to the government irrigation works, although carefully watched, and although the water-rate is fixed intentionally at a very low figure, will readily understand how great an engine of oppression might be framed out of the management of such a concern. It was accordingly provided in the case of the Orissa Company, that on the construction of the works being completed, the duties of the company's officers should be confined to the maintenance of the works, and that the distribution of the water should be undertaken by the Government. The company, in fact, was to sell the water to the Government, and the Government to sell it to the cultivators. All this complication, with the laborious negotiations that arose with the company, extending from first to last over several years, involving great delay in the commencement of work, and ending in an arrangement by which the Government accepted an expenditure over which it had no effective control: all this had for its object to save the Government from the responsibility of raising and spending directly one million sterling. Eventually the works were completed at a cost of two and a half millions, but they have not yet paid their working expenses. Orissa, except in very exceptional years, happily few and far between, gets as much rain as it needs, and no demand arises for water from the canals. Nevertheless, an undertaking which would be disastrous as a commercial enterprise, may be both proper and profitable for the Government to carry out. The direct return in the form of a water-rate is in fact an altogether secondary consideration. A failure of the crops involves the loss of the land revenue for the season, and the further liability for an enormous outlay to convey food to the famine-stricken districts. These are the direct obligations, apart from the loss involved to the people in addition to their inability to pay revenue, which it must always be the duty of the Government to endeavour to avert. That irrigation works, unlike roads, should in most cases yield a good return on their outlay, is a very satisfactory condition, but their primary object is to be an insurance, primarily against the horrors and losses of famine, and, further, against the resulting loss of land revenue.

The canals in Orissa, therefore, apart from their value as a means of assurance, are mainly useful for purposes of navigation, and in some parts the traffic on them is considerable. But the great province of Behar, very fertile and generally well supplied with rain, is yet liable to occasional drought, and a large canal system has been carried out there by which the waters of the River Sone, an affluent of the Ganges rising in the mountains to the south, are distributed over the country, irrigating about half a million of acres. The works have cost about two and a half millions and give a direct return in tolls and water

CHAP. XVIII.

rent of nearly three per cent. Altogether about seven and a half millions (Rx.) has been spent in Bengal on works of this class, in addition to a considerable outlay from year to year, provided from revenue. About one thousand square miles are under irrigation annually. But the actual extent of irrigation, here as elsewhere, in ordinary years is a very imperfect index of the amount of benefit that accrues in seasons of drought.

In North West Provinces.

The Irrigation works carried out in the great plains of the North West Provinces are among the most satisfactory records of British government in India. The first work of the kind was carried out about seventy years ago, a canal taken off the east or left bank of the Jumna, where it issues from the Lower Himalayas, which distributes a part of the waters of that river, till only a small stream remains at the tail or terminus of the canal to fall into the parent stream at Delhi. A second canal of larger size, taken off the right or western bank of the river, runs through a country—the greater part known as the Delhi Territory—which since the Mutiny has been transferred to Punjab. This was at first only the restoration of an older canal constructed under Mahomedan rule, which had fallen into disuse, a rude and imperfect work which has been realigned and practically reconstructed. The Ganges Canal, designed and constructed by Cautley and opened in 1854, is the most striking and original work of the kind yet constructed, from the great capacity of its channel and the magnitude and boldness of the head works, by which the canal has to be carried across the drainage of the sub-Himalayas for twenty miles, through, over, and under various affluents of the main river which in rainy weather are raging torrents of great volume. The Ganges Canal, with its branches, has a length of more than 4,000 miles, and conveys the waters of the Ganges to Cawnpur. The dam across the Ganges, at Hurdwar, which diverts the water into the canal is in great part a temporary work carried away every year when the river rises in flood, and renewed in the succeeding dry season. This is deemed to be cheaper than the construction of a permanent dam in a position of exceptional difficulty. Although in the times of lowest discharge the whole body of the river appears to be intercepted, a considerable stream issues from its shingle-bed a short distance below the dam, which, increased by the various affluents, soon becomes a large stream, and when a hundred and fifty miles of its course are accomplished, it rolls along a broad river as if it had not parted with any portion of its volume. At about this distance from the head another and permanent dam has within recent years been constructed across the bed, and a second, the 'Lower Ganges' canal, taken off from it, acting as a feeder to the first, and with its branches and subsidiary channels nearly 3,500 miles in length. These two works have together cost about six millions; with the East Jumna canal they form a network of water-channels spreading over the whole Doab, from the Himalayas to the junction of the Ganges and Jumna at Allahabad, driving away famine and insuring plenty. This is especially a country to protect, for the Ganges acts as a great drain to intercept the flow of waters from the Himalaya to the south, and having only a moderate rainfall in ordinary seasons, it is specially liable to drought. One of these great canals, a deep and rapid river, full in the driest season, its banks shaded by thick groves of trees in unbroken lines for hundreds of miles through a country in many parts bare of timber; such a phenomenon in a hot and thirsty land conveys a feeling of charm and refreshment, mental and bodily, which only those who have seen it can fully appreciate.

A second canal, called the Agra canal, of considerable size, finished twenty years ago at a cost of about one million, has been taken off the Jumna at Delhi, to irrigate the country on the right bank or south of the

CHAP. XVIII. river as far as Agra. The country north of the Ganges, Oudh and Rohilkhand, is not as yet protected by irrigation works on any extensive scale, but the rainfall over these regions is usually abundant. A considerable part of it comes under the influence of Himalayan moisture.

Altogether about $8\frac{1}{4}$ millions (of which the Ganges canal accounts for 6 millions) have been spent on capital account for irrigation works in the North West Provinces, which provide for about 3,000 square miles being irrigated every season. The net revenue from the sale of the water is over five per cent. on the capital outlay, but the irrigation on the more recently constructed Lower Ganges canal has not yet become fully developed, and a still higher return may be looked for; it needs hardly be added after what has gone before that this direct revenue is only the smallest part of the resulting benefit. The works would have been directly remunerative to the Government, even did they only cover their working expenses. The advantage to the country and people from them can hardly be overestimated.

In Punjab. The conditions of irrigation in Punjab differ from those obtaining in the North-West Provinces, so far that while here also the fertile districts towards the north, bounded by the Himalayas, need protection from occasional drought, and in all seasons are largely benefited by a plentiful supply of water, as the country extends to the south the average rainfall becomes more and more scanty, till at last the line of cultivation disappears in the Indian desert, where the wells, when found at all, are of a depth too great for use in irrigation, and husbandry is only practicable if water can be brought from a distance. Here then, also, irrigation canals are of inestimable value. Happily the great rivers of Punjab which, rising like the Ganges and Jumna in the perennial snow of the Himalayas, traverse the country from north to south, and flowing into the Indus make up the great volume of that river, offer the needful means for a great system of irrigation which has been in course of execution ever since the annexation of that country. The canal taken off from the right bank of the Jumna, transferred to Punjab after the Mutiny with the territory through which it flows, was indeed in full operation for some years before; it has been extended and improved, and pays about nine per cent. on the cost of construction; the accumulated profits on the work, after deducting interest and cost, amount to three millions. The first new work undertaken was the canal from the Ravi, opened in 1859 and completed at a cost of about one and a half millions. It now pays about 7½ per cent., and irrigates the great plain between the Ravi and Beas, known as the Bari Doab. The next great work undertaken was the canal from the Sutlej, which, at a cost of nearly five millions, irrigates the country between that river and the Jumna, including several Sikh States, which have contributed to the outlay, and is gradually extending agriculture into the thirsty districts to the south. The returns from this canal, as from all other works of the same class, have gone on increasing with the gradual development of irrigation, a process of time in every case. Opened in 1882, the return on the capital five years later was about 1½ per cent.; at the end of another five years it had risen to 7¼ per cent.

Another of the great rivers of Punjab has lately been utilised in the same way. A canal from the Chenab, a river with greater volume than the other three already dealt with, was opened for use in 1892. Over a million has been spent on this canal, which is still incomplete, but already 350,000 acres of waste lands to be irrigated from it have been allotted to colonists, whose migration from the more congested districts of the province will afford a very sensible relief to the agricultural community. The Jhelum and Indus rivers

CHAP. XVIII. still remain to be attacked, if it should be found that they admit of being dealt with in the same way. A canal from the Swat river, which falls into the Indus near Attock, in the extreme north of the province, recently constructed at a cost of 350,000 Rx., completes the list of the great hydraulic works in Punjab. Altogether about seven and a quarter millions have been spent on these, besides the contribution of more than one million to the Sutlej Canal from the native states interested, which already give a return of 6½ per cent., and with which 8,000 miles of main and distributory branches have been constructed. These are all canals taken off from the rivers as they issue from the gorges of the Himalaya. It would be impossible to give here any account of the various headworks by which the stream of waters are controlled and diverted; but their magnitude and solidity, and the boldness, ingenuity, and perseverance which have been applied to the task in each case, here as well as to the east and south, must command the admiration of all who have had the opportunity of seeing these great and original undertakings. Yet but few of their countrymen and practically none of their countrywomen take the trouble to visit them—among the most creditable records of what has been accomplished by Englishmen in India.

Inundation Canals. In addition to the canals constructed from the upper waters of the Punjab rivers, an extensive system of irrigation has been developed in the southern districts of the province by what are known as the 'Inundation Canals.' These are diversions of the waters in the flood season by cuts made through the high banks. The inundation canals are available therefore during only one season, and give only a single crop, and their operation is necessarily limited to the low country in the vicinity of the river; but the works are of a very simple and inexpensive character, and are extraordinarily beneficial and remunerative. The country round the city of Multan, where the average annual rainfall is only three inches, is a garden of cultivation carried out in this way.

In Sind.

The province of Sind, the basin of the Lower Indus, a practically rainless country, is cultivated entirely by artificial irrigation, mainly 'inundation' canals of the kind just mentioned. The conditions of this country closely resemble those of Lower Egypt, as do its products, but the Indus does not overflow its banks in the same way as the Nile, and artificial irrigation is necessary to produce any sort of crops. About one and a quarter millions has been spent on canals in Sind, which give a net revenue on that sum of nearly 12 per cent.

In Bombay.

In the province of Bombay the contour of the country, in great part irregular and uneven, and where the rivers are generally found running in valleys, is not favourable for the construction of canals, and the irrigation works generally take the form of tanks, or more properly lakes, to be filled in the rainy season and discharged by irrigating channels in the dry. A system based on the storage of water must necessarily be more expensive than the diversion of streams which give a constant supply; but in no part of India is artificial irrigation more valuable than in the Dekhan with its moderate rainfall, a slight deficiency in which at once creates a drought. The capital expenditure on irrigation works in Bombay has been about two and a half millions, one-third of this being on works still incomplete, and which have not begun to pay anything; the present return on the whole sum is about 5 per cent.[1]

[1] To those who desire further information on this subject may be recommended *Irrigated India*, by the Hon. Alfred Deakin, formerly Chief Secretary to the Government of Victoria, a book containing a detailed and very interesting account of these great and beneficent works.

CHAPTER XIX

RAILWAYS

CHAP. XIX.

Early history of Indian railways.

THE first beginning of railways in India was made in the year 1851 during the administration of Lord Dalhousie, under what is known as the guarantee system. The original scheme provided for the construction of three railways along what were considered the most important lines of communication for commercial, political, and military purposes:—1. The East Indian Railway, from Calcutta northward to the Ganges, thence along the course of that river to Allahabad, crossing the Jumna just above its junction with the Ganges, and so passing along through the Doab to Delhi, about 1,200 miles in length, to which was shortly added a branch of 250 miles from Allahabad to Jabalpur. 2. The Great Indian Peninsula Railway, from Bombay to join the East India Railway at Jabalpur, completing the communication between Bombay to Calcutta, with a branch to Nagpur opening out Central India and the cotton districts; and a southern line from Poona towards Madras, also traversing an important agricultural country. The total length of the whole concession was nearly 1,300 miles. 3. The Madras Railway, from Madras across the south of the Peninsula to the West Coast, to which was subsequently added (1858) a line from Madras to communicate with Bombay and the southern branch of the Great Indian Peninsula Railway. This third line was much less important than the other two, in fact, as experience has since shown, it had no claim to be selected as one of the initial undertakings; but the distribution was governed by the principle always assumed to be involved in the presidential system, that whatever was done for one Presidency must be done for the other two.

The first completed section of Indian railway—twenty miles of the Great Indian Peninsula—was opened for traffic in 1853; in the following year a section of thirty-seven miles was opened from Calcutta on the East India Railway. Further extension on the former line was at first slow, a difficult ascent having to be accomplished from the sea level of the table land of the Dekhan. On the East Indian, operations were carried on simultaneously in the North West Provinces and in Bengal, materials being transported up the Ganges to the former. Unfortunately no portion of this upper section was ready when the Mutiny broke out, but the line from Allahabad to Cawnpur was opened in the following year. The Ganges was reached from Calcutta in 1860; through communication was established between Calcutta and the North West Provinces in 1864, save for the large bridge over the Jumna; the whole line to Delhi was opened in the same year. The branch to Jabalpur was completed in 1867. Communication between Bombay and Calcutta was established by the connection of the two railways at Jabalpur in 1870. The third of the lines projected at the outset, the line from Madras to the west coast, of over 400 miles, was finished in 1862, and a branch therefrom to the table land of Mysore in 1864. The more important section from Raichur, completing communication with Bombay, about 300 miles, was finished in 1871.

The Guarantee system.

The guage of all these lines was five feet six inches, which was thus established as the standard guage for India. The capital was raised in each case through the agency of a joint stock company, to which a guarantee

CHAP. XIX.

was given of 5 per cent. on the capital outlay, and half of the surplus profits, no repayment being required of this guaranteed interest for the periods during which it might be in excess of the net receipts. To the company was entrusted the appointment of the engineering and other staff to be engaged, and the execution of the works. The Government, in consideration of this guaranteed interest, were to have complete control over the operations of the company, both as to design and expenditure in all branches. Power was taken to purchase the line at certain specified periods of time.

Further progress.

Following on these three railways four additional lines were soon afterwards undertaken on similar guarantees: the Eastern Bengal, 160 miles, from Calcutta to the Ganges; the Bombay, Baroda, and Central India, 460 miles; the Oudh and Rohilcund, 700 miles (further extensions were added later on); the Sind, Punjab, and Delhi Railway, from Karachi along the right bank of the Indus to Sukkur; onward by the left bank of the river and its tributaries to Multan; thence to Lahore and Delhi, a total length of 1,150 miles; also a small line in the south of India, begun in 1859, from Negapatam on the east coast to Erode on the Madras Railway.

Merits and defects of guarantee system.

The guarantee system as originally introduced was subject to the great defect that, under the terms of the contracts made, the Government covenanted to pay the guaranteed interest, not only upon all expenditure incurred, but on all the capital called up,[1] thus relieving the railway company from all responsibility for the cost of construction, and all incentive to economy, save that supplied by the prospect of an eventual share of

[1] Both conditions are prescribed in the contract, which was very carelessly drafted; in one clause it is specified that the interest shall be paid on the expenditure incurred, while in another clause the payment is extended to all capital called up with the sanction of government. The wider condition of course governed the adjustment of all the transactions arising.

surplus profits in excess of the guaranteed interest; but this prospect in the first instance and during construction was remote and contingent. The company had, therefore, a high incentive to make as large an investment as possible. The Government undertook to control the expenditure, but its efforts in this direction were at first very ineffectual. The controlling officers were inexperienced in the business and unacquainted with the proper method of conducting an audit, and their well meant efforts to secure economy were often applied in a way to create a good deal of friction, especially in dealing with the engineers engaged on the work—a body whose training and antecedents rendered somewhat impatient of control and economy, and who also began the undertaking without experience of Indian engineering. The result was that the first cost of these railways largely exceeded what would have been found necessary under a better system. But it is easy to be wise after the event. The guarantee system had these overruling advantages, that it attracted British capital to India, which so far has not been found forthcoming in any other way, save when the State itself is the borrower; and further, that after the contract was once made with the company, the work went on uninterruptedly to completion, free from all the delays and interruptions due to the vacillation of policy, which so far has appeared to be inseparable from the course of railway construction undertaken by the State, when the grants fluctuate from year to year according to the state of the financial balance-sheet. Under State construction these earlier lines would assuredly have taken a very much longer time to construct than was actually spent, and the enormous addition they have given to the administrative strength of the Government and to the prosperity of the country, would have been to that extent deferred. The advantages of the system have, on the whole,

CHAP. XIX.

greatly outweighed the disadvantages. Dear railways are far better than none; but in fact the extravagance of early days gave way in time to a better ordered system, and latterly the guarantee system has not been open to any reproach on this head.

Construction of railways by State.

It was, however, in view to the cheaper construction of railways that the Government of India undertook the construction of them by its own agency. The first State enterprise was the Rajputana-Malwa Railway, the first section of which, from Delhi and Agra through Rajputana to a junction with the Bombay-Baroda Railway at Ahmadabad, a length of over 700 miles, was begun in 1873 and completed in 1879. To this was added the Malwa branch, from Ajmir on the main line through Indore in Central India, descending into the Narbada valley to join the G. I. Peninsular at Kundwa, about 400 miles, making about 1,100 miles in all. Other extensions have been added, and the whole system now comprises nearly 1,700 miles. The Rajputana-Malwa Railway was the first constructed on the narrow or metre guage.

Introduction of narrow guage.

Railway construction continued for some years to make fair progress, partly by State agency, partly by guaranteed companies, some of the lines being on the standard guage and some on the metre guage. The lines constructed in Punjab (after the completion of the Sind, Punjab, and Delhi line), west of the Sutlej, have been made by State agency on the broad or standard guage. A beginning was made westward of Lahore on the metre guage, but the break was found so extraordinarily inconvenient during the Afghan war of 1878, that the line, so far as it had been completed, was converted to the standard guage, and no metre guage has been carried permanently beyond the Sutlej. The Punjab railways, of which the portions on the frontier are military lines made for strategic purposes, and from which no appreciable revenue is to be expected for a long time to come, have lately been extended through the passes of the Suleiman Mountains to Baluchistan and the table lands of Central Asia, under great engineering difficulties.

CHAP. XIX.

The great plain north of the Ganges, from the borders of Assam to the Jumna, has been occupied mainly by the narrow guage; the different lines have been made, partly by the Government, partly by companies.

The Dekhan and the part of India to the south of it have also been occupied by narrow guage lines—the Madras Railway excepted—constructed by the two agencies. The Southern of India Railway referred to above as one of the earlier undertakings, has been converted to the narrow guage.

Recent additions.

Two considerable systems, the Indian Midland and the Bengal-Nagpur with its branches, have lately been constructed by companies under a guarantee, both happily on the standard guage. The line from Delhi to Kalka, at the foot of the Himalaya, where the road to Simla begins, was made by a company under guarantee. A new line of 750 miles from Chittagong to Assam, inappropriately called the Assam-Bengal Railway since no part of it lies in Bengal proper, is now in course of construction by a company, the capital being supplied partly by the company on a guarantee, partly by the Government; this is on the metre guage. On the east coast of the Bay of Bengal, a line of 450 miles is in the course of construction from the Kistna to Kuttack, which was originally undertaken as a famine work; this is on the standard guage. It will eventually, if completed, give direct communication between Bengal and the east coast, but some large rivers have to be crossed involving great outlay for bridging.

Railways in Burma.

The railways in Burma are all State lines, and all on the metre guage; they comprise at present, the main line from Rangoon to Mandalay; a line from Rangoon to Prome at the head of the delta of the Irawadi river;

CHAP. XIX. and an extension of the main line from opposite Mandalay, along the right or west bank of the Irawadi to the frontier of Burma at Mogaung; about 750 miles have been opened; 150 more are in progress.

The foregoing comprise all the principal Indian lines. Altogether up to the spring of 1893, about 18,000 miles of railway have been completed, of which there are—

On the standard guage . .	10,346 miles.
On the metre guage . .	7,451 „
On special guages . . .	245 „

Almost the whole of these are single lines only. Portions of line only, mainly on the East Indian and the G. I. Peninsula, to an extent in all of about 1,050 miles, have as yet been doubled.

Evils of break of guage.

Two of the most obviously noticeable points brought out by any view of Indian railways, are the break of guage, and the diversity of agency employed in the construction of the different lines, both plain indications of the vacillation and want of definite principles of action which have marked the railway policy of the Indian Government. The metre guage was introduced with excellent intentions, to promote economy in construction, to make a given sum produce a greater mileage by laying light rails and permanent way to carry light rolling stock at a low speed. The same end might have been reached while yet maintaining the standard guage. The saving of cost in the narrow guage line, due to a narrower permanent way, is a quite inconsiderable item in the whole saving. In a flat country, and where the cost of land is trifling, the saving does not arise from placing the lines of rail closer to each other, but in using a light permanent way and a light rolling stock; these could have been provided equally in one case as in the other, while on the broad guage the stock is much easier to handle than on the narrow one, because it covers less ground for a given load, admitting of shorter platforms and goods yards. It may be objected, and probably was argued at the time, that if these lighter lines had been laid down on the wider guage, it would have been practically impossible to prevent heavy stock from being run over them; or that if the two kinds of stock had been kept separate, the stock of each part, heavy or light, being reserved for itself, there would have been equally in effect a break of traffic with all its inconveniences, just as much as if there had been a break of guage. Admitting this, still a great deal of the traffic might have been continuous and carried over the lighter road, the condition involved being a mere question of reducing speed, which surely could have been kept under regulation. With a uniform guage and permanent way, the lighter stock and permanent way could have been gradually replaced by stronger materials with the development of traffic. In Burma, indeed, where the railways are completely isolated from those of all other countries, the objection to the narrow guage does not hold good in this respect. The same thing may be said of the new Assam-Bengal railway, but as to both cases it may be asserted that in a level country there is no virtue in the metre guage, and that a wider guage (even if less than the standard) would have been as cheap and more convenient. In India itself, the Ganges, except in its upper parts, cannot be bridged within any measurable space of time; here then, also, the objection to a break of guage did not present itself at the outset, and the lines north of that river might have been laid down on the narrow guage, as a system separate from that established on the south of the river. But the ruling principle to be observed was violated by the construction of the Oudh and Rohilcund Railway on the broad guage. Moreover, the lines in upper Bengal are now in course of being connected with those to the westward, when there will be an extensive metre guage sys-

CHAP. XIX.

tem north of the Ganges, joining the extension of the Rajputana line, so that the metre and standard guage lines will be crossing each other at numerous points in North Western India, and all the evils of a break of guage will be manifested in an extreme form. The same intersection of broad and narrow guage lines already obtains in Southern India, but the broken surface of the Dekhan is especially suitable for the metre guage if it can be justified anywhere. It is remarkable that the mistake of first introducing that guage should have been perpetrated on the Rajputana Railway, one of the main lines of communication between Upper India and the seaboard, and over a section terminated at each end by a broad guage line. It is indeed a singular instance of mistaken judgment that India should be committed to all the irreparable evils of a break of guage by a government which had a perfectly free hand and a new country to deal with.

Vacillation of railway policy of Indian Government.

To appreciate fully the vacillation of policy which has marked the course of Indian railway administration, the various subsequent arrangements must be understood which have been made for working the different lines upon their completion. All the contracts with the guaranteed companies provided for the Government having the option of purchase at stated periods. This option was not availed of in the case of the G. I. Peninsula and Madras Railways, which on the expiry of the first period of twenty-five years, obtained a renewal of their contracts. In thus losing the opportunity of reducing the high and now unnecessary rate of guaranteed interest, 5 per cent., an opportunity which will not recur until 1899 and 1907 respectively, a fault of omission was committed which it is difficult to extenuate.

Extension of contracts granted in some cases.

railways purchased in other cases.

While extensions of their contracts were given to these two lines, the contracts with several others were determined. The Eastern Bengal Railway was acquired in 1884, and added as a working system to the narrow guage state line of that name, north of the Ganges. The Government has also undertaken the working of the Bengal Central Railway (125 miles), one of the few lines undertaken without a guarantee, but on which a guarantee was eventually granted; this line now forms part of the same system. The Sind, Punjab, and Delhi Railway was purchased in 1886, and incorporated with the Government North West system under the title of the North Western Railway, now comprising over 2,400 miles owned and worked directly by the Government, the most extensive system in India. The Oudh and Rohilcund Railway was purchased in 1889, and its management assumed by the Government.

To the Bombay, Baroda, and Central India Company, on the other hand, an extension of its contract was given on the old guarantee of 5 per cent. until 1905, and it has further been given a lease of the working of the Rajputana-Malwa State line, which had been worked as well as constructed by State agency. The combined system, broad and narrow guage, comprises about 2,350 miles, extending from Bombay to Cawnpur.

The East Indian Railway was purchased in 1880, and made over to a company to be worked under special arrangements which will be presently referred to. This company has also been given a lease of the new Delhi-Kalka line.

Amalgamations of different systems.

The Great Southern of India has been amalgamated with another company, the whole forming a concern called the South Indian Railway Limited, with a guarantee of 3 per cent. on the new capital, and 4½ on the stock of the old company, and a share of surplus profits when realised. The whole system covers about 1,100 miles, a considerable part of which consists of line, originally built on the standard guage, since converted to the narrow.

The Southern Maratha Railway, of 1,550 miles, is a

CHAP. XIX. system made up of various lines constructed by the company of that name, and various State-constructed lines made over to it for working, with a guarantee on the capital of 3½ per cent., and a charge on surplus profits.

The Bengal and North Western Railway, about 750 miles, similarly consists partly of lines constructed by the company of that name and partly of lines constructed by the Government, made over to the former for working. In Northern India also a comparatively small concern, the Rohilkhand and Kumaon Railway, of less than 60 miles, works a system of 300 miles of narrow guage lines, the greater part of which were originally made by the State.

The Bengal-Nagpur Railway, about 850 miles, is the property of the Government, in consideration of a contribution of nearly half of the capital, and a guarantee of 4 per cent. on the remainder. This is worked by the company by whose agency it was constructed. The Indian Midland, 750 miles, is on the same footing as the Bengal-Nagpur.

Diversity of system now obtaining.

Thus it will be seen that while the Government has bought several of the lines built by guaranteed companies, under the terms of the contracts, it has failed to take advantage of this option in the case of others; no reasonable explanation is forthcoming for this difference of treatment. Further, while the Government on the one hand has assumed the direct management of several lines originally constructed by companies, on the other hand it has made over to companies for working a considerable number of lines constructed by its own agency, the result being an extraordinarily complicated variety of agencies and conditions. The Indian railway system now comprises:—

1. Lines constructed and worked by the State.
2. Lines constructed by companies and worked by companies.

CHAP. XIX.

3. Lines constructed by companies but purchased and worked by the Government.
4. Lines constructed by the Government but made over to be worked by companies.
5. Lines constructed with State funds through the agency of companies and worked by them.
6. Lines constructed by one company but worked by another.
7. Lines constructed by native States and worked by those States.
8. Lines constructed by native States and worked by companies.

To sell a railway one day and buy another the next; to build a railway and then lease it to a company, and at the same time to take over another line on lease: these inconsequential proceedings are sufficient indication of the total want of systematic policy and good judgment which has characterised the railway administration of the Indian Government. But even more serious and harmful than past mistakes, is the lamentable want of progress exhibited at present in railway making. Less than 500 miles of new line were opened in 1892–3, and the additional work sanctioned for construction covers only 136 miles. This is as if railway making in India was regarded as having come to an end. It would be perhaps too much to say that railway construction is just beginning, but the total of only 18,000 miles completed in that great country is a figure which speaks for itself; there are still large tracts, highly cultivated and thickly populated, for which railways are practically non-existent, and which without railways can find no market for their produce. But everybody is agreed about the necessity of largely extending railway construction, and the Government professes itself to be most eager on the point; the difficulty is that it cannot make up its mind to a definitive policy which will

Stoppage in railway progress.

CHAP. XIX.

ensure a steady yet rapid progress without needless extravagance or foolish bargains. Not indeed that the bargains in the past can be so characterised. The guarantee of five per cent. was a not unreasonably high attraction to offer to the investor nearly fifty years ago, when the conditions of India and its trade were little known or understood. And if the rupee had maintained its gold value, the bargain would have proved to be a very good one for the Government, to which most of the earlier lines would now be returning handsome profits. As it is the present financial situation of the Government, as affected by its railway operations, is one of the most striking illustrations of the dislocation wrought in trade by the fluctuations in the value of gold and silver. The rupee being now worth only a little more than one half its value at the time when the capital raised was sent to India to make the railways, a return of nearly ten per cent. is now required to cover the guaranteed gold interest of five per cent. The loss thus incurred, as on every bargain struck before the depreciation of silver set in, is irrecoverable, unless the value of silver should be restored. But the same cause of loss cannot arise upon further transactions of the kind except in the improbable contingency of a still further fall of silver, which there is reason to hope has now touched nearly its lowest point, while of course there is no longer any question of a five per cent. guarantee; the latest contracts have been made at three per cent. on the capital outlay.

Effect of fall of silver on guarantee system.

Satisfactory position of railway finance.

The financial aspect of the Indian railways is highly satisfactory and encouraging. The annual account of receipt and expenditure for 1893–4 shows indeed a balance of a million and a half on the debtor side,[1] still further increased in the present year by the greater loss on exchange in payment of guaranteed interest. But

[1] A small part of this is due to substitution of terminable annuities for permanent interest, and is therefore in the nature of an investment.

the account is in the initial stage, burdened with charges on new lines which have not had time to pay. The frontier railways apart, which must always be worked at a loss, the average return on the capital outlay already exceeds 4½ per cent., although on several lines lately opened the traffic is still in a quite undeveloped state. The heaviest charge on the account, however, arises from the high rate of interest still paid to the Great Indian Peninsula, the Bombay-Baroda, and the Madras Railways, which will eventually be susceptible of large reduction. The burden arising out of the guarantee on the older lines from the depreciation of the rupee is one which it would be irrational to suppose will recur on any new engagements made, and in the development of railways is to be found the best prospect of strengthening the financial position of the government. In no other way can the exchange difficulty be so effectually met as by the stimulus thus given to the export trade. The benefit to India itself from railway extension will be incalculable. Every consideration therefore points to the urgency for replacing the present condition of hesitation and inaction by a policy of sustained and vigorous progress. The first condition required for securing this result is that the government should arrive at a speedy decision as to the machinery to be employed for carrying out the business in this way. At present, halting between a half-hearted desire to execute the work by its own agency and a disinclination to continue the guarantee system, it has brought the business almost to a standstill, for the annual grant made to State railways, besides that it cannot be certainly counted on, is utterly inadequate for the wants of the case.

State construction.

At first sight there might appear much to be said in favour of railway construction being carried out in future by Government agency. The Government can certainly borrow more cheaply direct than through the agency of a company under guarantee; it commands

CHAP. XIX.

the services of a staff of very able engineers, whose work is as economical as it is good. But while India and its people are highly prosperous, the Government itself is in a state of great financial embarrassment; the inevitable tendency to regulate railway expenditure with reference to the ways and means of the year would be fatal to the prospect of carrying out construction in this way with vigour and regularity. Every change in the state of the Treasury will be reflected in its railway policy; hesitation and vacillation—fits of energy succeeded by suspension of work, variation in the grants of work varying from year to year, almost from month to month; this has been the condition exhibited in the past and will certainly be maintained in the future. Nor is it desirable that a Government already overworked, should load itself with the burden of undertaking directly a laborious business of this kind. There is further great objection to the creation and maintenance of any more public establishments than are absolutely necessary. In most self-governing countries, indeed, the growth of these establishments is becoming a serious political danger. In India the danger assumes another phase of the same kind—that in a country where there is little public opinion and where amongst the English community the official element largely preponderates over the unofficial, the services should become too strong for the Government. But the first objection is the greatest of all, and it is conclusive.

Compared with joint stock agency.

The best and only satisfactory method for ensuring regular and sustained railway progress is by the employment of a separate agency, that is, to entrust the business to joint stock companies.

Terms to be given.

If this decision is arrived at, there remains to act upon it by fixing terms which shall be sufficient, but not more than sufficient, to attract English capital to the business. The Government have lately after much delay announced the terms on which they are prepared to entertain proposals for the construction of new lines. These terms, formulated as being those which must in future take the place of a guarantee, are: that the preliminary survey for a railway shall be undertaken at the cost of the State; that the land to be taken up shall be acquired by the Government, and given free of cost to the company; and that a rebate or discount shall be allowed to the new line for all traffic receipts brought by it on to, or received by it from the old line; this assumes that the new line will be an extension of an old one, as in fact almost every new railway must be. This rebate is obviously another form of guarantee. But it is one thing to lay down conditions, and another that they shall serve the desired purpose of stimulating railway progress, and it seems doubtful whether a guarantee simple in form and readily understood, would not be more attractive to the investor, while not involving any greater liability to the State than these somewhat complicated terms. The present state of the silver market is distinctly favourable to a guarantee, even in gold, because the fall which has occurred cannot in reasonable probability go further. If, however, the needful capital can be obtained without a guarantee other than the disguised one now proposed, by all means let the guarantee be dropped. How far the proposal will serve its purpose has yet to be seen. But in any case, if English capital is to be freely obtained for Indian railways, two conditions at least must be satisfied. The curious notion seems to pervade the official mind that the inducement which leads to the formation of companies is the prospect of a dividend on the part of the shareholders. Even if this were the cause, it is certain that the ordinary investor cannot afford to wait while the process of return is in course of development. This difficulty has been got over by an Act lately passed,[1]

[1] 57 & 58 Vict., Cap. xii.

CHAP. XIX.

under which it becomes lawful to pay dividends out of capital during the process of construction, which is in fact equivalent to loading the enterprise with a certain extra dead weight of expenditure, unproductive, but necessary under the circumstances. But investors alone do not get up railway schemes. The authorities in India and at the India Office have not apparently got to the points of understanding that, for this class of business as for any other, a special agency is needed, which must be paid for its services—the promoters who have to be responsible for raising the capital, and who, in order that subscriptions shall be forthcoming, have to underwrite or procure underwriters for the amount; and that they will not undertake this, with the risk or discredit of failure, without adequate return. There must in short be a lump sum provided at the outset for commission, under whatever name it be called, in addition to the actual cost of constructing the line. This consideration explains how it is that while in every mushroom South American Republic foreign capital is forthcoming for its railways, India fails to get any without a guarantee. But surely there is a mean between the state of things where every one from the Prime Minister or President downwards has to be squared—where the interests of the promoters are made the first, and those of the shareholders the last consideration, and the condition which those who conduct affairs in India appear to think reasonable and sufficient, that railway projects should be got up by the investing public themselves, simply with the prospect of ultimately getting a moderate interest for their money. The present state of Indian traffic returns shows that any well planned line, with the economical modes of construction now in force, can bear this loading of a reasonable profit to the promoters and underwriters who raise the loan, and of interest during construction to the shareholders, and yet return a good profit.

CHAP. XIX.

Railways should be constructed by companies.

But while new companies may be usefully established for raising capital and constructing new lines in various localities, the agency of existing companies may be employed to still greater advantage for carrying out the extensions required to the lines under their management. Hitherto the procedure in this respect has been in the last degree cumbrous and unnecessary. In the case of the Delhi-Kalka line, for example, which is obviously an extension of the East Indian, a company was got up to raise the capital and construct the line, which on completion was made over to the latter company on lease to work, the staff which had been got together for making the line being thereon dismissed, while the London board of the new Company is retained solely for the purpose of distributing the dividend to shareholders. Obviously this extension could have been carried out with greater economy and without this roundabout process by the existing company. A very pressing requirement at the present time is that the contracts between all the old companies and the Secretary of State should be so modified as to admit of his giving them borrowing powers for such extensions and the other approved works necessarily arising out of the development of their traffic.

Government acquiring ownership.

But while railway construction should be entrusted to companies, the advantage to the Government from the possession of the railways is so great that the condition of the right of eventual purchase will no doubt be provided in all future, as it has been in all past contracts. If to the condition of purchase be added a firm adherence to the wise policy now being pursued of paying off the purchase-money by terminable annuities, the State will eventually become the owner of this great and lucrative property free of encumbrance, a source of financial strength such as is presented by no possible mode of taxation.

On the other hand, if while State ownership of the

CHAP. XIX.

but not working the lines directly.

railways should be a cardinal point of policy, the first construction of the railways should not be undertaken by the State, still more desirable is it that the Government should divest itself of the working of completed lines. Over and above the disadvantages already stated as regards the first case, are those involved in the great and increasing burden of conducting a great railway traffic. Government management of a railway is shrouded in mystery. In the case of a private company the responsibility rests with the visible head; in the working of State lines it can never be known how far the blame for mismanagement and omission to make improvements is shared between the ostensible management and an obstructive controlling department at headquarters; the Government of India should not place itself in a position to appear responsible for bad administration in any branch. Moreover, an incurable defect attaches to government management in the constant movement of the executive officials from post to post, a condition incompatible with good administration.

All future contracts, then, should provide for the line being leased to the company which makes it, and the government may with great advantage also divest itself of the working of the lines which it still retains. The case of the East Indian Railway offers a valuable precedent on this head. The company, as reconstituted in 1880, has a working lease of the line with a capital of about one-fifth that of the original company, to cover the value of the stock taken over.[1] The profits on the working of the line are charged with the payments of the annuities due to the shareholders on the old stock, and with 4 per cent. guaranteed to the shareholders on

[1] The reconstitution of the East Indian Railway Company on its present basis, was practically the act of General Strachey, then a Member of the Indian Council and now Chairman of the Company; one of the many remarkable and beneficial measures due to the labours and genius of this distinguished man.

the new—or to be more accurate, with a rate of annuity equivalent to that interest; of the surplus, four-fifths goes to the government and one-fifth to the company. The working of this line is remarkable both for the large increase of traffic which takes place from year to year, and the extraordinary economy with which it is administered—the working expenses being less than 30 per cent. of the gross receipts, a result, it is believed, not attained by any other railway company anywhere. What that company now needs is the power to make the extensions which could be profitably carried out in various directions, and which are urgently required in the interests of the country. But the company has no borrowing powers; it is dependent on the government for the supply of increased capital for this purpose, being in this respect on the footing of a government line, and suffering equally with the government railways both in limitation of the supply of funds, and in the vacillation and uncertainty which attend the allotment of them. This allotment of late has been insufficient even for the purchase of the necessary additional rolling stock required to carry the increased traffic, while the work of extension is practically standing still. Great is the need that, as has been proposed, borrowing powers should be given both to this company and to all other guaranteed lines to enable them to carry out their needful developments when these are approved by the government, in the methodical and systematic way which alone is compatible with economy in construction, instead of with petty instalments of additional capital, doled out in varying sums and at uncertain intervals.

Reform necessary in railway administration. At India Office

Whatever reforms of system be introduced, and however much the government may divest itself of the burden of direct construction and management, the operations of the railways are so intimately connected with the financial interests of the State, that the government must continue to maintain an effective control

CHAP. XIX.

over them. An administrative agency of some kind will always be necessary; and in this respect also reform is urgently demanded. The existing procedure for dealing with this branch of public affairs sufficiently accounts for the blunders and vacillations of the past, and offers a conspicuous warning for the future.

The railway business of the Indian Government is naturally of a kind to be largely dealt with at home as well as in India itself, and the machinery of the India Office is singularly ill adapted for the purpose. The Secretary of State, coming with everything to learn to the charge of a department which is concerned with every branch of affairs, and unable to give more than a mere fragment of his time to the task, especially in these days of the interminable sittings of Parliament, can deal with the business in any one department only in the most perfunctory manner. The effective conduct of the business must perforce be left to the permanent staff, the head of which, as regards each department, is a Committee of the Council. Such a body, if suitable for reviewing the proceedings of others, is a bad form of agency for almost any kind of executive business; and especially inappropriate for the prosecution of railway business is a committee of old soldiers and civilians who come to it late in life, without any previous experience of the conditions with which they have to deal, and whose responsibility is nullified by the circumstance that their action ends with a recommendation to take action which is liable to be set aside by the collective Council. In a later part of this work a reorganisation of the India Office is suggested, which would furnish one responsible permanent head for this, as well as for the other departments into which it is divided, and with such a change there might be a reform in the mode of transacting business at the India Office, which now drives everyone who comes in contact with it to despair. But after all, Indian railway affairs

CHAP. XIX.

and in India.

in all their details must be transacted in India, and there the defect of procedure is even more glaring. Thirty years ago, when the departmental or cabinet system of Government was first introduced into the Governor General's Council, the Governor General himself took charge of the Public Works Department. With the rapid increase of business in all its details which took place after the Mutiny, the head of the Government soon found it impossible to superintend directly the Public Works as well as the Foreign Office, and the former was made over to one of the two civilian Members of the Council to hold in addition to one of the civil departments. In every other branch of the Government, law, army, revenue, finance, the Member of Council in charge was an expert in that particular line. In this case he was practically entirely ignorant of the business he was called on to administer, and grievously have public works interests suffered in consequence. It may be said that the same condition obtains in England, where all the ministers of departments are frequently changed, and always come and often remain from first to last quite ignorant of the business which they are nominally supposed to transact. But then in England the minister works in the light of day and under the constant criticism of Parliament; at any rate he has to assume a knowledge if he has it not, and in most cases to come to a decision; and he is aided by a permanent staff who spend their lifetime in the office. But in India, where it is the custom for business to be dealt with directly by the members of the government, singly or collectively, in a much more minute degree than obtains in England; that a minister should be entirely unversed in the business he is called on to deal with, is a condition unknown in any other branch of affairs. The head of the War Department is always a soldier; of the Finance Department a trained financier; of the Legislative Department a lawyer;

CHAP. XIX.

the revenue business of the Government is transacted by a civilian thoroughly trained and of long experience in that branch of affairs. It would be thought a monstrous thing to shift these ministers about among the different departments, but it is not more absurd to place an entirely untrained man at the head of so complex and extensive a Department as that of Public Works, which requires special knowledge and training just as much as any other. Moreover, under the traditionary rule always acted upon, that one of the two Civilian Members of the Council should be taken alternately from Madras and Bombay, the charge of the Public Works Department has usually fallen to the Councillor chosen from these provinces, apparently by seniority, who has possibly passed his life in the blameless discharge of duties connected with the law or revenue courts, who knows nothing of Indian affairs outside his own province, to whom the great problems of railway construction and administration have never presented themselves in any form, and who is unacquainted with the qualifications of the members of the large service at the head of which he is placed, and from which he has to make the selections for all the higher posts. The Indian Government have been fortunate in securing a succession of very able and experienced men for the post of Secretary to the department,[1] but ability and experience do not get full play in a subordinate position, and the Indian system suffers under the further defect that these officials are constantly changed. In England, the permanent under-secretary of a department will often hold that position for a great number of years, and so become the depository of great knowledge and experience; in India the secretary and other superior officers succeed each other every few months, the rule which superannuates them at the age of 55 years carrying a man off into

[1] It may be again mentioned that the secretary to a department in India holds a position corresponding with the permanent under secretary of a department at home.

retirement just as he has worked his way to the top of the service.[1] The present mode of administrating the Indian Public Works is indefensible. It is at the root of almost all the mistakes, blunders, and objectless changes of purpose, and especially the lamentable delays which have occurred to discredit the Indian Government.

A public works minister required.

An Act of Parliament passed in 1876 provided for the appointment of an additional member of the Governor General's Council for Public Works purposes; but the sanction given by this Act was only once made use of; the appointment first made under the Act was not renewed, and save during the exceptional period when a distinguished civilian, Sir Theodore Hope, had charge of the Public Works Department, the Public Works administration has been the least satisfactory feature of the Indian Government; with the increasing complexity and magnitude of the business to be dealt with, the need for reform becomes every year more urgent. The first condition for securing this is that a minister with the needful special knowledge and experience should be placed in charge of it. The objection to increasing the number of the Governor General's Council may be admitted. Even seven members are almost too many for prompt executive government. But if it be deemed inexpedient to prevent this increase by discontinuing to fill up one of the two seats reserved for members of the Civil Service, the same end might be secured by declaring the public works member eligible to sit and vote only when public works business was under discussion.[2] This would be

[1] It is a curious inconsistency in the Indian system, that the civilian in every branch is superannuated at a much earlier age than the military officer. If a major-general is considered to be physically fit for his post up to the age of sixty-two, it might be thought that a civilian could be kept to his work till at least the same age. A still greater age is not thought excessive for a Viceroy, the hardest worked man in the country.

[2] The addition of one word to the Act of 1876 would apparently effect what is desired; creating, instead of a member of the Governor General's Council 'for Public Works purposes,' a member 'for Public Works purposes *only*.'

CHAP. XIX. in harmony with the English system, under which all the ministers have not equal rank as members of the Cabinet, and it would be appropriate to the requirements of the case, the qualifications to be sought for in a public works minister being not necessarily of a kind to make his opinions of value on the other matters with which the Government of India has to deal. The essential point, however, is that there should be a minister qualified by his antecedents for the post, specifically responsible for the conduct of public works, able to speak and act with authority, and not compelled, as the virtual head of the department—the secretary, has hitherto been, to work through a more or less ignorant and incompetent superior, who signs the papers put before him and has no opinions, or only worthless ones, of his own.

and a public works board.

But this reform alone would not be sufficient. To secure the continuity of policy and progress which hitherto has been lacking in such a lamentable degree, some more durable governing body than a single man is necessary. In a general way, no doubt, and especially for vigorous executive action, government by one man is better than government by a Board; but in this case, where the interests to be dealt with are so various and complex, and in India especially where men come and go so quickly, the continuity of policy which above everything has to be aimed at can only be got by such an agency. Moreover, it is very desirable that the higher officers of the department should all be able to speak and act with authority. A Board, therefore, of which the minister should be chairman, and the three principal officers of the department, the Secretary to Government, the Director-General of Railways, and the head of the Irrigation Service, members, may be suggested as the machinery which should satisfy the needful conditions.

With the creation of a body of this sort, it would be

Railway accounts to be separated from general financial accounts.

possible to deal with the finance of railways and irrigation in a more satisfactory way than is possible at present. The railway transactions are now all brought into the general accounts of the country, and in a very unsystematic and confusing fashion. The fact is that the Indian Finance Department is attempting to combine two incompatible things—the English system of accounts and finance based upon annual grants and appropriation; and the accounts and finance involved in the working of a great property like the Indian railways and irrigation works. The system of yearly grants has been found highly inconvenient and impolitic applied to even the comparatively small expenditure involved in the naval defences of this country. To deal in this way with progressive expenditure already amounting to hundreds of millions is impracticable: the attempt must sooner or later be given up, and the sooner the better. Railway accounts and finance, at any rate, if not those of irrigation also, should be entirely separated from the general accounts of the country and dealt with, as they only can be properly, on commercial principles; and for this purpose alone a Railway Trust appears indispensable. The proposed Board would serve this purpose. Under this reform the net revenue receipts or expenditure, as the case may be, of the railways would be shown by one final entry in the general finance accounts of the year, as so much revenue or outlay. The capital raised for railway purposes should also be kept separate from the other loans of the Government, and grants made therefrom should not as at present be revocable. Only by separating railway finance in this way, from that of the general treasury, conjoined with the other reforms indicated, can fixity of purpose and methodical and economical progress be secured.

CHAPTER XX

FINANCE

[The unit used here, ten rupees (Rx), is that which is now adopted in the public accounts of India; a unit which twenty years ago was nearly equal in value to the pound sterling, and used to be treated in those accounts as actually representing that sum.]

CHAP. XX.

Finance accounts inflated by entry of gross receipts and charges.

THE gross revenue of India, as shown in the public accounts, is about 90 millions; the gross expenditure for the last two years has been still larger. Thirty years ago, when financial equilibrium had been restored after the losses and special outlay caused by the Mutiny, the revenue and expenditure were about 40 millions; twenty years ago they were about 57 millions. It would thus appear on a superficial view as if the public expenditure and revenue of India had increased during the last twenty years by more than 30 millions, and this has been assumed to be the case by some writers whose knowledge of the subject is not always on a level with the confident tone of the opinions they express upon it. This increase in the figures is in fact due to a large extent to the exhibition in a greater degree than formerly of all receipts in the gross on one side of the account as revenue, and all charges for collection and so forth as expenditure. But it is still more largely due to the inclusion, on both sides, of the State transactions connected with the Indian railways, which are practically a new item in the public accounts. The inflation of the financial accounts due to this cause will go on increasing largely from year to year with the development of these railways to such an extent as ultimately to render the other entries apparently insignificant—a distortion dearly purchased by the result. For even as a statement of the transactions which the figures profess to represent, they are misleading. In the accounts of 1893–4, the entry on the revenue side—about 20 millions in all—is made up of two items, $16\frac{2}{3}$rd millions of gross traffic receipts on the railways worked directly by State agency, the working expenses of these, $8\frac{1}{4}$ millions, being shown on the other side as expenditure; and $3\frac{1}{3}$ millions, the net traffic receipts of the railways worked by companies. The propriety of showing even the net traffic receipts as revenue is questionable, because at present there is a loss on the whole account, the guaranteed interest being in excess of the receipts. But at any rate the circumstance that the receipts of one railway are collected directly by the Government, and those of another through the agency of a company, is no reason for dealing with the items in a different way, the less so that the management of the railways is frequently changing hands. One year the Government buys a line and undertakes the working of it; another year it makes over one of its lines to be worked by a company. Clearly either the gross traffic receipts should be shown in all cases, or only the net traffic receipts. From the figures given nothing definite can be predicated until adjustments of the kind thus indicated as necessary are first made. As has just been pointed out, a new method is required for dealing with the financial transactions of the Government in regard to railways, in combination with the system of annual budgets. Apart from the financial distortion produced by the present mode of exhibiting the railway transactions, it seems misleading also to show miscellaneous receipts of the army and other public departments as revenue; they are merely recoveries of over payments made, and not revenue in the proper sense.

CHAP. XX.

This inflation of the finance accounts—the outcome of official purism—does not even satisfy the canon of accuracy, as representing the whole transactions of the Government, and is hardly more appropriate than would be the insertion in the accounts of a bank of all the cheques handed over the counter.

Net revenues and receipts compared.

In order to appreciate the relative improvement which has taken place in the finances, the net and not the gross revenue and expenditure for successive years must be compared. The following figures furnish this comparison for 1873–4 and 1893–4. It is not quite exact, because in the figures available for the earlier year, the loss by exchange (to be presently referred to) is shown in the lump sum, whereas in the later account it is distributed over the different heads under which the loss occurs. The comparison is, however, sufficiently complete for the purpose in view. It will be seen that the net revenue has increased from 39¼ millions in 1873–74 to 50¼ millions in 1893–94. This increase of 12½ millions has accrued at a fairly uniform rate of rather more than half a million a year. The land revenue has furnished a proportionate share of the total increase, while generally the increase in the different branches of revenue indicates a gradual and steady, but moderate, advance from year to year in the general prosperity of the country, a condition entirely borne out by the expansion of railway traffic and the statistics of the Indian trade. The increase in the salt revenue is accounted for partly by an increase in the duty, partly by increased consumption. It is practically the only obligatory tax in India, while from the facility of collection as an excise duty levied at the localities where the article is produced, or at the ports of entry, it is probably the least irksome form of taxation that could be devised. The most satisfactory item of revenue, however, as regards the people of India, is that derived from opium, it being not an impost upon them but an

Increase of revenue.

CHAP. XX.

INDIAN FINANCES

Net Revenue	1873–4	1893–4
	Rx.	Rx.
Land	18,138,300	21,381,500
Opium	6,323,400	4,809,500
Salt	5,647,000	7,840,600
Stamps	2,575,600	4,337,700
Excise	2,187,400	5,124,900
Provincial Rates	1,765,200	3,424,600
Customs	2,378,600	1,467,800
Assessed Taxes	28,500	1,677,500
Forest	231,300	752,600
Registration	60,100	203,700
Tributes Native States	768,500	792,000
	40,103,900	51,812,400
Assignments and Compensations	870,800	1,559,300
Total	39,233,100	50,253,100

Net Expenditure	1873–4	1893–4
	Rx.	Rx.
Interest	4,914,500	3,557,600
Post, Telegraph, and Mint	367,100	180,400
Civil Departments	8,463,500	12,923,500
Miscellaneous Civil charges	2,322,400	4,658,200
Famine Relief and Insurance	3,864,700	1,138,300
Construction of Railways charged against Revenue	32,800	77,100
Railway Revenue Account	1,414,700	1,597,000
Irrigation	610,600	536,700
Buildings and Roads	4,409,100	5,236,300
Army and Marine	14,217,400	22,588,400
Special Defence Works	—	342,000
Exchange	879,400	—
	41,506,200	52,524,700
Provincial and Local Deficits	465,300	478,800
	41,040,800	52,045,900
Deficit	1,807,700	1,792,800
Total	39,233,100	50,253,100

CHAP. XX

article of export paid for in cash. Unfortunately, from a merely fiscal point of view, the opium revenue shows great falling off; recovery is more than doubtful, and the loss accruing under this head will necessarily have to be made good by other imposts, direct or indirect.

Next to opium comes the revenue from stamps, $4\frac{1}{3}$ millions. The considerable 'provincial rates,' nearly $3\frac{1}{2}$ millions, are made up of various local cesses, among them a small percentage on the land revenue appropriated locally, tolls on roads and ferries, and other receipts realised locally and for the most part applied in the same way, but which are brought in the first instance to the credit of the imperial revenues. Provincial taxation must not be confounded with provincial finance, which will be referred to later on.

A long way behind the foregoing in amount come the assessed taxes, little more, and the customs a little less, than $1\frac{1}{2}$ millions. The falling off in the latter as compared with the receipts of 1873–74 is due to the abolition in 1883 of the cotton and other duties. The forests, under the care and good management bestowed upon them in past years, have begun to furnish a substantial and increasing addition to the general revenue, now amounting to $\frac{3}{4}$ of a million. The tributes from Native States, about as much, furnished under treaties made with them at different times, vary little from year to year. The fees derived from the registration of deeds, less than a quarter of a million, completes the list of revenue.

The 'assignments and compensations,' $1\frac{1}{2}$ millions, to be deducted from the total revenue, represent among other items the drawback allowed to certain native states for their share of duties levied, mainly salt, but principally assignments made in lieu of land revenue received.

These figures of the revenue of India tell their own story, and if we did not know the facts from other sources, would furnish an immediate indication of some of the most marked conditions of that country. Just as from the English Budget may be inferred some of the primary characteristics of the English as a people largely given to strong drink, great consumers and great producers of various commodities themselves, comprising also a very large wealthy class, so the Indian Budget is unmistakably concerned with the circumstances of a frugal people of simple habits, of whom very few are otherwise than poor and almost all are engaged in agriculture. The assessed taxes—the unfailing and almost boundless resource of the English financier—yield only about 1½ millions from 220 millions of people, indicating the almost entire absence of a middle class. The stamp duties tell the same tale, while generally the increase in the different branches of the revenue indicate a gradual and steady, but moderate advance from year to year in the general prosperity of the country.

The land revenue, the mainstay of Indian finance, is revenue only in a special and technical sense; it is really the rent of land, paid in most cases direct by the cultivator to the landlord, and the only rent paid by the former. Succeeding to the system under which, from time immemorial, the ruler of the country has been recognised as the owner of the soil, and the occupier as his tenant, the East India Company gradually substituted a money rent for the payment in kind obtaining under native rule, and rents fixed for a term of years in lieu of a certain proportion of each harvest from year to year. Unfortunately, through ignorance of the conditions subsisting on their first succeeding to the government, they went still further in the direction of fixity, and in the wrong direction. On the assumption of the government of Bengal by English officials, the mistake was made of taking the zemindars or farmers of the land revenue, whom they found in that

CHAP. XX.

position, to be the proprietors of the soil. Going to India with the aristocratic notions derived from English tenures, that the land must be held everywhere by the squire or great proprietor, the first English rulers of India took it for granted that the officials of the Mohamedan rulers whom they succeeded, to whom the land revenues had been farmed out, were the owners of the estates of which, at that time, they had charge, and these zemindars were declared to be the landlords of these estates in perpetuity, subject to the payment of the rents for which they were at the time responsible. This is what is known as the Perpetual Settlement of Bengal. Moreover while conferring these rights upon the zemindars, no action was taken to secure the rights of their under tenants; the profits from the rise in rents which took place with the advance in prosperity resulting from the establishment of peace, and its consequent increase of cultivation, were left to the zemindars, free to enrich themselves by rack-renting the peasantry; and it is only within recent years that the claims of the latter to a similar fixity of tenure have been recognised, and a system of tenant right established in the province of Bengal. In that part of India, therefore, which from the long period of settled government enjoyed by it, accompanied by the consequent influx of British capital, has attained to a greater advance in prosperity than any other part, the land revenue yields practically no increase; the land owners, with enormously increased incomes, contribute nothing of that increase to the finances. The advance in the land revenue during the last twenty years from seventeen millions to twenty millions[1] has accrued in other provinces. Fortunately, by the time fresh accessions of territory were acquired, a more accurate knowledge of the actual conditions of

[1] After deducting from 21½ millions shown in the table, page 329, the proportion of the assignments and compensations entered at foot thereof.

land tenure throughout the land had been arrived at. It had been discovered that the state was the owner of the soil, and the zemindar only the publican or rent collector; and the settlement of the land revenue was henceforth made directly with the cultivator—either collectively with the village for the land held by it, or with the individual peasant proprietor. The increase of revenue during the twenty years under review, is due mainly to the greater breadth of land brought under cultivation in the older provinces, and partly to accessions of fresh territory. But on the whole the assessment has actually become lighter, the proportion of the produce of the soil claimed as revenue or rent having been reduced from time to time. It should be added that the annual rate of increase hitherto accruing has for the present come almost to an end, the settlement over the great part of Northern India having lately been revised and fixed for a further term of thirty years.

Increase of expenditure.

Turning now to the expenditure side of the account, the first item, interest, shows the satisfactory result that, wars and famines notwithstanding, the annual charge for the public debt has been reduced during the twenty years under review by nearly 2,000,000*l.*; partly by the reduction of debt, partly by reduction in the rate of interest as the financial credit of the Government has rendered the conversion practicable. On the other hand, the account tells the same tale which is repeated in every country, of the greatly increased cost from year to year of both the civil administration and the army. But it should be explained that a large part of the increase is here apparent only, and is due to the ever growing burden of the loss by exchange. When the rupee was worth ten shillings, the Indian accounts were exhibited for financial purposes in sterling, the expenditure in India being taken at ten rupees to the pound. But when silver began to fall in value

CHAP. XX.

with respect to gold—about twenty-three years ago—this mode of dealing with the accounts ceased to be practicable; the sovereign now represented more than ten rupees, and it became necessary to introduce a definite charge to provide for the loss by exchange in the remittance to England of the silver required for the sterling payments to be made in that country. With the continued fall of the rupee the loss by exchange has gone on at an ever increasing rate. Twenty years ago it amounted to less than a million of tens of rupees. In 1893-4 it had reached to over 10 millions, and in the present year will be very much more. But, exchange allowed for, still there has been a very large increase of the charges both for the civil administration and army. What has happened in this respect in every country in Europe has happened also in India. The large increase in civil charges is due to the development of the civil administration in all branches, in pursuance of demands which every government finds irresistible and which grow in strength with every advance towards what is called civilisation. The increase is caused also in great measure by the rise in salaries of all branches of the Native Civil Service which has been taking place from year to year. The salaries of the English civil servants have meanwhile undergone no change, and the strength of the service has been largely reduced, although the boundaries of British India have been pushed forward to include large tracts of country on both the east and west. The cost of the home establishment also has somewhat decreased of late years—a fact which probably cannot be recorded of any other public department in London. And it is a remarkable and in one sense very satisfactory feature of Indian finance that, this loss from exchange apart, the total public expenditure during the last twenty years should have increased by only two millions—so that, if the rupee had remained at the old par of exchange, then other things

Loss by exchange.

Civil charges.

being the same, there would be at the present time, that is on the budget of 1893–4, instead of a deficit, a surplus of eight millions. The comparison is useful as indicating both the good management of the Indian finances and the tremendous liability placed on them by the fall of silver, a liability the further incidence of which in the future it is impossible to estimate, and which mocks all efforts at financial care and foresight.

Military charges. The military charges present the other great item of increase, from $14\frac{1}{4}$ millions to $22\frac{1}{2}$ millions; the exchange enters into this to the extent of 3 millions. It is partly due to the high pension rates arising out of the bad bargains made with the British officers of the old Indian army on its abolition, the full effects of which are now beginning to be felt; to an increase of strength in 1885 when 30,000 men (10,000 British and 20,000 native) were added to the army; and largely to the increased cost of military stores, ammunition, and equipment of all kinds. The modern cartridge costs almost as much as did the obsolete gun of twenty years ago. The greater care now taken of the British soldier, both of his health and comfort, also involves expenditure at all points, while increased allowances of all kinds have been granted to the native army to keep pace with the attractions of civil life, as the class which supplies the soldier becomes more prosperous. There is no prospect of any reduction under these heads, but rather a certainty of further increase. The pay of the British soldiers and non-commissioned officers serving in India is converted into silver at the current rate of exchange —they being the only class of the British in India who do not lose from the fall of the rupee, and the charge on this head will go on increasing with any further fall in that coin. Military operations and military precautions of all kinds tend to become continually more expensive, while it must be remembered that the army

CHAP. XX.

in India is now maintained at a very low strength with regard to the work it has to do even in peace time. It is moreover organised on a peace establishment only, and no machinery has as yet been provided for securing its expansion in case of necessity. A beginning has been made of forming a reserve, but only a beginning, and so far the measure can hardly be deemed successful; but effective measures for this purpose cannot be much longer delayed; the native army is now maintained with difficulty on its peace establishment, and at the outbreak of war recruiting might stop altogether if measures be not taken betimes to render the service more attractive.

Liability impending for exchange compensation.

On all sides, therefore, there are continual liabilities for increased expenditure; and one pressing liability in particular must soon be met. Owing to the fall of the rupee the position of the English public servant in India, civil and military, has for the last three or four years been becoming more acutely embarrassing. The status of what used to be known as the Covenanted Civil Service, the highest and most highly paid branch of the public service, has become thoroughly depreciated, and a remarkable exodus is now going on from it; men are retiring into private life just as the prizes of the profession are coming within their reach, because they find by the simplest calculation that the sterling[1] pension gives a better return than a nominal rise of salary in the depreciated rupee. To this class one great attraction, apart from the interest of the work and the sense of power it confers, has been that if the duties of the service were hard, and performed often in solitude and always in a bad climate, the life at least was one of ease and freedom from care about money matters. A man might live in comfort and yet lay by for his family. This attraction has disappeared, and the present members of the service are hurrying away from it to such

[1] A pension largely contributed to by deduction from their salaries.

an extent that there is already difficulty in securing men sufficiently experienced for the higher posts. But if this is the condition of the Civil Service *par excellence*, the class which fills all the higher posts in that country, that of the much larger class of public servants in other branches, Education, Post Office, Telegraph, Public Works, and others corresponding to the regular civil service at home, is still more serious. The pay of these has always been on a moderate scale, with only a small margin left after providing for the absolute necessaries of life in the East, which margin has altogether now disappeared. The officers of the army are in the same position. The public servant in India is placed at this disadvantage—that his official life there does not advance his interests to secure employment for his sons. The old system of patronage pure and simple was no doubt defective, even vicious in some respects, but at any rate it often enabled the public servant to put his sons in the way of gaining a similar livelihood, for the appointments given away were bestowed for the most part on the sons of public servants. The open competition system has put an end to this; but the public service is still practically the only career available for the sons of Indian officials, and to gain a place in this involves an education always expensive, and expensive in a special degree for those whose parents are living abroad. In any case the children must be sent home and educated there; the expense of sending a sick wife home, the loss of income caused by the breadwinner's own sickness, are more than mere contingencies. It was the means of meeting these expenses which it may be said alone made life in India bearable. Only if a man lived on rice and dressed in calico could he have met the fall in the rupee without loss; but his needs for the necessaries of life remain unaltered, while the price of everything has practically doubled. The result is that the life of the junior officers

CHAP. XX.

in India, military and civil, has become one of real poverty and hardship.

Nor have the necessities of the public servant himself only to be considered. The gravity of the present state of things, if unremedied, lies in its inevitable effect on the character of the administration. Indian officials are exposed to special temptations; it is not only unjust but dangerous that these should be increased. The present scale of salaries was established one hundred years ago to put a stop, not to corruption, but the irregular mode of emolument then in force. The Company was a trading body first, a governing body afterwards, and, under the lax views then held on the subject, their servants likewise were allowed to trade and derived almost all their emoluments from that source. This was put a stop to, and salaries were established on a scale, generous at the time and liberal for many years afterwards, with the result that the character of the Indian public servant became and remained absolutely pure. Reviled and slandered as are our Indian officials from week to week by an unbridled vernacular press, no suggestion of their corruptibility has ever been ventured upon; the charge would be too absurd to have any effect. But it is impossible to believe that this immunity can be maintained unless some remedy be applied to the hardship to which the Indian official is now subjected; when with his income practically reduced by one half, he finds it difficult to pay his way from day to day, and impossible to make any provision for his family or for old age. On all grounds, therefore, of justice to the present body of officials who were invited to enter the public service by expectations which have proved illusory, and to maintain the character and efficiency of the service in the present and future, a complete revision of the scale of pay with reference to the depreciation of the rupee is necessary. Something has been done in this direction after a not unnatural delay, but a far more complete and comprehensive measure of remedy will have to be carried out, and quickly; this involves a heavy additional charge. CHAP. XX.

Effect of fall in silver.

But while the government with its gold obligations is thus embarrassed by the fall of silver, and is in face of a position of financial difficulty which threatens to become still more acute, and in which it has only the consolation of being in no way responsible for the situation, nevertheless the fall of silver has not been without its compensations. It has not injured the tax-payer directly, and by stimulating exports has added to the trade of the country. Tested by every criterion for determining the condition of a country, the increase in internal traffic and foreign trade, and of the railway receipts, the capacity to buy and the capacity to produce, never were the people of India so prosperous as they are now. And if that country and its government were self-contained and without any liabilities to make gold payments, they might accept the present state of things with equanimity. It is not the silver-using countries which suffer directly by the fall in the value of silver. Indirectly indeed India does suffer through the discouragement given to the investment of English capital and especially in the check given to railway extension, the greatest present requirement of that country.

Stability of Indian finance.

Turning from the present to the past, one point comes out clearly from any enquiry into the subject—the remarkable stability of Indian finance. Wars have succeeded wars, and famine has followed upon famine, but the loans incurred for these account for only a small part of the expenditure involved. This was mainly defrayed from the revenue, year by year, and the debt incurred in the bad years was more than paid off in the good. The other special charges which have accrued of late years, as for the great works of harbour and frontier defence, have also been paid for, without borrowing, out of revenue from year to year. Few

CHAP. XX.

countries can show so good a record in this respect. Further, the financial condition has been even more satisfactory than appears on this view of it, in two important respects. First, as regards the so-called famine fund. The nature of this is frequently misapprehended. The liability of India to a recurrence of famine in some part or other of the country is only too well attested by the numerous visitations of that calamity during the historic period. A terrible famine occurred in Bengal in the latter end of the last century when many millions of persons perished; in 1833, the failure of the crops through the greater part of the North West Provinces created an enormous degree of distress and a great loss of revenue. In 1868–9 occurred the great famine in Orissa; the calamity falling on a roadless country, importing relief in the way of food became almost impossible. In later times the duty of conveying a food supply to the country affected by drought has been systematically undertaken by the Government, with a great mitigation of suffering, as in the famine of 1877 which extended over the part of Bengal north of the Ganges, but at an enormous cost. In 1877 a Commission was appointed, with Sir John Strachey—afterwards successively Lieutenant Governor of the North West Provinces, and financial member of the Government of India—at the head of it, to enquire into the whole subject of famine relief and to propose a definite system for coping with famines in future. Their report deals with the subject in a complete and comprehensive way. First, in place of a gratuitous distribution of food, they recommend the establishment of systematic relief works for the employment of the people whose crops have failed; and that only where the ordinary operations of private trade are insufficient to bring the supply of food to the famine-stricken districts, the agencies for this should be undertaken by the Government itself. But even still more important than an effective system

Famine relief fund.

of administering famine relief is the adoption of measures for preventing famine. Failure of the crops, indeed, can be averted only in those parts of the country where the configuration of the soil admits of the construction of irrigation works, but what would otherwise be famine may be reduced to the less terrible scarcity of food by improving the communications throughout the country, so as to furnish cheap transport. During the ten years ending in 1877, fifteen millions had been spent directly or indirectly upon famine relief. The Commission represented, therefore, that an average expenditure to this extent might be anticipated in the future, and that this indicated the necessity for providing a yearly surplus of at least one and a half millions in the prosperous years, in order that the revenue might suffice to meet the charge without a further increase of debt whenever famine should occur. This is the origin of the so-called Famine Relief Fund established in 1877, an action which embodied the intention of the Government to set aside one and a half millions yearly out of revenue to be applied to: 1. Relief works during the actual occurrence of famine. 2. The construction of railways and irrigation works in districts liable to famine. 3. Paying off debt in anticipation of the need for incurring fresh loans on the occurrence of famine. This sum was to be applied yearly out of revenue to one or other, or all, or any part of these objects; and the balance or surplus of the year was to be declared only after this sum of 1½ millions had been entered in the accounts as an item of the ordinary expenditure of the year. Thus supposing the sum to be wholly applied to paying off debt, then in ten years 15 millions would be paid off, and on the recurrence of famine involving an expenditure of that amount, and the contraction of a corresponding new loan, the net result would be to leave the public debt at the same figure as at the beginning of the operation: the

CHAP. XX. 15 millions borrowed would have been provided for out of revenue. So also if the $1\frac{1}{2}$ millions were devoted to railway making or irrigation works; the capital debt which otherwise would have been incurred for the purpose, would be *pro tanto* diminished, so that if eventually within the course of the ten years 15 millions had to be borrowed for famine expenditure, the sum total of debt obligations would not be increased, because 15 millions of railway capital which otherwise would have been borrowed had been provided out of revenue.

This is the operation of the so-called Famine Relief Fund. There was no fund in the proper sense of the term, as in the case of a bank setting aside a reserve; the operation merely expressed the determination to provide $1\frac{1}{2}$ millions a year before a surplus was declared as a charge of the year for one or other of purposes which properly are in the nature of capital expenses. But it is obvious that in order that the operation should be a real one there must be a surplus, or at any rate a financial equilibrium remaining after it has been carried out. If the result of entering the charge for this fund in the accounts is a deficit, the operation ceases to have any meaning. Expenditure on railways, for instance, cannot be provided out of revenue, when there is no surplus revenue from which to meet it; while if, as has happened in the present year, a loan has to be raised in order to provide for the ways and means of the year, it would obviously be a purposeless proceeding to go through the form of paying off debt on the one hand, and incurring a corresponding amount of new debt on the other. This explanation it may be hoped sufficiently disposes of the complaint which has been made by those who evidently did not understand the subject, that the Famine Fund has been abandoned. The fund, in the proper sense of the term, has never had any existence;

the action contemplated could from the nature of the case take effect only for so long as there was an available surplus, and must necessarily be suspended in a year of deficit. The allegation made in certain quarters, that inasmuch as extra taxation was imposed for the purpose of creating this fund, it is a breach of faith to apply the proceeds of that taxation to any other purpose, hardly needs a serious reply. Had the total expenditure of the country remained at the same amount from year to year, then when the necessity for obtaining this surplus no longer existed, the taxation imposed to produce it might have been remitted. But in lieu of a surplus there is now a deficit which more than absorbs these proceeds. The contention that in this or any system of finance the proceeds of any particular impost are ear-marked, and applicable to meet only one particular item of expenditure, would be raised only by persons unacquainted with the elementary principles of the subject. It would be as rational to contend that when a man takes a ride, so much of the distance covered is to be credited to the rider, and so much to the horse.

It was never contemplated that this annual provision for famine relief should be made perpetual. The Famine Commissioners reported that 20,000 miles of railway would suffice to ensure the means of cheap and speedy transport of food into every part of India liable to be affected with drought, of which 10,000 miles were already completed, but that even 5,000 more would go far to remove all further risk of serious difficulty in the supply of food to any part of any district in the whole country. Since that report was written 8,000 more miles of railway have been opened, and although this addition includes some lines on the frontier carried out for other objects, still the particular 5,000 miles which were most pressing from a famine point of view have been constructed. It may be said, therefore, that India

CHAP. XX.

has now been made safe in that respect; in proof of this, the failure of rain in Behar which occurred in 1888 and again in 1891, which was nearly equal in extent to that which occurred in 1877, and in consequence of which full preparations were again made for meeting a famine by a scheme of relief works, nevertheless produced only a severe scarcity, and the whole outlay of public money found necessary for purposes of relief was only between three and four lakhs. During the last thirteen years, since the report of the Commission and the establishment of this so-called Famine Fund, only about a third of a million has been spent on actual famine relief; the rest of the surplus set aside under this head has been appropriated—5½ millions to new railways, 1¾ millions to irrigation works, and 5½ millions to paying off debt. The total operations of the fund, therefore, have amounted to about 13 millions, and with that expenditure it may be said that the necessity for further outlay of the kind has come to an end. The scheme of famine protection has been carried out to the contemplated extent; the liability of the Government to incur a great expenditure on the direct relief of famine, in the supply of food or relief works, no longer exists.

Net surplus in recent years.

The Indian revenue during the eleven years ending in 1891–2 shows a balance of surplus of 8 millions; if to this be added 12¾ millions spent on Famine Relief operations,[1] an outlay which any other government would have paid for by raising loans for the purpose, the virtual surplus during this period has been nearly 21 millions. This is not a bad record. A period of deficits has now been entered on, due to the fall of silver, but as regards the finance of the future, a new and very satisfactory element of Indian finance arising

[1] Three millions more have been charged to the same account in succeeding years, but as there have been deficits in these years of nearly the same amount, the money was not provided from revenue and is therefore omitted from this statement.

Financial bearing of the railways.

out of the State railway operations has to be considered. This has already been referred to in some detail in the preceding chapter. The Indian Government possesses in the railways it owns already, and others of which it may become the owner, a highly valuable and rapidly improving property. The general result of the railway accounts shows at present a deficit, or net charge over receipts, of one and a half millions a year; but, as has been explained, this is mainly due to temporary causes which should soon disappear. The military frontier lines, indeed, which account for a small part of the loss, are not, and probably never will be, directly remunerative. But of the commercial lines owned by the Government, or of which the interest on the capital is guaranteed, some have been lately opened, and are not in full working order; all of them promise to be remunerative in the early future. The most important of the older lines are paying good dividends, although the cost of converting these into the gold guaranteed interest still imposes a charge on the revenue, but this rate of interest should be largely reduced when the Government purchase the lines on the expiry of the contracts now running. But further, the Government is not paying only the yearly interest on its railway capital account, it is, in effect, buying up these railways by the substitution of terminable annuities for the fixed annual interest. The increased charge constitutes therefore an investment, by means of which the Government will eventually become the owner of this great and valuable property. To this extent the finance accounts are actually better than they look, so far as that the future is being provided for in the present; and the nominal deficit of the year to that extent disappears. Whether the tax-payer in the present should be called upon to this extent for the relief of obligations in the future must be a matter of opinion which does not admit of being definitely determined one way or the

CHAP. XX.

other; but considering the liability under which the Government of India is placed to meet possible calls in the future for military and political purposes, calls to be met from a revenue which, if steadily improving, is still inelastic, and not readily susceptible of large or rapid augmentation—the form of insurance exhibited by this gradual discharge of existing liabilities will probably be deemed not to err on the side of excessive prudence. At any rate, the financial conditions which admit of even a limited outlay on railway construction, and the process of extinguishing the railway debt being regularly carried on, cannot be otherwise than intrinsically sound. There is indeed just now a dark shadow thrown over the situation by the loss in exchange, which threatens to become ever larger, and the consequences of which it is impossible to foresee, or for the Indian Government of itself to provide against, and which may baffle all the efforts dictated by prudence and foresight. Yet, on the other hand, the danger may pass away again. Another great discovery of gold, and it might be dissipated as quickly as it arose. Not that the matter need be left to chance. There is of course a definite remedy. This is not the place for an essay on bimetallism, but so much at least may be said, that it is not the silver-using countries which suffer alone, or suffer most from the fall in value of that metal, a fact slowly but surely forcing itself on the comprehension of even the most prejudiced and hard of understanding. As soon as the conversion of the English treasury to sound economic principles is accomplished, a currency reform to relieve both England and India of present difficulties will come within measurable distance of accomplishment.[1]

Loss by exchange.

[1] When Sir William Harcourt complacently announces that he pins his faith upon a gold standard for England and a silver standard for India as the only sound currency basis, and spurns the bimetallic 'nostrum,' one is reminded of the address of M. Diafoirus, senior, in *Le Malade Imaginaire*, when in recommendation of his son, Dr. Thomas Diafoirus, he says: 'Above everything, what I admire in him—in which he follows my example—is that he is blindly attached to

CHAP. XX.

Fiscal resources available.

No one familiar with India would lightly entertain the idea of additional taxation to meet the difficulty, although that country is more lightly taxed at present than it has been at almost any previous time. But one source of revenue, free from the objections apparent to every other form of impost, is to be found in the restoration of the cotton duties. The history of this case is still so fresh in recollection that it is not necessary to recapitulate it. That the tax has not yet been imposed is due, not to any consideration for the people of India, but simply to the supposed exigencies of party government at home. The principle involved, however, goes far beyond one of pure finance. It opens up the larger question, whether the government of India is to be conducted in sympathy with the interests and feelings of the people of that country, or in accordance with the small and shifting policy of party needs; as to which it may be said that, unless the steps lately taken are retraced, an injury will be done to the good faith and character of the British Government of India, which may and probably will lead to far reaching consequences.

Provincial Finance.

Provincial finance, how far practicable.

We have so far been dealing with the revenue and expenditure of India as a whole. The different provincial governments have also certain financial responsibilities, involving a system of provincial or local finance, as it is termed, of which some account may here be given. First it should be explained that this is something quite different from what might be inferred from the published records. For example, to the general account showing the revenue and expenditure of all India, a supplementary account is attached, professing to show the distribution of the different heads of re-

the opinions of our forefathers, and that he altogether objects to listen to the reasons and experiences of the pretended discoveries of the age, touching the circulation of the blood and stuff of that kind.'

CHAP. XX.

Misleading form of provincial accounts published by India Office.

ceipts and expenditure among the various provinces into which British India is divided; and at first sight it might appear as if the Indian system of finance were primarily provincial, and that the imperial finances were built up simply by collecting together the several financial operations of these provinces, and so arriving at a general account for the whole country; that is, as if the general surplus of the year was the sum of surpluses contributed by the various provinces after deducting the deficits of those provinces which do not pay their way. Such a view, although thus favoured by a superficial aspect of the accounts as presented,[1] would be however wholly erroneous. It may be observed that this distributed account contains, besides columns for the different provinces, a column with the heading 'India, General,' in which are entered the operations of the departments—post office, telegraph, &c., directly under the Government of India, with which the Provincial Governments are not concerned. This heading, 'India, General,' also comprises the operations of various smaller provinces which are not provided with separate columns of their own; and several items of revenue, of which salt, two millions, is the highest, are placed in that column, because the collection was effected in one or other of those smaller provinces. The railway receipts, also, shown in this column, are the receipts of the railways which are administered directly by the Government of India. On the other hand, the different provinces are not charged with military expenditure. The mode of showing this is indeed especially misleading, it is not all placed in the column 'India, General,' but is distributed between that and the columns for Madras and Bombay. As a matter of fact, the expenditure is all incurred by the Government of India and accounted for in one central office, and

[1] See, for example, the tables from p. 98 of the *Statistical Abstract of British India* for 1892–3.

afterwards distributed under these heads. This mode of exhibiting the military expenditure, which is one of the last surviving relics of the old Presidency system, is thus absolutely inaccurate. The military expenditure shown under 'Madras' is not merely the military expenditure incurred in that province, but includes that incurred in Burma, Mysore, and several other provinces; the amount of military expenditure shown under 'Bombay' is equally inaccurate.

This account therefore gives no indication of the financial position of any one of the provinces. In order to arrive at an estimate of this, it would be necessary that all the general charges—as for the post office, &c., should be distributed among them. Many other adjustments would need to be made. The sea customs are collected at the seaports, but obviously the provinces in which these seaports are situated are not entitled to the whole of these duties. So also Bengal is credited with the revenue derived from all the opium manufactured in the north and east of India, because the administration charges of all the opium agencies of those parts are entered in the Bengal column. Bombay again is credited with the profits of the excise duty levied on the opium exported from the port of Bombay, none of which however is grown in the province of Bombay. The railway accounts are equally misleading as any indication of the conditions of provincial finance. The railway transactions, *e.g.*, shown under 'Punjab,' do not refer to the railways within that province alone, but to the transactions of the great system of frontier railways known as the North Western Railway, which extends throughout Sind and far into Baluchistan beyond the limits of the Punjab province.

Even if it were practicable to make this general adjustment of revenues and charges over the different provinces on a rational basis, no equitable distribution could be arrived at of the military charges. The troops

CHAP. XX.

massed in Punjab are a protection to the whole of India, and admit of Bengal being denuded of troops; but how much of the cost of the Punjab garrison should be charged to the defence of Bengal it is obviously impossible to determine. Even if this and all the other adjustments could be effected, there remains the interest on the public debt, for which no sort of provincial allocation is practicable. It is quite impossible to predicate of any particular loan that it was contracted on behalf of any particular province or provinces.

Decentralisation of Indian Finances impracticable.

The practicability, therefore, of establishing any system of provincial finance based on total revenues and charges, such as has been proposed at different times by politicians and writers with the view of decentralising the labours of the Indian Government, disappears at once when the matter is looked into. The interests and obligations of the different parts of the country cannot be separated or distinguished from each other. And this being so, nothing useful is indicated in this direction by the so-called provincial accounts now published. The figures given in the different columns in which the items are distributed do not represent the respective claims and responsibilities of the different provinces; the columns to which these names are given merely represent the geographical distribution of the different agencies through which the financial business of the Government of India is conducted, and through which the revenues are collected and the expenditure defrayed. Even so there is in most cases nothing provincial about them. The revenue and expenditure, for instance, shown under 'Bombay' represent the revenue and expenditure which pass through the books of the Accountant General at Bombay, and so with the other provinces. But the different Accountants General of provinces are imperial officers belonging to one of the departments acting directly under the Indian Finance Minister. Even where the fiscal officer concerned belongs to the local service, as the collector of excise or opium, his proceedings are regulated entirely by the financial department of the supreme government, and the intervention of the local government in the business is purely formal. In short, the figures exhibited, although they may be serviceable to the Finance Department itself, fulfil no useful purpose as regards the public; they are simply calculated to mislead the inquirer, and might advantageously be omitted from all future returns.

But provincial governments should have financial powers and responsibilities.

But although a system of provincial finance in the sense indicated is from the nature of the case impracticable, that the different provincial governments should be without any financial responsibility has always been a grave defect of the Indian administrative system. As was pointed out in the former editions of this work, these governments, with all the high-sounding apparatus of governors and councils provided for some of them, were really nothing more in fact than the administrative agents of the supreme Government. But while they had no interest in financial economy, they had a strong interest in obtaining the largest possible share of the public money each for their own province. This condition of things was thoroughly unsound and provocative of extravagance, and a practical reform of it was urged in the earlier editions of this work, the following extract from which explains the case as it then stood, and indicated the sort of form by which the needful object could be effected:—

'Thus, in effect, the general finance department is dependent rather on the forbearance and loyalty of the different provincial administrations for securing adherence to its estimates, than on the action of its own officers. The law invests the Supreme Government with the most complete authority in regard to every kind of expenditure, but there is practically no means of enforcing it, for the only effectual check against an

CHAP. XX.

abuse of their opportunities by the local authorities must necessarily be reserved for serious cases of financial insubordination. Small breaches of rule cannot be treated with this gravity, and they will always be condoned by public opinion. That a body, which in all its outward forms appears little removed in dignity and importance from the Supreme Government of India, should in reality have none of the attributes of a government, but be merely the executive agent of the central authority, is a relation hard to be distinctly apprehended by the public either in England or India, while it is one which the subordinate authority continually chafes under, and struggles to escape from. Unfortunately, the efforts at liberty are made only in one direction. The Supreme Government is perpetually embarrassed by the occurrence of expenditure which it has not authorised, or which it would fain avoid, while no spontaneous efforts are made to assist it with additional revenue. The provincial governments have a direct and very lively interest in obtaining for their share the largest possible amount of the public expenditure. Their dignity and importance, and their popularity both with the public and with the services, will be enhanced by a liberal expenditure, as will also indeed their administrative efficiency and the prosperity of the country, while the local press will always be ready to applaud any instances of outlay incurred for local purposes against the wishes of the supreme authority. On the other hand, the provincial government has no immediate interest in increasing the revenue, for any addition made will not appear in any tangible form to the credit of the contributing province, but will be merged in the general revenues. Nor is it only, or even mainly, in matters of new expenditure that this embarrassment is created. No doubt the sentiment of obedience is usually sufficient to restrain the local authorities, even although there may not be the distinct means of enforcing it. But it is, perhaps, rather in cases where reduction in existing expenditure is desired that the Government of India feels most distinctly its financial isolation. In such cases retrenchment has usually to be carried out, not only with the co-operation of the provincial governments, but often against their vigorous opposition. On these occasions the Government of India finds itself on one side, and all the local authorities arrayed on the other; while the latter, regarding the effect of expenditure merely as it increases their administrative efficiency, and being in no way concerned with the financial result, are always armed each with abundant reasons why reduction is impossible, or why, at any rate, it should not be applicable to their own province in particular. These ill-regulated financial conditions sufficiently explain the unsatisfactory relations so often obtaining between the supreme and subordinate governments, particularly those of Madras and Bombay, where the panoply of councils and ministerial officers with which they are surrounded renders their legal financial status especially incongruous, and because the privilege which they possess of corresponding directly with the home authorities often commits the Indian Government to expenditure against its own wishes. The same thing occurs more or less in every other quarter. There is everywhere manifested the same desire to secure administrative efficiency with the same indifference about the provision of the needful means. Thus India, in its financial aspect, is a federation of a most defective kind, in which there is no proper distribution of responsibility, and where, from the nature of the case, the interests of the central and local authorities are liable to be constantly opposed. The remedy for this state of things is to be found in that re-adjustment of the financial system already advocated, under which the contribution to be paid by each province to imperial pur-

CHAP. XX.

poses should be limited to a fixed sum, and the balance of its revenues should be available for its own expenditure. Another practicable arrangement would be, while retaining certain sources of revenue as imperial, to place others at the entire disposal of the local government, with the proviso that certain branches of expenditure which are now defrayed from the imperial exchequer should henceforth be met from these local revenues. Under either method the provincial government would be invested with a distinct financial responsibility and interest in financial success; and while such a redistribution would not only lead the way to new methods of taxing, it presents the only effective plan for putting a stop to the administrative extravagance which is the cause of the present financial embarrassments. None but a very strong government could resist the continued pressure put on it from all parts of the country for increased expenditure in every branch of the service, and the Indian Government has often been in its financial administration exceedingly weak. But let the provincial governments be thrown on their own resources, and they will soon learn to limit their wants by their available surplus; and that zeal for material progress which is now so often found in company with a lofty disregard for the ways and means of effecting it, will no doubt be succeeded by a more business-like and sober temperament.'[1]

System adopted for securing this.

The method of provincial finance which has been actually adopted carries out the principle thus advocated. Any attempt at decentralisation, in the sense of creating a system of provincial finance complete and self-contained, the budgets and accounts of which, when brought together, would make up a general budget and account for the whole of India, is impracticable for the reasons already given. What has been done is this.

[1] *Indian Polity*, 2nd edition, p. 439.

To each province there has been credited a fixed part of certain items of the revenue collected within the province, against which is charged all the purely civil expenditure of the province; the surplus, if any, arising on this account, is held to be at the disposal of the local government. The apportionment of revenue so made is purely arbitrary, and varies for the different provinces according to their relative prosperity. But generally these hypothecations comprise about one-fourth of the land revenue and the excise, three-fourths of that from stamps, seven-ninths of the assessed taxes, three-fifths of the forest revenue, and certain differing shares of the other items. Irrigation revenue, also, is brought into the account; for example, in the North West Provinces the provincial account is charged with interest on the capital cost of the works at 4 per cent., and credited with the net revenue derived from them.[1]

Provincial contracts.

The arrangement thus set up between the supreme and each provincial government in no way affects the mode of conducting or exhibiting the public accounts. These are still wholly imperial, and the revenues received and payments made on whatever account are still recorded as such. There is no setting aside any part of the monies, either in the way of establishing separate stocks of coin, or even of an account. Nor are the provincial governments absolved from the rules requiring the sanction of superior authority—the Government of India or the Secretary of State, as the case may be—for all new establishments, or for increasing the salaries of members of existing establishments when those are in excess of a certain specified amount. Nor does this apparent hypothecation of the

[1] This debit of interest on capital is a purely paper entry; the cost of these works has been long ago defrayed, partly out of revenue from year to year; what remained as capital debt created has been merged in the general debt accounts of the empire.

revenue appear in the public accounts; the transactions in question are recorded in a supplementary account, such as that which a landowner might keep with his agent in respect of a particular estate, on the understanding that the surplus income from this, after all expenses were paid, should be available at the discretion of the latter for the improvement of the estate; or the account which a man might keep with his wife, if while himself paying all the family bills he agreed that any surplus arising on a certain fixed part of his income set aside for housekeeping, should be at her disposal to spend as she might wish. The practical effect of the arrangement is, that whereas formerly all proposals of a provincial government for increased expenditure of any sort were simply made on their merits, unaccompanied by any suggestions for finding ways and means, the burden of which fell wholly on the central authority, the provincial government is now bound to show that means are available from the balances accruing on the provincial accounts. Or, in cases where the expenditure is of a kind not involving the necessity for reference to higher authority, the provincial government can employ the available surplus arising in the province at its own discretion. This is especially the case in regard to public works, including such railways as are now placed virtually under provincial management.

These provincial contracts, as they are called, which are made for a term of years, thus give to the provincial governments a strong interest in keeping down unnecessary expenditure, because the larger the balance accruing on the contract, the more they have available for provincial purposes to spend at their discretion. It should be added that the Government of India necessarily claims the right, in case of urgent necessity, to levy contributions on the provincial balances in aid of the imperial exchequer, a claim obviously just and reasonable. The provincial governments must take their share in bearing the financial strain caused by the fall in the rupee, or any similar difficulty. Such an emergency has twice arisen since the system was introduced. CHAP. XX.

This explanation indicates the need of the entries shown in the Budget to record these provincial agreements. In the account of 1893–94, for example (p. 329), a deduction of Rx478,800 is made from the total imperial expenditure, in order to arrive at the net charge of the year. The reason for making the entry will be readily understood from what has gone before. The expenditure of a provincial government is part of the imperial expenditure, and is shown under the respective heads of the services concerned—civil administration, public works, and so forth. But a debtor and creditor account is kept with each province, the proportion of revenue allotted to it being shown on the one side and the provincial expenditure on the other; and upon this account a balance has, in the course of time, arisen to the credit of each province. If a provincial government were to spend in a year exactly the amount credited to it in that year, this balance would be unaltered, but such a precise identity between receipts and expenditure can never happen in practice. If, then, the provincial expenditure in a year is more than the proportion of revenue it is entitled to take credit for, the excess must involve a reduction to that extent of the balance at credit of the province. But the liability of the imperial government being to that extent reduced, the total of the imperial expenditure should be correspondingly reduced. Similarly, if the provincial balance increases during the year by an excess of receipts over expenditure, although only that expenditure which has been actually incurred can be detailed in the public accounts, yet this increase to the provincial balance forms a new liability which must be

Adjusting entries in finance accounts.

CHAP. XX.

added to the total expenditure of the year, although as it has not been actually disbursed it cannot be distributed over any particular heads of service.[1]

The introduction of these provincial contracts, by making the different subordinate governments shareholders with the Supreme Government in financial profits and interested in maintaining economy, has constituted a valuable administrative reform. They can still have no concern with army expenditure, nor with the public debt, the operations connected with which are for the most part conducted in England; and many other general charges can be dealt with only by a central authority; further, the portion of the revenues to be allotted to a province, must, as has been explained, necessarily be determined in an arbitrary way. But with their powers even thus limited, the different provincial governments are for the first time invested with the attributes attaching to the name. What is now required is to carry the change still further in the direction of giving them greater and independent authority to deal with matters of expenditure, especially in regard to charges for establishments. It may be added that a similar delegation of authority to the Supreme Government in this respect is greatly to be desired. At present the Governor General in Council cannot sanction a pension of five rupees a month, but must refer the case to the India Office. Great is the waste of time and money involved in such references, but the love of centralisation is to be found in every bureaucratic body, and the practice of requiring them will perhaps not be readily abandoned.

Further powers should be given to provincial governments, and supreme government.

[1] The case may be illustrated by the analogous case of a landed proprietor who we may suppose agrees to allow his Scotch and Irish stewards each 1,000*l.* a year for the up keep of his estates in those countries respectively. The one spends 1,300*l.* in the year, anticipating his allowance by 300*l.*: the other spends only 900*l.*, carrying forward 100*l.* to next year. The landlord's actual cash outlay is thus 2,200*l.*, but in making up his accounts for the year he would deduct 200*l.* in order to arrive at his virtual expenditure as compared with his income. So with the Government of India *vis-à-vis* to the Provincial Governments.

CHAPTER XXI

THE HOME GOVERNMENT OF INDIA

CHAP. XXI.

Earliest jurisdiction by Court of Directors.

The body of merchants styled the East India Company derived their authority from charters given by the Crown, the first of which was granted by Queen Elizabeth in 1601. These were renewed with modifications at various times, the last of them being a charter granted in 1752 by King George II. Under these charters the Company had in course of time undergone various changes from its original form, and was invested with authority to raise troops, to carry on war, and to occupy territories in India and the Eastern Seas. The first statutory recognition of British India is contained in the Act of 1773,[1] by which the administration of India was vested in a Governor General and a Council at Fort William, in Bengal. This Act however did not touch the home administration of the Company, which remained under its ruling body, the Court of Directors, until the passing of Pitt's bill of 1784,[2] known as the Regulating Bill, which created the Board of Control over Indian affairs, an organisation which lasted until the abolition of the rule of the East India Company in 1858. This body was to consist of not more than six Privy Councillors, three of them being the two principal Secretaries of State—the whole number then existing—and the Chancellor of the Exchequer. Three of the members constituted a board, the senior of them, in

Board of Control.

[1] 13 Geo. III, C. 63. [2] 24 Geo. III, C. 25.

CHAP. XXI.

the absence of a Secretary of State or the Chancellor, was to preside. All the commissioners might sit in Parliament. The Board was vested with full power and authority to direct and control all operations and concerns which in any wise related to or concerned the civil and military governments and revenues of India. The inclusion of the Secretaries of State and the Chancellor of the Exchequer provided for the business of the Board being brought when necessary under the view and within the control of the Cabinet. But the active and practically the sole control of affairs rested with the nominated commissioners, whose salaries were chargeable to the revenues of India.

The provisions of the Act of 1784 regarding the Board of Control were slightly modified by the Act of 1793,[1] in which the first Commissioner named in the Letters Patent constituting it was declared to be the President of the Board. It was also provided that two Commissioners might be appointed from outside the Privy Council, and that the Secretary might be a Member of Parliament, so that his office became a party appointment. Under this change the collective action of the Board appears to have become little more than a fiction, and it consisted virtually of the President alone, who was always a member of the Cabinet, with the parliamentary secretary as his mouthpiece in the House of Commons, if he was a peer. In the India Act of 1833[2] no specific number of Commissioners was laid down, and the qualification of belonging to the Privy Council was omitted: they might be 'such persons as His Majesty shall think fit to be and who shall accordingly be styled Commissioners for the affairs of India.' Accordingly, after the passing of that Act the number of Commissioners was reduced first to four and later to two, including the President; and in 1841 and afterwards only a single Commissioner (the President of the

[1] 33 Geo. III, C. 52. [2] 3-4 William IV, C. 85.

Board) was appointed, the first to hold the office under these conditions being Lord Ellenborough, who filled it for a few months until appointed Governor-General of India.[1]

From 1841 therefore the Board as a matter of fact had ceased to exist, although the officer who exercised its functions was still styled President of the Board, this being one of the numerous legal fictions which abound in our administrative system.

Procedure for exercising control over Company.

Means of exercising the control contemplated by the Act of 1784 and succeeding Acts were very fully provided therein. Not only was the Board given full access to all the records and correspondence of the Company; the Court of Directors were also required to supply copies of all orders and despatches sent to India within eight days of sending them, and all despatches from India immediately on the receipt of them. No order could be sent to India without being first submitted to the Board for approval; full power was given to the Board to make any alterations in the despatch, which the Court were bound to send in its altered form after, if they so desired, an exchange of opinions thereon; and if the Court failed to frame despatches within fourteen days, the Board might itself frame the despatches which the Court was bound to send on. Further a 'Secret Committee' of the Court, limited to three members (in practice to two, the Chairman and Deputy Chairman,) was constituted and sworn to secrecy, through which Committee the Board might send secret orders to the Government of India, which the Secret Committee was bound to transmit as from themselves. Similarly, any despatches from India marked 'Secret' were to be recorded at the India House in the Secret Committee, and delivered to the Board without being seen by the other Directors.

Secret Committee.

[1] He had held the office also on two previous occasions under the old conditions.

CHAP. XXI.

It is a remarkable illustration of the illusive effect of form in constitutional affairs, that although these provisions which transferred all real power and authority from the Company to the Crown were clearly set forth in an Act of Parliament and repeated in succeeding ones, the circumstance that the Court of Directors was still maintained as the ostensible ruling authority and the actual channel of communication between the Governments in India and at home, nevertheless sufficed entirely to disguise from public attention the actual state of things. For the period of three-quarters of a century during which this system remained in force, it was popularly supposed that the Court of Directors were alone conducting and controlling all the affairs of India. Sir Charles Napier and his brother biographer denounced the Court and some of the Directors by name in virulent terms for withholding prize money claimed to be due to the former for the conquest of Sind, a proceeding for which a single member of the Cabinet was immediately responsible, and with which the majority of the Court had nothing to do, and no official knowledge of. Similar ignorance obtained generally among the English public. Much public astonishment was expressed when Sir John Hobhouse stated before a Select Committee of the House of Commons that the invasion of Afghanistan in 1838 had been carried out wholly by his orders as President of the Board. Great is the force of official shams.

Patronage reserved to Court of Directors.

But while the minister whose individuality was concealed by the apparatus of a board was thus generally omnipotent in the direction of Indian affairs, his powers were limited in one important respect. The Board of Control could not increase salaries or grant allowances or gratuities, except on the proposal of the Court first made and after reporting the matter to Parliament—a condition which placed a salutary check on jobbery in appointments. And the Company were left for a time their monopoly of trade to the East; the monopoly was restricted by the Act of 1813 to trade with India, while in 1833 their trading powers were abolished. And to the Court was left all patronage of appointments to India; the nomination, subject to the approval of the Board, of the Governor General, the Governors of Presidencies and Commanders-in-Chief, and all first appointments to the civil and military services. This patronage was the great object of a seat on the Court, a position gained, not by meritorious services or personal distinction, but through election by the proprietors of East India Stock, the canvass for which, always long pursued, often through many defeats in order to obtain eventual success, was as degrading as such a pursuit must be. The goal once reached, the Director received his share out of the general fund of nominations to the Indian services, which was equally distributed among the collective body, the Chairman and Deputy Chairman of the Court (offices filled in rotation) getting however a double share. This was patronage pure and simple, bestowed without any divided responsibility, and for the most part entirely on private grounds. A Director might sometimes give his nomination to the son of a distinguished officer, but no instance is on record of the Court collectively awarding a single nomination to the relative of a public servant in recognition of his merits. And the bestowal of nominations naturally followed the order of value; sons and nephews were appointed to the Civil Service, or if they were not clever enough to pass even the very limited test of qualification laid down for that service, then to the well paid Cavalry. Next in value came direct appointments to the Infantry, and, lastly, for those who had the least personal claims, nominations to the Company's Military College at Addiscombe, the cadets from which supplied the Artillery and Engineers—services in which promotion was excep-

Addiscombe and Haileybury.

CHAP. XXI. tionally slow; while the cadets who failed to come up to the standard for those services were appointed to the Infantry. The educational arrangements of the Court were in strict keeping with the relative directorial interests; Haileybury College, where the young civilian was educated, was maintained on a reasonable scale of comfort, and equipped with a very able staff of professors, while a shower of prizes descended on the students. At Addiscombe the cadets were badly lodged and insufficiently fed, while the place was altogether lacking in the appliances for military training as for recreation; there was no riding school or gymnasium; not even a fives court. A high standard of work was maintained at the top of each class, owing to the competition among the cadets to gain places in the Engineers or Artillery; but although the hours of study were inordinately long, leaving to the industrious cadet absolutely no time for exercise, save a little perfunctory drill, the standard of qualification for the Infantry was of the lowest, and might be reached after two years of continuous idleness. No medical examination was imposed on candidates for the Army, and it was an illustration of the Company's system that the Military Secretary at the India Office was a senior clerk on the establishment who had passed his life peaceably in London. But indeed there was nothing in the composition of the Court of Directors to qualify them for the government of India in any part of its affairs, and all the arrangements connected with it indicated the inadequacy of such a body to the duty. That the result was not unsuccessful on the whole for many years was because they interfered so little with the actual administration of India, and because the conditions of that country developed a body of statesmen and soldiers equal to the task. But although the action of the Court and the Board of Control was generally that of a drag on progress, this obstruction was not necessarily exercised on the side of real caution. There is no evidence to show that any warning was ever given by these bodies, or any sense exhibited of the danger of denuding the older provinces of British troops with the extension of their territories, or of the continual expansion of the great overgrown homogeneous Bengal army; and it was the rule of seniority strictly maintained by the Court, not only in regimental promotion, but in succession to commands, which as much as anything contributed to the decadence of the Indian military system and the catastrophe of the Mutiny.

Abolition of Court of Directors and Board of Control, and appointment of Secretary of State and Council of India.

In 1858 the Government of India passed from the East India Company to the Crown, and the administration of the Court of Directors came to an end. The Act of Parliament passed in that year[1] after many and long debates abolished the Board of Control, and invested the home government of India in a Secretary of State with a Council. The constitution of this Council was especially the subject of protracted discussion in the House of Commons, in which the leading members of both sides took a prominent part. It was ultimately decided that the Council should consist of fifteen persons, of whom eight were to be appointed by the Court from their own body, the other seven by the Crown. Vacancies arising in the first class were to be filled up by election of the Council, vacancies in the second class by the Crown. The major part of the Councillors were to be persons who had resided ten years at least in India, and who should not have left India more than ten years before appointment. The appointment of a Councillor, who was ineligible to sit in Parliament, was to be held during good behaviour, but he was to be removable on an address by both Houses of Parliament. Business was to be transacted by the Council collectively; all

[1] 21 & 22 Vict., C. 106.

CHAP. XXI.

despatches to India were to be signed by the Secretary of State, to whom also all correspondence from India was to be addressed. Power was given to the Secretary of State to override the decision of a majority of his Council, his reason for so doing being formally recorded, when any members of the Council present might also record their opinions. The machinery of the Secret Committee was maintained, but its powers were concentrated in the person of the Secretary of State, who was authorised to send out secret despatches to the Governor of India which would not be seen by any of his councillors; similarly, despatches from the Government of India marked 'secret' were to be seen only by him, and were not to be communicated to the Council. The Act further provided that no grant of any part of the Indian revenues could be made without the concurrence of a majority of votes at a meeting of Council.

Changes made in Council.

These provisions are still in force, but some modifications have been made in the constitution of the Council. In 1869 an amending Act was passed [1] putting an end to the election of a portion of the Councillors, and providing that all appointments to that body should be made by the Secretary of State instead of by the Crown. The Members of Council were to be appointed for ten years and to be ineligible for reappointment, save for special reasons to be set forth in a minute by the Secretary of State to be laid before both Houses of Parliament. Members of Council appointed before the passing of the Act were to be eligible for pensions on retirement after ten years' service therein. It was explained in the debates on the measure that this provision was introduced to encourage retirement, and so to admit of fresh appointments being made of men of recent Indian experience.

In 1876 another amending Act was passed,[2] under which the Secretary of State may appoint not more

[1] 32-33 Vict., C. 97.

[2] 39 Vict., C. 7.

than three members to the Council for life, with pension after specified length of service, such members not being subject to the condition of ten years' previous service in India, the reasons for such appointments to be set forth in a minute laid before Parliament. The object of this change was explained by the introducers of the Bill in both Houses to be to admit of the appointment of lawyers to the Council; the provision has been applied also to admit men of English financial and banking experience and unconnected with India. By an Act passed in 1889[1] the number of councillors was reduced prospectively from fifteen to ten.

Reduction in numbers.

Effect of the change.

It might appear at first sight that the change of government introduced in 1858 was merely one in name. The Crown—that is the British Government for the time being—had possessed for three-quarters of a century the means of exercising complete control over the affairs of India. All, therefore, that was apparently effected by the change was to bring the member of the Cabinet who had charge of Indian affairs into more direct communication with the permanent body which shared the administration with him, and as regards this body to substitute for the old and vicious system of election by the holders of India stock, direct appointment by the Government, a change calculated to secure in a much higher degree the appointment of distinguished and experienced men to the Council. But, as has been pointed out more than once in this work, in order to appreciate the full effect of the administrative changes effected by a change in the law we must go behind the verbal provisions and examine its effect on the actual course of procedure. The law gave the President of the Board of Control (a body which latterly had no existence) power to override completely the Court of Directors if he chose to exert it. But the law also prescribed that the initiation of business

[1] 52 & 53 Vict. C. 65.

CHAP. XXI.

should ordinarily rest with the Court; and in public affairs it is the man who initiates who has the real power. The Court received the despatches from India in the first instance, discussed them and submitted to the Board the drafts of the despatches which they proposed to send in reply. The President of the Board might alter these drafts or substitute others in the place of them. But to do this constantly or even frequently involved a power of work as well as a power of will seldom, if ever, to be found combined in a man working single-handed, a busy Cabinet Minister, who, even if zealous and industrious, could not give the whole of his time to the business of his department, but who was often indolent, and always came to it profoundly ignorant of the matters to be dealt with. Add that while the Court had a large office and an able permanent staff, the President of the Board had only a small office; further, that the responsibility of overriding the Court was exercised only in secret, and that he would receive no credit for any proceedings taken, and it will be readily understood what course the business under such circumstances would naturally follow. The President indeed sometimes intervened with great effect by placing business in the Secret Department and so removing it from cognisance of the Court—sometimes with disastrous effect, as in the case of the invasion of Afghanistan in 1838. But generally the conduct of business rested with the Court. Their proceedings however being subject to the cognisance and approval of the Government, they were divested of all legal responsibility for the consequences.

Necessity for a Council.

The change in the law, therefore, by entirely altering the course of procedure, has necessarily brought about a fundamental change of system. The Secretary of State is now publicly responsible for everything; he is addressed in name by the Indian Government, and signs all the despatches issued from the India Office.

The rapid communication now established between the two countries, the greater public interest taken in Indian affairs, and the larger quantity of business to be transacted in this country in connection with the finances, the prosecution of railways, and indeed with every department of affairs, involve the constant interposition of the home authorities; the proper organisation of the Home Government becomes, therefore, a subject of extreme importance. The less the Government in India is interfered with the better; but interference of some sort is unavoidable at every point. Apart from the large amount of business connected with India which has to be transacted in this country, the constant disposition evinced by sections of political parties to interfere with the Indian administration involves the necessity for a strong and efficient representative agency in this country; not merely a responsible official with access to information, but an instructed and experienced department to deal with it. For the conduct of the Colonial Office little more is needed than the power of mind capable of dealing with the matters set forth in official papers containing little that is special or technical in character, or that cannot readily be understood by any well educated person. And the business of the Colonial Office is comparatively unimportant, for the colonies in regard to which any direct action can be taken by the British Government are few and small. But as to the competency of any man suddenly appointed to the duty, however able and well educated he be, to deal adequately with the questions arising out of the Indian administration; if we consider how those who have passed a lifetime in that country and taken the largest share in its administration are yet sensible of the imperfection and incompleteness of their knowledge of it, we may understand the absolute insufficiency of any man who, perhaps when past middle age, finds himself

CHAP. XXI.

charged with the administration of affairs strange, complex, and multifarions as are those of the Indian Government, to which he comes not only ignorant, but about which he has probably never before given a serious thought. The impossibility of entrusting the control of Indian affairs to a single party official will therefore be at once apparent. The power which some statesmen so placed have exhibited by exceptional industry and ability, of mastering at any rate the elementary subject matter of the business of the Indian department is indeed as remarkable as creditable to themselves; but the ordinary politician transferred to that office from the respectable discharge of routine duties of some department requiring little more than nominal control, who perhaps owes his elevation to talent in debate, a talent which, while it necessarily carries with it great weight in this country, may yet be unaccompanied by business habits or industry; such a man going to the India Office, often late in life, will not unnaturally shrink from the great and distasteful labour involved in the attempt to overcome his absolute ignorance of the very elements of the subject he has to deal with. Still more will he be likely to evade the task when party exigencies leave him only a shred of his time for the purpose. This ignorance may be concealed from the public to a certain extent by the written answers prepared for him which he reads out in reply to questions put in Parliament; and if in the unavoidable personal communications he has to hold with officials from India and others, he keeps to vague generalities, he may hide it to a certain extent from those with whom he has to do business, and so may not only enter upon but give up charge of his department, utterly ignorant of India, its people, and affairs. And not only does party government involve vacation of office just as perhaps the minister is beginning to get a glimmering of the business of his department; it often happens that the Indian Minister is changed even during the short life of a Government, by promotion, as it is called, to some higher office, or at least to some post which brings him more prominently before the public, and enables him to take a more active share in the business of his party. It would be thought an absurd thing if any member of a government were eligible to be made Lord Chancellor, although without any knowledge of the law, but the mode of selection adopted for the India Office is really not more absurd. It is, however, a necessary condition of our system of parliamentary and party government; but except among a certain class of politicians, in the view of whom ignorance is a positive qualification for high office, and who would wish to have nobody with knowledge and experience interposed between India and their desire to make experiments upon it, the necessity for maintaining a permanent Council or body of some sort unconnected with the ebb and flow of party politics, will be universally recognised, and the constitution of this body will equally be considered a matter of importance. The number of councillors was fixed at fifteen in the first instance, in order to admit of its being fairly representative of knowledge and experience gained in the different parts of India and of the different interests to be dealt with; and making allowance for the proportion of dull men who will always find their way into such a body, it is certainly not too large for the purpose. Whether the Council, as established, is turned to the best account will depend on the procedure laid down for its working One of the most important points to be provided for is the protection of the people of India, the tax payers, from the infliction of improper and unfair charges. This was, no doubt, the object aimed at in the provision of the Act of 1858, that 'no charge should be placed upon the revenues of India without the sanction of the majority of the Council.' But this check is practically

CHAP. XXI. rendered nugatory by the power given to the Secretary of State to deal with business alone in the Secret Department. In the days of the East India Company the Chairman and Deputy-Chairman of the Court of Directors were associated with the President of the Board of Control on this Committee; but now the Secret Department of the India Office is removed entirely from the view of the whole Council. And thus while the sanction of the majority of that body is required to the granting of a gratuity or a pension of a few shillings a year recommended by the Government of India on behalf of some humble applicant, a Secretary of State may order, and has ordered, military operations to be undertaken by the Government of India, involving an expenditure of millions of money, not only without the sanction, but without even the cognisance of his Council. This is a flagrant defect of the system which was certainly not contemplated by the framers of it, and which calls urgently for remedy. The Secretary of State should undoubtedly have power to override his Council. It could not be allowed that the policy of the British Government should be liable to obstruction by any other body than the Parliament which places it in power; but the interests of India demand that the Cabinet should at least be placed in possession of the opinions of those who are best qualified to judge of the effect of any measures proposed which will involve a financial burden on India; and while it should be recognised that in dealing with measures involving military operations, secrecy is a necessary condition, and that the maintenance of secrecy is not compatible with deliberation of a large body; yet, on the ground of justice to India, and to prevent rash and ill-considered action, the reconstitution of at least a part of the Council as a Secret Committee is undoubtedly required. At present such of the clerks as deal with the secret business of the India Office are placed in a more responsible and important position in the Council; they can at least make representations regarding the measures dealt with in these despatches, while the Council itself may be in absolute ignorance about them.

Existing procedure should be reformed.

Further, the practical efficiency of such a Council depends largely on the mode in which it is employed. The assumed purpose of a Council is to advise, but its effective action for this purpose depends on the point at which, in the course of deliberation, its advice is recorded. The Council of India is divided for working purposes (under statutory provision) into Committees for dealing with the particular subjects coming before them, judicial, financial, military, revenue, political,[1] and public works. The members as a rule serve each on two committees, and are occasionally transferred from one committee to another. In the case of orders to be sent to the Government of India, the most important class of business, the procedure followed is that the Secretary of the Department concerned first takes the orders of the Secretary of State on the case, often in the way of preparing a draft reply and submitting it for approval. The draft after being seen and perhaps amended by the Secretary of State is then referred to the Committee for opinion. Here their criticism comes in; they may suggest alterations, or even prepare and submit alternative draft despatches of their own. But the Secretary of the Department is not the Secretary of the Committee, although he attends their meetings. If they do not like his way of putting a case they must put it themselves; but four or five men sitting round a table cannot write a letter. To set a case in motion therefore under such circumstances, in the way of proposing a new line of action, involves a degree of volition which few men so placed are likely

[1] The political department of the office also deals with the secret despatches, but without the cognisance of the political committee, its immediate superior.

CHAP. XXI.

to exercise, and in fact the result fully illustrates the fact that in administrative business the outcome is determined by the procedure, and that the man who initiates practically governs the situation. The Committee therefore may object or obstruct, but they cannot direct. The subsequent stages of business are of the same tenor, but the power of criticism is even less distinctly present. The papers, after passing through Committee, and if approved by the Secretary of State, are made available for inspection by the rest of the Council, and then brought up before a meeting of that body and formally passed, with usually little or no amendment. And regard being had to the innate indolence of most men, especially of old men, and to the natural disinclination (in itself a creditable feeling) of men experienced in business to appear obstructive, it will be understood that the experience and judgment of the Councillors are to say the least not turned to the best account. A strong man may assert himself and make his influence felt—a strong man will always do this in any circumstance—but he must go out of his way to do it. Add that of individual responsibility there is none, opinions being expressed collectively both in Committee and in Council, and it will be recognised that the Indian Council as actually constituted is not as efficient a body as it should be, and that its procedure at any rate needs to be reformed.

Anomalous position of Councillors and Secretaries.

Further, the India Office has lately undergone an important change. Formerly, except in the military branch, the Secretary of which since the Mutiny has been an officer of the Indian army, the Secretaries of Department have been simply senior clerks of the establishment promoted to the higher position—in most cases men of great ability, but whose knowledge of India was gained in London. Of late years, however, retired Indian officials of distinction have been appointed to some of these posts. It is illustrative of the change which has come over the course of an Indian career, that whereas formerly the successful civilian on returning to his native land after holding high office in India would buy an estate and set up as a country gentleman, and possibly get also a seat in Parliament, he is now satisfied to supplement his small savings and modest pension (a great part of which he has provided himself by contributions from his salary) by accepting a subordinate appointment in the India Office. The result is, that the departmental secretary is often a man of higher official standing as well as of more recent experience than the Councillors to whom he is is subordinate. One secretary of a department came to the post from being Lieutenant-Governor of Bengal, the most important office in India after that of Governor General. Another was for five years a member of the Governor General's Council; a third conducted the great administration of Burma during and after the critical time of annexation. These gentlemen have not only a wider record than any of the Councillors, they have had greater experience than most of them, and having the initiation of business and direct access to the Secretary of State, they must naturally have greater influence than the Councillors. Yet, while the latter are so far responsible that they are the statutory advisers of the Secretary of State, and have the power of recording opinions which may be, and sometimes are, made public, the secretary is not responsible for his advice; technically he is only a civil service clerk.

Councillors should be placed in responsible charge of departments.

Clearly there is not room for both councillors and departmental secretaries of the new stamp, and an organic improvement indicated by these considerations would be to give the members of the Council specific administrative duties and responsibilities by placing them severally in direct executive charge of the different departments—in fact, to reconstitute that body on a footing similar to that of the Governor General's

CHAP. XXI.

Council in India. That Council, as has been explained in a previous chapter, was in the first instance merely a consultative body, and in that capacity very inefficient. Its advice when given came too late in most cases, and the burden of initiation imposed on the Governor General became at last so heavy with the increasing amount of business from year to year, that his Council had to be reconstituted on new lines dictated by experience. The members of that Council are indeed still spoken of as the advisers of the Governor General, and so they are in the same sense in which the Chancellor of the Exchequer may be said to be the adviser of the First Lord of the Treasury. But they, with the Governor General, form the Government of India, and each member has responsible charge of one of the departments of the State. By reorganising the duties of the Council of India in the same way, the experience and ability of its members would be utilised much more fully than at present, and much better effect would be given to the intentions of the Act of 1858 as indicated in the debates on the subject.[1] The Secretary of State, while bound generally to abide by the decision of the collective body, and having the benefit of their advice in that collective capacity, would still retain his full responsibility and his power of over-ruling their decisions when necessary.

A change facilitated by recent reduction of Council.

The recent reduction of the number of the Council from fifteen to ten members favours the change. The reasons alleged for proposing the reduction were indeed audaciously insufficient. The Bill was brought up for second reading in the House of Commons after midnight, and pressed forward on the ground of the relief that it would give to Indian finance. The sum to be saved was 5,000*l.* a year; if, as the Under Secretary in

[1] This was the system proposed by Lord Palmerston, who when introducing the first of the two Bills brought in, explained that his provision of a Council of eight members only would admit of each member having charge of a department.

charge of the Bill implied, the prospect of effecting that saving furnished an unanswerable case, a still stronger case lay for abolishing the whole Council. The only reason Lord Cross vouchsafed in the Lords was that he thought he should do better with a smaller council, and that the members of that body themselves were favourable to a reduction; but in what way that opinion was recorded he did not explain, or whether it was the opinion of the more active and able minority, who found little benefit from the presence of venerable colleagues who had long ceased to take any active interest in Indian affairs. The indecent haste in which the Bill was hurried through both Houses on such a flimsy pretext was in painful contrast with the care and consideration with which the constitution of the Council was discussed in both Houses during the session of 1858. For a consultative body which should bring a reasonable amount of varied experiences gained in various parts of the country and in different branches of affairs, fifteen is certainly not too large a number; while among the objections to the reduction must be noted the loss of any new accessions to the Council while it is in course of being carried out. For an administrative body, however, a smaller number would be sufficient; although this view of the case does not seem to have occurred to the Secretary of State when proposing the reduction. Six or seven councillors at least would be required under the proposed system, for the charge of the different departments, and some others might usefully be employed on purely consultative business. On the change being made, the position of departmental secretary would revert to its former status, and these posts would in future be filled as before by promotion of the senior clerks of the office. There is nothing in the reform here suggested which could not be carried out under the statutory provisions of the Act of 1858; but the tenure of office of a councillor might advantageously

CHAP. XXI.

be reduced to less than ten years, a change which would involve the passing of an amending Act to that effect.

Caution against undue interference with Government in India.

The Council of India thus reorganised would undoubtedly be a much more efficient body than the present. An objection might perhaps be raised to the change that it would be too strong; that able and experienced men coming to it after holding high positions in India and placed in charge of the different departments of the India Office might be tempted to try to direct the administration of that country from their new position; to press their own views against those of their successors in India. This is certainly a possible danger. Hitherto the India Office, recognising that its proper function is that of a court of review, and that India can be properly governed only by the Government in that country, has as a rule laudably abstained from direct interference in administrative details. This statement may perhaps create surprise in India, where undoubtedly there is often a feeling of soreness at the supposed tendency of the India Office to interfere in matters which should be left to be dealt with on the spot; but everyone who has watched affairs dispassionately with a knowledge of what has passed on both sides of the water, must recognise that the Secretary of State for the time being has usually been scrupulous in maintaining this dividing line of the respective functions of the two authorities. There have indeed been exceptions to the rule, as in the case of the reorganisation of the army after the Mutiny, when a quite impracticable scheme was sent forth from the India Office cut and dried to be carried out in India. These and similar attempts to transfer the initiation of affairs from India to England, have served to bring the more clearly to light the soundness of the policy of abstention; and as the procedure of the Council would continue to be of its present corporate character, and the proposals of the different departments in every case would come under the review of the whole body before the proceedings reached the stage of final orders, it may be trusted that a sufficient check would be exerted over any tendency of the departmental officials to interfere unduly with the executive functions of the responsible authorities in India.

The maintenance of this principle, that India must be administered by the Government in India—with the development lately set in motion of local institutions, the advancement of the people of that country to a larger share in its administration through the expansion of the legislative councils, and their extended employment in all branches of the public service—becomes now more than ever of vital necessity, and makes it superfluous to discuss the proposals put forward from time to time for the replacement of the existing Council of India by a larger body. Anything in the shape of an assembly debating in public is from the nature of the case out of the range of serious consideration. Indians could not be brought to this country to serve on it, at any rate in sufficient numbers to be representative of the people of India; and the idea that persons so placed, whether Englishmen or Indians, should be in a position to advance opinions, still more to carry resolutions for the result of which they would not be wholly responsible, will not be entertained by anyone who has the most elementary acquaintance with the conditions of that country, or of representative institutions. If, in the dim and distant future, the time should ever arrive when a parliament of any sort is possible for India, it must be set up in that country and not in this.

CHAPTER XXII

GENERAL CONSIDERATIONS

CHAP. XXII.

Political aspect of India.

THE salient features of Indian administration have now been passed in review, and various points have been brought to notice in regard to which the present system calls for amendment and reform. One question especially of great interest and importance is naturally suggested by the enquiry, how far that system, with the development which may be indicated as necessary from time to time, will be suited to, and sufficient for, the wants and circumstances of India in the future, and what modifications of it are likely to be required or brought about in the course of events. Over and above the special circumstances arising out of its connection with England, India now presents this singular political aspect, that its people have been put in possession of a degree of personal liberty as great as is enjoyed by any nation in the world, but liberty not associated with the usual accompaniments of self-government or of representative institutions, save only to the limited extent to which these have been introduced for municipal purposes. The government of a country so circumstanced must necessarily be delicate and difficult; and among the special elements of difficulty at the present time is the appearance on the surface of Indian society of a new class—a class which has no affinity with the landed aristocracy or the natural rulers of India, or the mercantile, or the agricultural communities; which has never before occupied a position of any importance; a

Full personal liberty without free institutions.

Difficulties resulting.

Agitation set on foot.

class which is the product of our system of free education, and which, while constituting a numerically insignificant minority of the whole population, lays claim to be accepted as the people of India, and, with the assistance it is endeavouring to secure from an uninstructed section of English politicians, is entering on a course of political agitation, vague, unreal, and inpracticable in its aims, but which, unless directed into a rational course, may bring about trouble and danger to India. The vast majority of the people of India, on the other hand, although the agitation now being got up among a section of the small English-speaking class necessarily excites among them a vague feeling of unrest and expectation, are still politically in an elementary condition to which no part of Europe furnishes anything analogous. The questions which we are told exercise the minds of the people of India, such as the expansion of the legislative councils, the constitution of the Civil Service, and so forth, are at present absolutely beyond their apprehension. Their notions of the nature of the Government they are ruled by are of the vaguest. To them the Government is represented by the three or four district officials with whom they come in contact; these they see to be acting under higher authority, but as to the nature of this they have only the vaguest notions, while of the government in England, with its parliament and political parties, they have no more conception than of the composition of the solar system. Representative institutions, franchises, voting, elections, the simpler political questions which are coming to be understood by all classes in Europe do not enter even in the most remote way into their thoughts. This is a class of whose wants and feelings little or nothing is heard in the so-called political discussions now going on in India; yet it outnumbers the other class by thousands to one, and it is mainly in their interests that the government has to be conducted.

CHAP. XXII.

Encouragement received from certain classes of English politicians.

Simultaneously with this movement in India a greater degree of interest has become awakened here in the affairs in that country than was formerly felt about it—an interest however not necessarily based on knowledge. The class of persons who profess to take India under their patronage is made up for the most part of minor politicians whose reputation is associated with eccentricities or fads—persons who are not taken seriously at home and are of little account in English politics, except so far as they are weighed by their voting power, and whose defective judgment and unfitness for the position they would endeavour to assume are sufficiently shown by the attitude which they have taken up. They have thrown themselves into the hands of the small party of agitators, taking them at their own valuation as what they profess to be, the representatives of the people of India. These gentlemen have not made the elementary discovery that the class with whom they have associated themselves not only have no sort of claim to be so accepted, but that the interests of those who compose it are to a great extent antagonistic to those of the general community. The movement in question derives its impulse from a section of the educated class of one nationality, the Bengali, whose domination if established would be in the highest degree obnoxious to the other nations of India. The aims of those who have set this agitation in motion find expression in the proceedings of the so-called National Congress, and form the continued subject matter of the vernacular press. The character of this press is not generally understood even by Englishmen in India, and to the English public it is probably absolutely unknown. It is unlike the press of any other country in that it is not divided by party lines to represent various sections of the community; with a few honourable exceptions it is all cast in the same mould, and animated by the same spirit—the desire to disparage and discredit the

The vernacular press.

Indian Government and render it odious in the eyes of the people. Not only are the actions of that Government continually misrepresented, and its officers denounced and reviled, the most insidious attempts are made to arouse the feelings of the masses by appealing to the prejudices which have been affected by previous legislation. Even the abolition of *sati* by the Government of Lord William Bentinck in the early part of the century is not too far-fetched a topic in time or reason to be continually dragged in; while the legislation of the Government of Lord Lansdowne restraining the premature consummation of child marriages is denounced week after week as being an unjustifiable interference with caste and religious observances. The press in its present form originated in Bengal, and although it has now spread over the whole country its impulse is still given from that province. The unanimity with which any topic calculated to disparage the Government is taken up and made the subject of accusation and abuse week after week until it gives place to some new topic, shows the power of combination with which the business is conducted. In face of this persistent misrepresentation and abuse, often taking the form of rank sedition, the inaction of the Government, although superficially magnanimous, is to say the least imprudent. A Government by a handful of foreigners, which is possible only while it has the respect and confidence, if not the regard of the people of the country, runs a great risk when it is thus from week to week persistently held up to obloquy and hatred, while the English public servants are denounced as being selfish, unjust, and tyrannical, and hating the people over whom they are placed. These papers are contemptible as literary productions and the circulation of many of them is extremely small, but the number of copies sold would be a very incorrect index of the number of readers; and although the mass of the people of India

CHAP. XXII.

are still quite uneducated, the subject matter of these newspapers, which is the only thing read at all, undoubtedly filters down to the classes below the readers and cannot but in the long run tend to produce serious mischief. Of this the Government of India is well aware, for it has received many warnings on the subject from various quarters; that it abstains from moving in the matter is not because of any doubt as to the action which should be taken, but from the uncertainty felt whether this would be supported by the authorities at home. The remedy would be really of the simplest kind but for what has gone before. The Government of Lord Lytton passed an act to restrain the press, which had then for the first time become markedly seditious in its tone; the Act provided that a paper after being warned would be liable to suspension, and the legal sanction thus obtained for action was found amply sufficient to prevent the necessity for any action being taken—not a single case of proceeding under the Act took place. Nor was any harm done to anyone. These truculent writers do not in the least mean what they say; they have sense enough to know that if the British Government were overthrown, their class would not be gainers; politically they are but as mischievous children, quite unfit to be left without control. And if the matter had been allowed to rest nothing more would have been heard of the matter in India. Unfortunately the Act was repealed, in deference to a party cry raised in this country. The repeal was perfectly unnecessary, even as a means for giving practical effect to the object in view, because under the provisions of the Act it might be suspended by notification of the Government in any part of India; and this suspension might have been extended by degrees to the whole country. Such however being the past history of the case, the Government of India is unable to take any action unless it can first be secure of the sanction of the Government at home.

The remedy therefore must wait for the appearance of a Secretary of State with the courage to act in opposition to the small section of politicians who are unable to see that the platitudes about the inherent right of every people to a free press are not applicable to the case of India, and that the poisonous literature now being circulated without let or hindrance threatens to create a great political danger. The people of India, generally docile and tractable, are credulous to a remarkable degree and liable to unreasoning outbursts of excitement, and if they were brought to believe that their rulers are really what the native press declares them to be, passions might be aroused and a movement set up fraught with tremendous consequences. Not only is repression of this uncontrolled seditious writing necessary for the safety of the country, it would be hailed with satisfaction by all the more respectable and sober-minded classes, many of whom are at present the victims of the systematic terrorism and blackmailing pursued by the vernacular press. For the Indian, the official equally with the private gentleman, is politically timid; he will not assert himself to resist this tyranny; he looks only to the Government for relief from the nuisance, and wonders that this scandalous press should be so long tolerated.

The National Congress

The so-called National Congress, which comes more under notice in this country than the writings of the vernacular press, although also thoroughly disloyal, is less mischievous, because of the absurd character of its proceedings. They always set out indeed with a profession of loyalty to the British Government, but the resolutions they embody are distinctly aimed at rendering that government impossible. The self-elected delegates who make up that body are in great part pleaders in the Law Courts, and ex-students from the Government College in want of employment, a class yearly increasing under our system of free education, the

CHAP. XXII.

class, in fact, which works the native press, with which the Congress is in close alliance. For chairman some foolish politician is chosen, or, when one can be found to come forward, a native of position who has a grievance against the government. The proceedings do not include discussion or debate, but a number of resolutions, prepared beforehand by a self-constituted committee, are passed by acclamation, and are usually carried forward with additions from year to year. Among the most favoured resolutions are those for the repeal of the Arms Act which forbids the carrying of arms without a licence, an amusing one to emanate from a class peaceful and unwarlike beyond the people of any other country, and which has never furnished a soldier to the army under either native or British rule. Of a piece with this resolution is that in favour of a 'widespread system of volunteering such as obtains in Great Britain.' No reason is advanced why volunteering, which is unknown to any country in this continent but England. and is not allowed in Ireland, should be applied to India, a country where the people are votaries of one or other of two great religious faiths, each of which evokes the most passionate prejudices and excitement causing of late dangerous riots, repressed without great bloodshed only because the rioters were unarmed; where the agitation against such an innocent practice as the killing of kine has recently been made the subject of widespread feuds. That in India, of all countries in the world, volunteering should be seriously proposed, sufficiently indicates the political sense of the persons who compose this annual gathering. As for practical politics, the resolutions declare for a great reduction in the salt tax, a doubling of the minimum income exempt from payment of income tax, increased public expenditure on all branches of public education, and reduction of the fees in the schools and colleges. In fact, taxation is to be reduced, public expenditure is to be increased, and legislation generally is to be in the interest of the class which practically contributes no taxation whatever. This, with the proposal that the small body of English public servants should be replaced by natives, embodies the political aspirations of the members of the Congress. And yet there are to be found politicians in this country who not only accept these crude and foolish utterances as the voice of the people of India, but have not made the discovery that they do not represent the aspirations of any considerable portion of the educated classes as a whole, or the upper ranks of native society. For it would be an entire mistake to suppose that while there is this apparent unanimity among the party who run the press and the Congress, and while their schemes are framed entirely in view of their own interests, these make up the whole or even a large portion of the more respectable classes in India. Happily there are plenty of educated native gentlemen, even in Bengal, who regard the proceedings of the Congress with disapproval; but political courage and independence of character are virtues which have not yet taken root in India. In their dread of being singled out for obloquy by the vernacular press, the more respectable classes of the community abstain from any combination or counter agitation. The other section on the other hand have grown bold with impunity, and the class of Bengalis who lead the movement are adepts in the art of agitation. The funds are supplied by one or two rich native gentlemen, the wire-pullers provide all the accessories, down to the telegrams sent from time to time to a certain class of London newspapers to give the movement a factitious strength and importance. At the last meeting held the president in opening the proceedings assured the meeting that 'every one of Ireland's Home Rule members was at their back in the cause of the Indian people.' That the section of Indians whose agitation takes this form should be

CHAP. XXII.

secure of the hearty support of the Irish Nationalist party is only what might be expected; unfortunately this sympathy is shared by other members of the House of Commons who do not necessarily desire to embarrass the Government, or to encourage the growth of difficulties in any part of the British Empire, but whose knowledge of India is of the elementary kind which leads them, as has been said, to take the small party of agitators at their own valuation, and to suppose that they represent, as they profess to do, the wishes and aspirations of the people of India at large.[1] While public opinion is of this ill-instructed sort, there is danger of parliamentary interference in the affairs of that country of a very mischievous kind. The House of Commons as a whole being unprepared, and for the most part indifferent about debates on Indian questions, a small section of the House may and does succeed in carrying resolutions, striking at the root of the Indian administrative and financial system. This would not be very mischievous if such resolutions were regarded as the mere expression of opinion on the part of those who support them; but the claim is made that they should be acted upon as if they had the force of law. We have only to compare the effect of such action with the elaborate procedure enforced in regard to English finance, the debates in committee, the formal resolutions which follow in the whole House, and the incorporation of these in a Bill carried through its successive stages before they can take effect, to appreciate the monstrous assumption made in such a claim The

Intervention of parliament in Indian affairs.

Resolutions of House of Commons.

[1] In a recent debate, a highly respectable member assured the House of Commons that the rejection by the Government of the Resolution of the House in favour of simultaneous examinations for the Civil Service, had disappointed the 'expectations of countless millions of our fellow subjects.' It would be a far less absurd exaggeration to say that the one desire of the millions of the working classes in this country was the abolition of the duty on the higher brands of champagne; and yet men who make foolish remarks of this sort claim to be taken as advisers regarding the government of India.

humblest local taxpayer even, would have greater protection than the government of India. An English town council cannot add an additional furlong to its street tramways without a Bill formally carried through both Houses, but yet forsooth the vote of a scratch majority in a thin and tired House of Commons is to be accepted as sufficient authority for tampering with the whole administrative and fiscal system of India, and possibly throwing them into utter confusion.

And their ill effects through timidity of ministers.

For the lamentable results which have ensued, and may yet follow if this contention is to be accepted, the blame rests with successive Governments of both parties, from their weakness in suffering such resolutions to be taken seriously. No doubt in the ordinary course of legislation, when votes are taken from time to time at various stages of debate, the action to follow must be governed by the decision of the majority, whether small or large. In such cases there can be no counting of heads; a vote is a vote, whether carried by a large or a small number. But the time has come for recognising that the Indian administration must not be placed at the mercy of the erratic dictates of a chance majority. There might be occasions when a Resolution of the House of Commons would be the most solemn and unmistakeable expression of the voice of the English nation, but it is the duty of a Government before taking extreme action, to make sure that it really has this high authority. To treat all such utterances as having equal force is either political pedantry or political cowardice. It may be said indeed that although a Resolution of the House of Commons may be foolish and ill considered, still that a Resolution of the House can turn out a Government. No doubt it can, if directed to that end; but on all recent occasions when India has been made the sport and playground of the faddists, there has been no question of making these divisions a test of confidence in the Government. The men who carry one or other

When authoritative,

CHAP. XXII.

and when not.

of these snap votes would be quite powerless to carry a vote of that kind; and if on a late occasion the Government, instead of taking the feeble course of throwing on the Government of India the burden of deciding against the simultaneous examinations, had at once announced their intention of ignoring the Resolution, sensible men and reasonable politicians on both sides of the House would have rallied to their support in sufficient numbers to bring out the numerical insignificance of those who would make India the vehicle for introducing rash experiments which they would be quite impotent to force upon their fellow countrymen at home.

Still more important is it to recognise that India should not and must not be subjected to treatment which the House of Commons would not venture to adopt towards the smallest self-governing colony, and that while that country is not and will not for an indefinite time be fit for representative institutions, it must nevertheless be governed in accordance with the wishes of its people so far as they can be ascertained, and are compatible with the maintenance of British rule. If this principle had been kept in view we should not have had Opium Commissions forced on India to ascertain at great expense to that country what all those whose judgment is worth considering knew already, that the objects which the faddists were aiming at would not only result in throwing the Indian finances into confusion, but would involve an unwarrantable and tyrannical interference with the habits and customs of the people of that country, especially of the class which forms its most powerful bulwark of defence, and which, if it were alienated from our rule, would soon render that rule impossible. Nor should we have seen the Indian tariff played fast and loose with in the interests of certain classes in this country; the discreditable episode of the cotton duties would not have occurred—an episode which by causing a widespread belief that Indian policy is dictated in the interests of political party rather than in the interests of the people of India, has inflicted a grievous blow on our character for good faith.

Danger of undue interference with Government of India.

Another point lately brought into prominence is the difficult and anomalous position which, under recent action taken in this country, the Indian Government is coming to occupy. In the view of the people of India, that Government appears vested with the highest power and authority in its executive capacity, and all the other attributes of a great government; while for legislative purposes it presides over a body in which the people of India are now largely represented. This is the outward appearance of things, actually of course the condition is quite different. According to the law the Government of India is merely a delegated agency for carrying out the policy and instructions of the Government at home, and the legislation entered upon by the former is subjected to the full control of the same authority. So far the law has made no change in either respect from the state of things always in force. The legal position of the Government of India still remains what it was in 1784, and although a numerous council has taken the place of the single English lawyer who from 1833 to 1854 represented the legislative element in that Government, its legislative proceedings equally with its executive action remain, as they have always been, subject to the control and approval of the Government at home. This is of course a necessary condition of the case. The Home Government and the British Parliament have the same full rights over every portion of the Queen's dominions; but wherever representative institutions have been granted, these authorities abstain from exercising almost all of the rights they by law or precedent possess. Their powers and rights remain dormant. But in India, where no such institutions exist, the ultimate power must reside somewhere, available for exercise in an active form. And unfortunately, while

CHAP. XXII.

everywhere else their exercise of authority by the imperial government has greatly lessened, if it has not altogether ceased to be employed, in regard to India the control has become more stringent and minute. The change which has come about is not in the form of law, but in the strain put upon the application of the law. Until quite recently the initiation of all legislative measures has rested with the Government of India, although it has had to submit its proposals for legislation to Her Majesty's Government as represented first by the Board of Control and afterwards by the Secretary of State. These proposals sometimes met with opposition and may not always have been accepted, but it is only now that the Home Government has for the first time begun to employ the power given it by the letter of the law, not only to initiate legislative action itself, but, in deference to the outcry of a small fanatical, ill-instructed section of its supporters, to force on the Government of India the obligation to carry out legislation to which the latter is distinctly opposed.[1]

False position occupied by that government in consequence.

This change in the policy so long wisely pursued, a policy by which alone India can be safely governed, has placed the Government of India in a false position. Not only must that government carry out measures to which it is opposed, it must in loyalty to Her Majesty's Government profess to approve of those measures. It has not even practically the means of recording a protest in the form of resignation. The members of the government at any time are all serving under different tenures; some may be just entering upon their term of office, others on the point of closing it, so that the sacrifice involved in resignation would be very unequal. Moreover, there is no analogy between the conditions of Indian and English political life. Here, if a party or individual minister resign, they pass over

[1] We may refer especially to the proceedings taken in connection with the Indian Cantonments Act.

to the other side of the House, but still exercise a potent influence over the course of affairs, to the direct management of which they will in all probability eventually return. Members of the Indian Government, if they resign, would retire into obscurity and uselessness. Occasions indeed might arise when it would be their duty to refuse to obey orders from home, accepting their recall if ordered. It is impossible to lay down a precise line at which disobedience to improper orders, given at the dictates of a rash and unscrupulous political party at home, might become a duty to India; but generally they will best consult the interest of the people of India by remaining at their posts, and putting a drag in the last resort on such unwise and high-handed proceedings.

Interference especially inopportune at present time.

This objectionable departure from the policy hitherto maintained, has been especially inopportune at the present moment, just when the expansion has taken place of the Indian Legislative Councils. The false position into which the Indian Government has thus been thrown in being called upon to carry a measure through the enlarged council to which they are obviously opposed, might under a persistence in such a course soon make their position untenable. Nor must the fact be lost sight of, that the Secretary of State has lately taken the unusual course of over-riding the unanimous opinions and advice of his own council, a course which the spirit of the law only justifies in cases of imperial importance. That India should be kept altogether outside party politics is perhaps a counsel of perfection, but it is the obvious duty of ministers to minimise, so far as possible, the effect of party government, and when they quote parliamentary authority for interference in the ordinary course of Indian administration, to be sure that it is the real voice of Parliament which they are obeying. They must, in fact, exercise more political courage; there must be no repetition of

CHAP. XXII.

such scandals as that of a minister forcing legislation on India, against the wishes of the local government, at the bidding of a small section of political faddists, or of his prohibiting the introduction of fiscal measures desired by all the people of India who are capable of forming an opinion on the matter, on the plea that these are opposed to sound economic principles—fishing for parliamentary votes on the hypocritical profession of inculcating sound economics. India is held by the right of conquest, and the form of its government is absolute; but these conditions should at least not be offensively obtruded.

Summary of case.

To recall what has been said, the present condition of India politically is, that the fullest measure of personal liberty has already been given, and so far as can be foreseen, the grant of political power will follow as fast as it can be safely conceded. The administration is mainly Indian already, and is rapidly becoming still more completely so. Hitherto the expansion of native agency has proceeded most largely in the judicial line; the employment of Indians in high executive posts is only just beginning, and is still in the experimental stage, but the experiment must be pursued *pari passu* on both lines, if the great change is to be safely carried out. With an executive staff consisting of British officials, a purely native judiciary, if animated by the spirit shown by the vernacular press, might bring Indian administration to a deadlock. Indian native officials are politically timid, and peculiarly susceptible to the influence of press criticism, and if not actually siding with the party of sedition might yet be a feeble instrument with which to make head against it.

Material prosperity of India.

In material respects, India, as compared with any previous state, is now extraordinarily prosperous. Weighed by every practicable test, internal and external trade, the increased production and consumption of commodities, the accumulation of the precious metals, above everything the growing railway traffic, the India of the present day, although still according to English standards a very poor country, is by comparison vastly more wealthy than it has ever been before. But two elements of danger and difficulty in the social condition of the country are coming into prominence, to qualify the satisfaction with which the situation might otherwise be viewed. As the ruthless wars which were the chronic condition of India in past times have been succeeded by the present era of internal peace, while famine no longer sweeps away the population over widespread tracts of country, and while simultaneously the elements of sanitation have been introduced, almost everywhere the population tends to increase faster than the increase of cultivation and the improvement of the soil, and to press with growing force upon the means of subsistence. It is easier to point out the evil than to apply a remedy. The religious customs of the country favour early marriages, and emigration on a scale sufficient to be effective is practically out of the question; but the case has to be stated to show that even a peaceful and beneficent rule is not without its concomitant drawbacks.

Qualifications to be made.

Excessive growth of population.

Next, apart from the pressure of population on the means of subsistence, in many parts of the country a social revolution is taking place, not the less momentous because in silent operation, arising out of the increasing indebtedness of the agriculturist, and involving the transfer of the land from the simple peasantry which have held it from time immemorial to the professional money lender, in redemption of loans borrowed at exorbitant interest. The process is favoured by the procedure of our law courts, which with their rigid enforcement of bonds entered into, even by those ignorant of their purport, the highly technical system of pleading allowed and the facilities afforded for costly appeals from the one court to another, are utterly

Cultivators in course of being displaced from the lands.

CHAP. XXII.

unsuited to the understanding and circumstances of the agricultural classes.

It is a curious inconsistency in our policy that while in Ireland so much attention and labour should have been directed towards attaching the cultivator to the soil and creating unalienable tenant right, and while philanthropists and economists should be aiming to introduce the same conditions for the agricultural classes of Great Britain, we should have admitted, indeed encouraged, this social revolution to set in silently on India and work the havoc which it has already created. Some special remedial legislation has been applied, as for example, the Dekhan Raiyat Act, to check this evil. But a larger and more general process seems necessary, nothing less in fact than complete abolition of the sale of land for debt. It would be also a great advantage to the unfortunate peasantry affected, if in all suits arising out of loans made on their land or crops, the agency of professional pleaders were disallowed, and the parties to the suit alone were heard in person. The importance of dealing with this great matter in a thorough and comprehensive way cannot be too strongly insisted on; the class concerned make up the great mass of the people of India, and apart from the claims of justice, the foundations of our rule rest upon their contentment.

Remedial action required.

It is notable that the vernacular press are generally silent upon this social revolution. The agitators, the money lenders and the pleaders whom they employ, are closely allied; they belong to the 'white-clothed' class whose interests, in many respects, are directly antagonistic to those of the people of India.[1]

[1] The Congress does indeed pass an annual resolution, 'that fully fifty millions of the population, a number yearly increasing, are dragging out a miserable existence on the verge of starvation, and that in every decade several millions actually perish by starvation; and humbly urge once more that immediate steps be taken to remedy this calamitous state of affairs.' This resolution—dovetailed among others proposing the establishment of volunteers, the creation of a medical profession, the abolition of taxes, and increased expenditure on education and other things—does

Assumed drain of wealth from India.

The complaint is often made that our foreign domination drains India of its wealth. The wealth at any rate is the creation of our rule; we found India poverty stricken as it always had been before, and as doubtless it would still be if we had not appeared on the scene. The drain of wealth which consists in the large payments which have to be made to England, is of course a fact, but we must distinguish between the two sources of this drain. By far the larger part consists in the payment of interest on the English capital invested in India. In this respect India is in the same position as almost every other country in the world, and has all the advantages derived from a borrower under such circumstances. Borrowed money is the source of her wealth. The greater part of this capital has gone to make the railways which have enriched India more than anything else, and brought about her present prosperous condition; among other things the great tea and jute industries in particular have been established entirely by British capital. The interest India pays on this represents but a very small portion of the benefit which she derives from it. There is, however, a drain of another kind, but smaller in amount, for the pensions paid to English officials, the savings taken away by Europeans of all classes, and that part of the cost of the army which is defrayed in this country. This last item is obviously a necessary condition of the maintenance of a stable government of any sort in India; the most truculent of the agitators who are for replacing the English civil service straightway by natives, have not yet advanced to the point of suggesting that the British army should be withdrawn. The other items

touch the matter, but can hardly be said to deal with it in a very practical or useful way. A town council would not be held to gain credit for good sense or philanthropic spirit by placing a minute on its proceedings to the effect that a large number of the English people were suffering from poverty, which Her Majesty's Government should take immediate steps for putting an end to.

CHAP. XXII.

are no doubt a drain in the actual sense of the words, but that this should be cause of complaint involves the absurd assumption that without English rule exercised by English officials, India would have attained of itself to a state of internal peace and prosperity. Those people must have a very slender acquaintance with Indian history or with the Indian people who can suppose that there is the smallest foundation for such a belief; or that if the *pax Britannica* had not been established in India, that country would not either still be the prey of intestine feuds, such as desolated it before our rule, or have again become the spoil of some warlike invader from the north. All that can be said is that a good government by foreigners is more costly than would be an equally good government by the people of the country. So it would be cheaper for a man to cure himself when sick, if he knew how to do so, than to call in a physician. And the fact needs to be plainly stated that the capacity of the Indians to govern themselves has yet to be established. We must not mistake what may be merely a facility for adaptation, and imitation, and proficiency as agents working under supervision, for original capacity. The assumption that all the races of the earth possess the same natural power, and that the backward ones may by training and propinquity be readily brought up to the level of a higher civilisation, has yet to be established.

Political instability of India if left to itself.

Even now the internal conditions of the country present no elements of political stability. India is still a congeries of nations which although mixed up together in a bewildering degree, and undergoing a rapid fusion in their superficial aspects under British rule, are yet so widely different from each other that generalisations are apt to be delusive and misleading. The difference between the various peoples, between, for example, the martial frontier races and the Bengalis or the people of Madras, is far greater than that which is found between any two races or classes of Europe. But this at least is clear, that the ascendency of the class, now so disloyal and so noisy, which is claiming to succeed us, and which puts forward the impudent claim that every English official constitutes a wrong done to themselves by keeping one of their class out of office: that the ascendency of this class would be utterly abhorrent to the greater part of the people of India, and that as they are simply the artificial creation of British rule, so they would be the first to disappear from the surface if that rule were withdrawn.

English rule not necessarily popular.

Attractive character of Indian people.

That this rule should be popular is hardly to be expected, nor probably are the English themselves individually popular; but if the people of India do not like us, it is impossible to help liking them. They differ, as has been said, from each other so widely, that generalisations are apt to be delusive and misleading; yet there are some characteristics which the English in India will recognise as common to all, especially their good temper, sobriety, industry, patience, and power of self-denial, their kindness to children, their loyalty to family ties. We must all too admire the gallantry of the warlike races, and few can leave the country without carrying away memories of disinterested gratitude shown for good offices done, ties formed of mutual affection with those who have nothing more to look for from our friendship; feeling a degree of interest in India and its people which only long acquaintance with it and them could give; and hopeful that if wisely governed a prosperous future is before them.

INDEX

D D